The Palgrave Macmillan Series in International Political Communication

Series Editor

Philip Seib
Annenberg School for Communication and Journalism
University of Southern California, USA

Aim of the series
From democratization to terrorism, economic development to conflict resolution, global political dynamics are affected by the increasing pervasiveness and influence of communication media. This series examines the participants and their tools, their strategies and their impact.

More information about this series at
http://www.springer.com/series/14418

Jowan Mahmod

Kurdish Diaspora Online

From Imagined Community to Managing Communities

Jowan Mahmod
Uppsala, Sweden

The Palgrave Macmillan Series in International Political Communication
ISBN 978-1-137-51346-5   ISBN 978-1-137-51347-2   (eBook)
DOI 10.1057/978-1-137-51347-2

Library of Congress Control Number: 2016950224

Cover image © Worldspec/NASA/Alamy Stock Photo

Printed on acid-free paper

This Palgrave Macmillan imprint is published by Springer Nature
The registered company is Nature America Inc. New York

In loving memory of my father
Mahmod Mola Ezat

Acknowledgements

The chapters in this book have their origin in my doctoral thesis, completed in 2012 at Goldsmiths, University of London, UK. The book has been supplemented with new material collected during my stay in Kurdistan (Iraq) in 2013–2015. My first and foremost thanks go to Professor M.I. Franklin, my research project supervisor, for her guidance and patience, and for asking important questions and motivating me to continue exploring new ideas. I would like to extend my thanks to my viva voce examiners, Professor Dawn Chatty and Dr. Dan McQuillan, who kindly praised my work and were the first to encourage me to publish this book. I would also like to express my sincere appreciation to Professor Philip Seib for supporting and believing in the value of this work. I am grateful to my late friend Dr. 'abh' Anthony Burnes-Howell, for his tireless encouragement and discussions about my research, challenges, and ambitions. Special thanks also go to Professor David Romano for providing with help when needed. The book has started and ended with the encouragement and motivation of other close friends. Thank you. I want to take this opportunity to sincerely acknowledge all participants who have made this work possible. Their passionate conversation about matters close to their hearts was admirable. I want to express my appreciation to Tadgh O'Sullivan for providing editorial assistance. Finally, my eternal gratitude goes to my family for their patience and support over the duration of this exacting task.

CONTENTS

Abbreviations and Key Terms

AKP	Justice and Development Party
BNP	British National Party
CFR	Council of Foreign Relations
CPJ	Committee to Protect Journalists
Daesh	Islamic State of Iraq and al-Sham (Arabic acronym)
DTP	Democratic Society Party
EU	European Union
Gorran	The Movement For Change/Change List
HDP	Peoples' Democratic Party
HRW	Human Rights Watch
IS	Islamic State
ISIL	Islamic State of Iraq and the Levant
ISIS	Islamic State of Iraq and Greater Syria
KDP	Kurdistan Democratic Party
KRG	Kurdistan Regional Government
KRI	Kurdistan Region of Iraq
NGO	Non-Governmental Organization
Peshmerga	Armed forces of the Kurdistan Regional Government (KRG) that covers northern parts of Iraq
PKK	Kurdish Workers' Party
PUK	Patriotic Union of Kurdistan
PYD	Democratic Union Party (Syria)
UNHCR	The UN Refugee Agency
YPG	People's Protection Units (Kurdish forces in Syria)

PART I

Multiculturalism in Imagined Communities

CHAPTER 1

Introduction

INTRODUCTION

This book sets out to describe how the imagined community is being weakened in the age of new media. The argument offered here is that the new information and communication technology is increasingly challenging the imaginings of belongingness based on ethnicity, identity, and the nation-state that have been constructed largely through traditional media such as television, radio, and newspapers. Access to the new information and communication environment has increased people's ability and willingness to express their opinions and be heard inside and outside their nations, far beyond anything witnessed before. These voices demonstrate a consciousness that confronts the imaginings of a nation and which the governments around the world are trying to reinforce through "multi-culturalism has failed" debates in Europe to the assimilationist violence in the Middle East and North Africa and elsewhere. The aim of this book is to show how new media can work in a different way, namely, against the grain of national order, and, instead, creates a space that fosters counter-national dynamics and formations that are punctuating the imagined community. If we think of new technology as a tool, which is not only changing social relations, but also exposing existing ones that have until now been concealed, we are only writing a "rough first draft" of history in this early twenty-first digital century.

© The Author(s) 2016
J. Mahmod, *Kurdish Diaspora Online*, The Palgrave
Macmillan Series in International Political Communication,
DOI 10.1057/978-1-137-51347-2_1

The "imagined community," as coined by Benedict Anderson (1983), is a community that rests on the idea that people share common traits and beliefs based on their ethnic and national ethos. It is imagined because people who have never met live according to the notion that they are united and alike, and, by definition, are different from people outside the ethnic group. The imagining does not imply that the nation-state is false or unreal, but rather, it refers to the popular processes shaped by—and in turn shaping—political and cultural institutions. They produce a consciousness in which nations, national identities, and national homelands appear as natural. Owing to this imaginary element, nationalism has a strong social psychological dimension (Billig 1995). It is especially through traditional media that the nation-state has been able to present itself as a singular and coherent culture with related identities, by pitting symbols, speeches, and images that strengthen the identity of the Self against the identity of the Other. Therefore, the construction of the imagined community is also a by-product of the identification of "us" and "them."

This "us-making" requires sharp boundaries in terms of nationalities between countries. In multicultural and diverse societies, such distinctions are made by using terms like "majority" and "minority," which serve to separate the dominant national group, who belong together, from the given minorities (Appadurai 2006; Thangaraj 2015). In accordance with these ethnic, religious, and gender lines, people are, in terms of their national identifications, demarcating themselves by differentiating themselves from others. It is the task of this book to analyse these rigid conceptions of identity, which are underpinning much of the discrimination, conflicts, and crises we see around the world, by proposing important aspects which contribute to commonalities across ethnic boundaries.

In order to capture such subtle and abstract procedures, the book turns to diasporic people and their online activities. Diasporas are intriguing to study as they pull ethnic identifications out of the space of the nation-state and move from one single nation to multiple entities (Anthias 1999; Ang 2001). Migrated people, in general, pose a threat to the homogeneous nation-state and "call into question the idea that a people [must] have a land in order to be a people" (Boyarin and Boyarin 1993, p. 718). The Kurdish diaspora makes a valuable case to study for a number of reasons. Kurds are among the largest stateless diasporas in the world (van Bruinessen 2000), whilst also being one of the most active diasporas in Europe (Baser

2011). Diasporic Kurds, victims of assimilationist policies and persecution in Iraq, Turkey, Syria, and Iran, have been settled in Europe since 1960s, and are still a considerable community there. This means that a growing number of Kurds belonging to second, third, and fourth generations are born outside Kurdistan and live within two or more cultures. What implication does this have for Kurdish identity and belongingness? I argue that Kurdish diaspora—an increasing number of individuals who live within multiple cultures, speak multiple languages, and live through transnational practices (Portes et al. 1999)—are confronting the boundaries by which nations and majority groups define themselves.

Homi Bhabha (1994) has argued that the homogeneous period of the nation's imagined community cannot eradicate the discontinuities that minorities and diasporas convey. However, the implications also work in the opposite way; the national narrative of a country challenges the displaced cultures and people and their homogeneous notions of constituting a people away from home. To phrase it differently, the narrated *scripts* that people carry with them are disputed by other national scripts. The idea of scripts as coined by Kwame Anthony Appiah (2005) is valuable as it helps us grasp how collective identities come with socially produced ideas of how certain types ought to conduct themselves if they want to stay put. Scripts suggest how to act if we happen to be, for example, Germans, Swedes, Kurds, Christians, or Jews (Appiah 2005). They are "narratives that people use in shaping their projects and telling their life stories" (Appiah 2005, p. 22) to remain within their group, whether ethnic, religious, or gendered. Because diasporas are more mobile than people rooted in one nation, their scripts are more prone to be contested, negotiated, and rewritten. Such blurriness is even more enhanced when diasporas are involved in transnational practices. These transnational engagements consist of social and practical links and active networks and organizations that cross at least two geographically and internationally distinct places.

The disruptions of scripts become particularly evident and easier to observe when we look at the new communication environment online—a space where people gather from all over the world to interact. These articulations are important as they intermingle the more explicit "us" and "them" from the offline environment. The Internet has therefore paved the way for nuances and contradictions that diverge from homogeneous narratives produced by the nation through traditional media.

Conjointly, these triangulated set of processes—new technology, diaspora, and transnationalism—could be one of the most powerful instruments in terms of creating a momentum to understand the diaspora consciousness that exceeds what the nation-state and traditional media have allowed. Diasporic consciousness is an evolving element of such cross-border living. In his work, Paul Gilroy (1987, 1993) explains double consciousness as a specific consciousness among the African diaspora that is shaped into a multifaceted cultural and social intermingling between Africa, Europe, and the Americas. Such a diasporic consciousness challenges the everyday reproduction of "national consciousness," the latter being a way of life lived in the world of nations (Billig 1995). However, the redefinitions that diasporic Kurds are engaged in online, break from the duality of homeland-settlement country and move beyond both the national consciousness and the double consciousness. In order to discover these in-depth and latent contestations, I argue that only by qualitatively digging deep below the surface of migration movements and diasporic experiences, and into their daily conversations and doings, can we move beyond myopic viewpoints and look to the periphery to understand the world around us and where we are headed.

The approach pursued here has benefited greatly from critical interdisciplinary tools developed within post-colonial, media, and feminist studies. The purpose is to open up new perspectives by adopting an interdisciplinary and comparative approach, "even perhaps, at the risk of hubris, post-disciplinary" (Morley 2000, p. 4). Nevertheless, by adopting a more complex tactic, specified later, this book attempts to offer a deeper understanding of "the issues at stake in what I take to be one of the most central political questions confronting us, as we attempt to construct a viable cartography of the world in which we now live" (Morley 2000, p. 4).

Against this backdrop, the reason for this book's existence is twofold. Firstly, and in relation to scholarship in general, it aims to fill a gap in the literature on diaspora and new media. The complex nexus of diaspora, new media, and identity includes contestations and reconfigurations that to a great extent have gone unnoticed by researchers and policymakers. The analyses developed here address new tendencies among (Kurdish) diaspora by going well beyond first-hand sequels and instead looking into the messy, intense, and contradictory statements that inform important contemporary socialities. Following on from this, new light is shed on the Internet and how it is challenging the notion of national consciousness, a dynamic which diaspora and media studies to date have largely failed to acknowledge.

The second reason is related to the political debates in Europe given the migration and refugee crises in the aftermath of recent ethnic conflicts and civil wars in the Middle East and North Africa. With the increase in voluntary and (in particular) forced migration, ideas about identity, belonging, and home need to be reconsidered in order to rethink citizenship policies, which, in many contemporary societies, have come to define nationality in terms of its ethnic, rather than civic, meaning. Much of the rhetoric used in public speeches in Europe demonstrates a need to reimagine European societies by bolstering the view of "us and them," which, in turn, has provided ample fuel to European nationalist and far-right movements. I will elaborate these two reasons further in the following two sections.

The Academic Default: A Critique

Two idioms can be identified within the academic writing on diaspora and new media. I argue that despite an important discourse that has been developed over the years, diaspora has remained trapped within the duality of homeland and the settlement country. Part of the problem lies with the difficulties of finding a suitable definition for a people who were forcibly displaced. Numerous accounts of the concept have emerged over the last decade, to the degree that the concept of diaspora itself has become a diaspora in an ocean of semantics (Brubaker 2005). While diaspora initially defined victim diasporas, such as Jews and Armenians displaced by persecution and war, it has more recently been used as a catch-all phrase to speak of (and for) all population movements (Cho 2007). Old, classical, and victim diaspora are intermixed with new, transnational, trade diaspora. That said, the issue at stake in the many disparate definitions is not so much about who is and who is not a diaspora, but rather, it involves the merging histories and realities of these different groups, which, in turn, overlook the existential question. As Gijsbert Oonk (2007) argues, the definition of diaspora cannot only be answered by making a comparison between different ethnic diasporas, often based on their ethnic origins, but, rather, it needs to be based on the *causes* of migration. The question is not simply about who travels, but when, how, and under what circumstances (Brah 1996).

The terms "old diaspora" and "new diaspora" (Mishra 2007; Spivak et al. 1996) reflect the different historical conditions that created them.

While I argue that an initial contextualized distinction is important, it can at the same time trap us in endless binaries, and—even more problematically—it completely ignores the changing and fluid processes that identities and cultures undergo. If identity and culture are not universally fixed, which is the post-modern position often reiterated and recognized in diaspora studies, the identity of the old diaspora must also undergo changes in the modern and developed societies they are settled in. To complicate the discourse of diaspora further, I argue that old diasporas morph into modern and transnational diasporas. While diasporic people emerge and are attuned to historical discourses, they live in hypermobile and transnational spheres. Adopting capital and skills, and developing their consciousness that now consists of multiple cultures, they are able to rearticulate themselves, which is evidenced by the mobility and practices they are engaged in. Declining to recognize the evolving nature of diaspora may indirectly suggest an essentialist conception of identities. This, in turn, also denies the ability of diasporic individuals to travel with their passport and return to a (new) home established within the settlement country. These perspectives need to be articulated in order to endorse the fluid processes which certain post-colonial thinkers (Bhabha 1994; Gilroy 1993; Hall 1992) have engaged in exhaustively. This means that we need not approach diasporas as characterized by the contingencies of long histories of wounds and blisters, but as a condition of subjectivity (Cho 2007).

The second idiom, which can also explain why much work stops from arriving at such new outlooks, is the belaboured "imagined diaspora." Like nations, diaspora has grown into the idea of imagined diaspora. The term is an extension of Anderson's concept, which proposes that people have created an imagined landscape where they produce myths and dreams of the homeland to which they belong and will one day return. Although the passion among diasporic people, evident from the way they speak of themselves, their histories, and homeland, is still present among many of them, academic scholarship has to a great extent been trapped within a discourse of imagined communities, imagined diaspora, and imagined identity, thereby look past whatever is new about the emerging transnational consciousness. One possible explanation of this could be that conventional models of diasporic studies, offline and online, have focused largely on the collective trauma of losing a homeland and facing discrimination in the settlement country, which has resulted in scholars turning to the digital space where the diaspora has been able to reconnect with the country of origin. Embedded in these analyses is the matter of how temporal concerns (histories) interact with spatial considerations and how trauma can be a defining feature in con-temporary diasporic formations.

Within the context of Kurdish diaspora, the term "imagined" may be to a greater extent explicable, as they lack a nation-state. The imagin-ing of a homeland has indeed been a stark element in the Kurdish dis-course as Kurdistan is frequently referred to as a country, using terms such as "South," "North," instead of "Iraqi" and "Turkish" Kurdistan. However, while the Internet may allow for homogenization through renewed ties with the homeland and strengthened national identities, it is also giving way to diversification among ethnic groups, in turn allowing marginalized individuals to discuss and deconstruct identity in ways not possible before. To some extent, what some scholars describe as trans-nationalism and hybridity have been antithetical in terms of the realities described.

Therefore, the theorizing of imagined diaspora begs three questions. As Anderson has already identified the national community as an imagined construction, in what way does the imagined diaspora differs from this? Secondly, if diasporic people are subject to hybrid mixed cultures (Bhabha 1994; Gilroy 1993; Hall 1993) and are active between different nations under the label "transnationalism" (Glick Schiller et al. 1992), how does this affect or interfere with the imagining of national communi-ties? Thirdly, if the imagined community was able to construct and main-tain itself through systems of traditional media, how does the new digital media differ, and what are the implications for the condition of these imaginaries? Reviewing large parts of the academic literature, it looks as if Emily Ignacio's (2005) critical question, "What happens when the images and discourses of a nation—identities, culture, and gender—do not just circulate within national boundaries, but cross frontiers into a transnational space by anyone, regardless of authority?" (p. 3) has been left unanswered.

What happens with national systems and notions when the power to discuss them has moved from the prevailing authorities to the people? What happens to the imagining of ethnic, national, and gender common-alities when similar experiences bring together people to discuss and share the same interests? What befalls the notions of belonging and home when diasporic individuals are born outside their origin country, or leave it at an early stage in life, and acquire more cultures than the one they were born into? When the traditional living together in one place is interrupted by new ways of living and interacting, it raises multiple questions about old conceptions and new structures, which this books endeavours to discuss by drawing from the conversations between Kurdish individuals in diaspora, online and offline.

The arguments in this book depart from earlier works that emphasize that diasporas have strengthened their identities through transnational activities. For example, the research on Kurdish diaspora and media has concluded that Kurdish identity has been reinforced by second- and third-generation Kurds who are presently growing up in Europe (van Bruinessen 2000; Alinia 2004; Curtis 2005). It is said that they tend to be more interested in Kurdish national identity and politics than their parents. There is no reason to argue against these accounts, as there are numerous occasions where dispersed people gather, share important matters, and mobilize at critical times thanks to the rapid and ubiquitous development and use of communication technologies. However, it would be a mistake to view the new technology as simply facilitating or speeding up communication, thus connecting people and strengthening national identities. While the intensity of nationalism is present online, it also complicates the nexus between space, place, and identity. As Arjun Appadurai (2006) argues, "collective imaginings and imagined collectivities, in the era of cyber technologies, are no longer just two sides of the same coin. Rather, they frequently test and contest one another" (p. 24).

IDENTITY CRISIS IN EUROPE

The second motivation behind this book is related to the "failure of multiculturalism" discourse in Europe and the identity crisis that have appeared in the early twenty-first century, and how diversity and belonging are understood. Although multiculturalism at one stage had a certain intellectual and social currency, it has had a bad press in recent years (Karim 2006; Turner 2006). Leaders from the most powerful European countries—Germany, France, and the UK—have all lamented multiculturalism and questioned its viability. Chancellor Angela Merkel, Nicolas Sarkozy, the former President of France, and Prime Minister David Cameron have, in public speeches, indicated that they do not believe that different cultures and communities can conveniently coexist in a given society. They have portrayed the idea of multiculturalism and the dominant values of their nations as conflictual (Merkel has pointed to "Germany's Christian values" and multiculturalism's "absolute failure"; Sarkozy has said that, "We have been too concerned about the identity of the person who was arriving and not enough about the identity of the country that was receiving him"[1]; and Cameron has argued that "we have tolerated segregated communities to behave in ways that run counter to our values,"[2] or, as he a few years earlier stated, "the creed of multiculturalism" amounts to a deliberate "weakening of our collective identity.")[3] The phrasings confirm what Stuart Hall (2000) had discussed earlier, namely, that the heterogeneous formation of "Britishness" grounds the United Kingdom as an "imagined community," and that the homogeneity of British culture has been exaggerated, thereby disregarding the reality that there are different ways of being British (Hall 2000).

Other nations that have taken part in the coordinated attack on multiculturalism include the Netherlands, Denmark, Belgium, Sweden, and Austria, who all question the ability of migrants to integrate and replace their own values with those of the dominant nation. Concerns arise from the conflicting politics of ethnic difference: the riots in France in 2005 and 2007 by urban youngsters with origins in North and West Africa against the police raise questions about the relevance of the French non-ethnic and secular republican model (Hsu 2010).

In the aftermath of the recent humanitarian disaster in the Middle East, the crisis in Europe has been exacerbated. For example, an image of a line of people crossing a field through Slovenia to Europe was described in the following terms: "The extraordinary aerial photo of a column of refugees and migrants tramping through the fields of Slovenia may come to symbolize the moment the EU began to fall apart."[4] The UN Human Rights Commissioner, Zeid Ra'ad Al Hussein, warned against the language used by many politicians, stating that phrases such as "swarms of refugees" were dehumanizing.[5] The warning came after the British Home Secretary Theresa May controversially stated that mass immigration made it "impossible to build a cohesive society."[6] Furthermore, Al Hussein has argued that discussions and disagreements over the resettling of these refugees are being used by those who argue that even the smallest minority is a threat to the idea of the national purity of the state. The nation-state has increasingly been reduced to a fiction of its "ethnos," thereby acting as a last cultural archetype (Appadurai 2006).

A possible reflection of the warning against "swarms" and the striving to close the European borders could, for example, be the pondering of how many of "them" are *here* among "us" and, furthermore, who is among "us," and who are among "them" (Appadurai 2006) when refugee exodus and terrorist attacks took place simultaneously. Who is really a Muslim, a terrorist, and a refugee? Attackers who are of Arab origin, or nominally Muslim, incite fear in a wholly different way from the "white wolves" like Anders Behring Breivik who killed 77 people in Norway in 2011. Furthermore, the refugee movement into Europe has been presented as the greatest challenge to the continent since the Second World War,[7] and specific questions have been asked about how Europe could protect its borders from the massive refugee and migrant influx on the one hand, and terrorist attacks on the other.

The migration problem had once again monopolized media coverage in Europe, reigniting earlier debates on multiculturalism at an EU level, for years one of its most contested issues (Seeberg and Eyadat 2013). Mainstream conversations on the refugee crisis, order, and stability have been added to discussions of the burqa, mosques, terrorism, and other migrant issues repeated in the "failure of multiculturalism" debates.

What Is the Problem?

The sheer volume of debates in the media circulating in the aftermath of each of the terrorist events taking place in Europe has made the concept and even the condition of a multicultural society unsettling in many of these countries. By combining three specific idioms in British discourse— multiculturalism as a single doctrine, the fear of Islamic colonization, and the cultivation of separatism—the fear factor has become stronger (Vertovec and Wessendorf 2010). The play on national victimhood and the fear that Western culture is under threat with a need for European borders to be protected have intensified these debates to the extent that it has become difficult to argue—from any political position—that multiculturalism is viable for social unity and diversity in different societies. The debates taking place in different nations are all pointing to a condition that has given rise to the condition of *worrying* about the fate and future of *our* society (Hage 2003). The aspects of worrying and caring are of particular interest here, as they serve as zones that pose sober questions concerning the "nature" of the nation and its relationship to its citizens.

What is entirely absent from these debates are the dynamics of different cultures. Discussion of the comprehensive research and scholarship on migrants and the fundamental processes of change and fluidity are completely missing in the media (Blommaert and Verschueren 1998). Furthermore, the problem with essentialist discourse is that identity is wholly defined by culture, which is assumed as explaining migrants' behaviour. Put differently, cultures are indicative of why migrants act the way they do without consideration of gender, class, and other socio-economic factors.

The book serves to show how migrants—the Kurdish diaspora in this case—confront these fixed notions of us and them, Self and Other. The main part of the Kurdish diaspora experienced forced displacement, like many of today's migrants who have left their countries, seeking refuge in Europe and elsewhere. Through a detailed exploration of diaspora Kurds and their online and offline activities, I will present the changing discourse of Kurdishness in two locations, Sweden and Britain, thereby demonstrating that they have adopted new notions of who they are and where they belong. These explorations blur the clear-cut relationship between ethnicity, belonging, and homeland, which are usually pronounced in the public sphere. The case study of the Kurdish diaspora is a fascinating journey, which demonstrates both the challenges and the difficulties they undergo as migrants in a new country, as well as the richness of living hybrid transnational lives, which has attributed to them a multiconsciousness that goes beyond imagined diasporas and communities. These processes of socialization into a new homeland by migrants are not uncomplicated, but they are important to explore in order to understand how and when cultures and identities undergo changes, and why they are less inclined to change.

Given that the reality of conflict zones around the world results in increased migration, with 1 in every 122 humans either a refugee, asylum seeker, or internally displaced (UNHCR 2015),[8] migration itself will not go away in a hurry. Europe has not presented any serious ambition to meet the new migrants who have attempted to settle in Europe. The book, therefore, hopes to be an example of how further research can be conducted in order to understand forced displaced people, thereby addressing key questions concerning multiculturalism and integration, both theoretically and practically.

THE STRUCTURE OF THE BOOK

Against this background, to fully engage with the myriad abstract fluctuations that transnational diasporas bring with them, a comparative approach is needed that takes into consideration (1) the components of the experiences of migration and the policies of settlement countries, (2) the components of diasporic formation (gained through ethnographic studies), and (3) its online and offline sites.

The book is divided into three main parts. Part I—Multiculturalism in Imagined Communities—consists of Chaps. 1, 2, 3, and 4. Chapter 2, "Multiculturalism Debates, Policies, and Concepts," identifies key issues in European multicultural societies and their policies. The purpose is not to delve into the policies and citizenship models of each European nation, but to identify key terms that have generally been considered as problematic by political leaders, and how the relationship between the nation and its citizenry is understood. Particular attention is paid to Britain and Sweden, as they make up a central part of the case study. Chapter 3, "Nations, Diaspora, Identity, and Alternative Explorations," presents the theoretical context in which each key concept is explored, within the frameworks of post-colonial, post-modern, and feminist thought. Pending a detailed discussion of diaspora, the text emphasizes the importance of defining diasporas with due care and careful contextualization. Central ideas are drawn from prominent post-colonial thinkers such as Stuart Hall, Paul Gilroy, Gayatri Chakravorty Spivak, and James Clifford, who lend themselves to understanding how certain essentialist ideas are conveyed through public discourses. I deploy post-structural and feminist ideas to clarify how identity can be envisioned in order to allow it to be truly contested and deconstructed. By using concept of scripts—the idea that ethnicities and nationalities come with certain written texts regarding how to act—I discuss how people make choices between different cultures in terms of deciding to be, or not be, who they are. This is coupled with Judith Butler's concept of "performativity," which supports the mechanism of doing and undoing identities or, in other words, their national, ethnic, or gender scripts. Performativity helps to elucidate how identity is changing character in the production between subjectivities and in dialogues. Chapter 4, "State Struggles in the Middle East and the Kurdish Diaspora," describes the case study, Kurdish diaspora, by providing a background account of the conflicts in Iraq, Turkey, Syria, and Iran where the Kurdish populations are settled, thus explaining why Kurds have been pushed outside their countries and have become diaspora. Again, the intention is not to offer an exhaustive survey of Kurdish history, which is well presented in many scholarly works, but to show the complexity of the "Kurdish question." Following this is a lengthier section on the Kurdish populations in Europe.

Part II in the book—Arriving on the Scene—presents the empirical Chaps. 5, 6, and 7, consisting of online discussions and further informed by the data gleaned from offline interviews. In a detailed exploration of the exchanges online, I examine how Kurds in diaspora deal with critical issues that are related to homeland, settlement countries, identity, and belonging. They have been members of an online community, which, for years, has given them the opportunity to discuss, contest, revise, and strengthen their sense of Kurdishness in a completely different way as opposed to face-to-face interactions. I had the chance to ask more specifically about their online experiences, impacts, and views. This multisited and triangulated approach has led to significant new insights about how Kurds view themselves and the societies from they come from and in which they are now settled.

Chapter 5, "Is it OK?—Challenging Gender Roles explores how young Kurdish women and men in Sweden and the UK deal with renegotiations of gender roles, sexuality, drawing from both their cultural norms and novel values they have adopted in the new country. Young Kurdish females have, in particular, taken a distinct role in contesting older norms of how to behave and act as a Kurdish woman. While they have occasionally been stigmatized and "othered" in Europe, that is, in relation to "honour killing" debates, they have talked back against a Western discourse as well as engaged with Kurdish traditions and norms regarding how they should act. However, it is evident that some elements of Kurdish culture are not available for renegotiation, while others are constantly contested.

Chapter 6, "Am I a Kurd?":—Deconstructing Kurdish Identity, explores the deconstruction and reconstruction of the Kurdish identity. Shifting the gaze from the "external other" to "internal othering," I examine the different layers of Kurdish self-identification. These include differentiations between, respectively, the Kurdish diaspora and homeland Kurds, different European Kurdish diasporas, between old and new diasporas that migrated in different phases to Europe, and various generations of Kurds and their relationships to old and new media.

In Chap. 7, "My Kurdistan Chapter": Kurdish Repatriation, new material was gathered when I had the opportunity to speak with Kurdish repatriates in Kurdistan in 2015. While feelings of guilt combined with career interests and the wish to contribute to the Kurdish society were a strong incentive to return to the homeland for many people, the feeling of being a foreigner, in contrast, became too overwhelming. That said, diasporic Kurds seem to have found ways to live and work between different nations. These interviews shed additional light on how Kurds through new experiences break from their respective imaginaries of who they are and where they belong.

Part III—Consciousness, Information Technology, and New Direction—composes of Chap. 8, "Towards a Weakened Imagined Community," and Chap. 9. I explain why the double diaspora consciousness needs to be extended to a multi-consciousness in light of new information and communication technologies and diasporic transnational practices. A particular consciousness among the Kurdish diaspora has grasped their fluidity, from being an old victim and classically diaspora, to new, transnational, and even cosmopolitan diasporic figures that cross borders, work, and live between different communities. These individuals do not imagine their communities; they are managing them. To conclude, I attempt to outline the possibilities and uncertainties that migration, diaspora, multiculturalism, and citizenship entail.

Notes

1. The Telegraph, "Nicolas Sarkozy declares multiculturalism had failed," February 11, 2011.
2. BBC News, "State multiculturalism has failed, says David Cameron," February 5, 2011.
3. The Economist, "In praise of multiculturalism," June 14, 2007.

4. The Telegraph, "We are watching the death of open frontiers in Europe," October 26, 2015.
5. Guardian, "Refugee rhetoric echoes 1938 summit before Holocaust, UN official warns," October 14, 2015b.
6. Request More, "Refugee rhetoric reminiscent of pre-Holocaust senti-ment—UN human rights chief," October 14, 2015.
7. The Atlantic, "The Global Refugee Crisis," October 14, 2015.
8. The UN Refugee Agency, "Worldwide displacement hits all-time high as war and persecution increase," June 18, 2015.

CHAPTER 2

Multiculturalism Debates, Policies, and Concepts

INTRODUCTION

While this book deals with how changing identities can be understood among transnational (Kurdish) diaspora people and how new technology can increase our understanding about implications and impacts, the questions are in the spirit of a wider context of multiculturalism, socio-political ideologies, and migration movements that have occupied much of the debates in recent years in Europe, and beyond. As mentioned in Chap. 1, and as will be further developed in Chap. 3, nations are presented as natural entities and they are continued to be reinforced through technologies and public debates (Anderson 2006). The attempt here is to describe the discourse around issues, such as forced marriage and honour killing, in Europe, in order to encircle underlying problems with different approaches.

Culture, identities, nations, and belonging are continuously being redefined, in particular in this digital age, but much of the migrant debates have strengthened the binary of Self and the Other. While an increased cosmopolitan outlook has developed through transnational links, multiculturalism policies continue to view migrants to engage in a one-way course that breaks their links with their roots (Karim 2006). The recent responses by European leaders to the question of integration demonstrate ideas about multiculturalism as a "natural" relationship between nation and its citizens, without giving much consideration for the transnational

© The Author(s) 2016

J. Mahmod, *Kurdish Diaspora Online*, The Palgrave Macmillan Series in International Political Communication, DOI 10.1057/978-1-137-51347-2_2 practices by which migrants and diasporas live their lives (Karim 2006). The pending presentation of the case study describes how these transnational activities may look, including challenges and constructive outcomes. But before that, we need to look closer at what the public debates entail and why they have stirred much contentious announcements about the end of multiculturalism.

MULTICULTURAL VERSUS MULTICULTURALISM

It is useful to make an initial distinction between "multicultural" and "multiculturalism." Multicultural is the particular status of the multiple cultures living in one society, while multiculturalism refers to the different ways, strategies, and policies that are created to manage the diversity in a given society (Gunew 2004; Hall 2000). Multiculturalism can therefore be seen as being composed of a set of political ideas (Modood 2013). Although the debates and awareness of the multicultural society are fairly recent, the phenomenon itself—the state of diversity and group difference—is a feature of most societies (Kelly 2002). While an increasing number of people see minorities as part of a national problem in European societies, often connected to economic deflation and crises and a threat to the national culture, this has recently led to a rise of far-right and racist parties (Alibhai-Brown 1999, in Kelly 2002). This has also been the case for many of those societies where a discussion of multiculturalism may be absent but the societies are effectively multicultural and multiethnic.

The Middle East and North Africa are distinctive regions with diverse histories and complex societies, and each nation has its own political, cultural, and religious specificities (see Burayidi 1997), where minorities are excluded from the public sphere and denied identity recognition at best, and their existence at worst. Almost every day the news media agencies bring to the front pages the stories of maltreated groups and ethnic and religious conflicts in different regions of the Middle East and North Africa. All over the world, there is a growing crisis of recognition that characterizes the relation between citizens and formal institutions. When the old structural societies meet the new hypermobile technologies at the intersection of globalization, it has rising implications for the question of the identity-citizenship-nation nexus. We can, therefore, see that these equivalent arguments about intolerance and discrimination are also made even when migrants are generally considered as being from the same religious or cultural group. Minority groups in this part of the world have been viewed as not fitting into the society because they have different habits, values, and views. The internal diversity of all societies and their division into different social groups, and the adoption and readoption of external components and their irregularities, are so comprehensive that it is indeed difficult to distinguish anything specific in terms of assumed national identities (Cardus 2010).

However, the issue of diversity has become particularly acute in Western *liberal* and *democratic* societies committed to equal representation. Kymlicka (2010) argues that the "rise and fall" discourse in the context of European multiculturalism is a specific historical phenomenon that emerged in Western democracies in the late 1960s. More importantly, multiculturalism was part of a wider human rights revolution within the context of ethnic and cultural diversity. Before the Second World War, ethno-cultural and religious diversity in the West was characterized by illiberal and undemocratic interactions. Hence, before what has been termed "citizenization" (Kymlicka 2010), racial ideologies openly expressed the superiority of some people and cultures and their right to control others. The framework of human rights, including the oppression of, for instance, women and homosexuals, puts forward an important reason to ask why cultural diversity has been seen as an obstacle to the development of European society (Verschueren 2000). What is it in the European conception of its fabric that makes the construction of diverse European identities problematic? It remains a crucial task to understand why tensions in Europe are intensified within several well-established democratic societies, and, simultaneously, why is there a strong protection of identities that are recognized to varying degrees. Racial segregation is not an option, even if until the early 1970s cafés in Antwerp had signs saying "Interdit aux nordafricains" (Verschueren 2000), even if segregated communities do exist in some corners of European cities. In a similar vein, assimilation is no longer de rigueur, perhaps because we have realized that contemporary migrants no longer break ties with their home society, but, instead, "build social fields that link together origin and settlement" (Glick Schiller et al. 1992).

There is a comprehensive body of literature on the topic of multiculturalism, in particular, in the field of political philosophy (Taylor 1994; Gutmann 1994; Kymlicka 1995; Modood 2013; Parekh 2000), but the task here is concerned less with its philosophy and more with the meaning of multiculturalism when politicians, media, and the public speak about it. So, what is it that multiculturalism is trying to achieve? What does it promise its citizens? For a concise description I refer to Stephen

Castles who explains that the essence of conventional multiculturalism has involved "abandoning the myth of homogeneous and monocultural nation-states [and] recognizing rights to cultural maintenance and community formation, and linking these to social equality and protection from discrimination" (2003, p. 12). Principally, the main concern with multiculturalism, as implemented through different types of representation, education, health, popular culture, public institutions, and so forth, has been to promote tolerance and respect for different ethnic groups and their rights (Morrell 2008). The crux of the politics of multiculturalism has been to meet the demand for recognition, which is, in turn, a matter of acknowledging individuals and their identities in different ways (Appiah 1994), and emphasizing the distinct makeup of each ethnic group.

But two significant problems have arisen, even within nations upholding the noble idea of tolerance for diversity, and these problems express themselves most clearly via the rise of far-right movements across Europe. The first is the expectation that migrants must assimilate wholly, subsuming themselves to all aspects of the "host state's" national culture, and the second is the view that migrants will remain migrants, perpetuating their own distinctive culture to the detriment of the host state. These problems are diametrically opposed, but both center on intolerance. Culture has become a euphemism for "race" as something inherently irreconcilable (Burdsey 2007).

Since the late 1990s, policies and debates have been observed and interpreted by commentators as a retreat from multiculturalism, with a new approach to diversity under the name of civic integration (Borevi 2014). This civic approach is considered to be significantly different from that of actively integrating immigrants into economic, social, and political mainstream, "muscular" defence of liberal democracy, as expressed by the British prime minister (Banting and Kymlicka 2012).

Identical Diversity: Different Multiculturalisms

Some scholars (i.e. Grillo 2000) have distinguished between "weak" multiculturalism where cultural diversity is acknowledged in the private sphere, while migrants are expected to assimilate in the public sphere, and a "strong" variant that defines the recognition of cultural difference and political representation in the public sphere. A skim through multiculturalism policies across European countries allows us to analyse their variations. The aim here is not to rehearse at length all the policies and citizenship rights adopted by each country. Rather, it is the identity dimension of citizenship that is in focus, with each example providing a contextual reading of the policy design that a country has employed and which, in turn, has contributed to the crises between the state and its migrant citizens. Of course, integration and multiculturalism comprise a spectrum of practices and policies that can be considered as "weak" or "strong," or somewhere in between.

In a comparison between Britain and France, the former is often considered as belonging to the strong model of multiculturalism, while France is viewed as rather weak. To illustrate this, Grillo (2000) refers to the French response to headscarves and the British way of dealing with Sikh demands to wear turbans. The National Assembly in France decided in 2004 to ban headscarves in public schools, and in 2010 to outlaw the wearing of "clothing intended to hide the face" in public spaces, imposing a fine or even jail sentence for offenders. The former President Sarkozy declared, "The burqa is not welcome in France because it is contrary to our values and contrary to the ideals we have of a woman's dignity."[1] The burqa garment has also been an issue in other European countries. While some other countries, such as Belgium and the Netherlands, have passed similar laws on veiling and the burqa, which have been coupled with questions of integration and citizenship, other countries such as the Britain, Germany, and Denmark have eschewed such decisions at the same time that political leaders have announced their disapproval of veiling. The case of the burqa demonstrates a number of concerns that go to the heart of these debates and the nexus of multiculturalism, gender, and national identity.

Clothing that projects the image of an oppressed woman has been one of the sources of national drama, as it does not conform to an open and liberal democracy. While the bill in France avoided mentioning any specific communities or religions, it was general knowledge that it mainly aimed at Muslims. The burqa garment and an increase in the number of immigrants have sparked discussions that centred on fear for the future of French values and culture. The main difference in past and present discussions about the veil is that banning the burqa cannot be legitimized in the name of *laïcité*, which is the French equivalent to liberal state neutrality (Joppke 2013). It was stated that "If *laïcité* is threatened, French society is threatened in its unity and in its capacity to offer a common destiny" (Assemblée Nationale 2009, in Joppke 2013). While opponents have emphasized the small number of women who wear the burqa or niqab, the majority of the French population favoured the ban: 70 % of the French public supported the ban

(Joppke 2013). The French authorities, in other words, blamed most of the problems, including Islamic fundamentalism and a growing ghettoization, on the headscarf (Bowen 2007). Simultaneously, French sociologists have repeatedly argued that ghettoization and segregation have little connection to religious commitments (Rattansi 2011). The actual reasons for segregated Muslim communities were referred to in the French government's decision as intentionally providing accommodation in poor suburban areas to migrants who were encouraged to go to France in the aftermath of the Second World War (Rattansi 2011). As such, there was no bona fide intention to support migrants in integrating into French culture. On the contrary, the children of immigrants were encouraged to learn their "languages and cultures of origin" in order to accelerate a return to the homeland (Rattansi 2011).

Hence, the criticism of multiculturalism has not merely been presented in the context of political violence, but also engages with sexual repression (Modood 2013). Many of the critical voices within the debate on multiculturalism have addressed honour-killings, forced marriages, and wearing of the burqa, which are all linked to the oppressed female body. However, the veil ban concerns more than a piece of clothing; it is the body of the woman used as a signifier of cultural, religious, and ethnic differences (Yuval-Davis 1997). The problem with such an approach is that it creates a double bind for Muslim female citizens in France and elsewhere, as they are effectively caught between two cultures. What is often overlooked in the discussions is the recognition that migrant women, who belong to minority or marginalized religious groups, are continuously in a process of negotiation of their multiple affiliations (gender, faith, families, and new and old homelands) and are placed within a tight space for action (Shachar 2015). That said, female migrants and their garments take cue as visible markers of a much wider struggle over power, identity, and difference (Shachar 2015). The focus on Muslim women's veiling has contributed to further politicization of the matter, and different camps understand the practice of veiling, and the practices of non-veiling, as a declaration of "loyalty" and "belonging" (Shachar 2015). This is the double bind that women are trapped within.

Besides France, Germany is one of the European countries that is generally considered to have experienced difficulty in embracing the idea of multiculturalism. Germany has a history in which foreigners remain foreigners (*Ausländer*) without full political rights. This can be compared to ethnic German immigrants (*Aussiedler*), newly arrived from the former Soviet Union, who receive full social and political rights based on their "inborn" link to the nation (Spevack 1995).[2] Blood-and-soil nationalism has informed German identity for all of the modern era. This means that Germany is reluctant to grant full citizenship rights to refugees and guest workers. This was evident when the shortage in labour recruitment from Italy, Spain, and Greece in the 1960s required Germany to import labour from other non-European countries, such as Turkey. During the period of sustained economic growth, Germany did not consider the social effects the migration would have on local communities (Eccarius-Kelly 2008). A common expression among politicians, "arrive today, leave again tomorrow," underlined their expectations, and only decades later did Germany recognize that the question of political and social integration of migrants needed more attention from policymakers (Eccarius-Kelly 2008).

The countries that first identified themselves as multicultural were societies that had long historical experiences of immigrants and were even built on immigration, such as Canada, Australia, and the United States (Modood 2013). This essentially means that in these countries, migrants were seen more as prospective co-citizens and that the nation was seen as multiethnic. One of the leading scholars on the subject, Tariq Modood (2013), states that the sign that a society had become multiethnic or multicultural concerned not only demographics and economics, but also the perception that new challenges emerged that required new political agendas.

While some countries such as Denmark, Germany, and Austria have employed integration strategies that are viewed as compulsory and assimilationist, other countries such as Britain and Sweden have adopted civic integration policies that are more voluntary and pluralistic in form (Banting and Kymlicka 2012).

Multiculturalism in Britain and Sweden

In Britain, discussions about racial differences have taken place since the 1960s but the pronounced crisis of multiculturalism started in 2001, according to Modood (2013), with the advent of a number of events: David Blunkett became Home Secretary, there were riots in some northern English cities, and the 9/11 attacks took place in the USA. In particular, the riots and the rise of terrorism, which some felt were supported secretly by many Muslims, resulted in heightened criticism of multiculturalism as well as signalling a changed political climate (Meer and

Modood 2009). The new criticism came overwhelmingly from pluralistic centre-left individuals who had initially been sympathetic to identity politics and the redefinition of progressive forces, but who now argued that multiculturalism had led to more segregation than racism. For example, Farrukh Dhondy, an Asian one-time Black Panther who founded multicultural broadcasting on British television, mentioned a "multicultural fifth column" that must be excluded, arguing that the state funding of multiculturalism should instead focus on defending the values of freedom and democracy (Modood 2013). From early 2000, it became increasingly common to hear about the challenges that Britishness faced given Muslim cultural separatism and self-imposed segregation. Multiculturalism had failed because it had not encouraged minorities to be truly British (Baldwin 2004, in Modood 2013). These critical voices reached a new peak after the London bombings of July 7, 2005 (7/7). A central concern within these debates was the fact that most of the individuals who were involved were born or brought up in Britain.

Despite this, the trials of suspects in the 2005 London transit bombings, resulting in numerous court dismissals, meant that little has been done to resolve the confusion about government policies to recognize local imams as representatives of British Islamic communities (Hsu 2010). The proposition from British authorities has essentially been that migrants did not integrate well enough and should work harder to become more British. More specifically, the identification of multiculturalism's failure referred to the ghettoization of immigrants, unsatisfactory economic integration, poor educational outcomes for children, high dependence on welfare, continuation of illiberal traditions among immigrant groups, which referred to limited rights and liberties of girls and women, and political radicalism, especially among Muslim youth (Banting and Kymlicka 2012/2013). The new view on multiculturalism was implied in the 2004 introduction of citizenship ceremony for new nationals, including an oath of allegiance to the queen and the guarantee to respect freedom, rights, and democratic values (Phillips 2007). Citizenship test, which demonstrated skills of language and life in the United Kingdom, was established one year later. The rhetorical retreat was hence appearing before 7/7 (Phillips 2007).

The role of history in both national identity and the state of multiethnic Britain was one of the most emphasized points in the Parekh Report on *The Future of Multi-Ethnic Britain*, published in October 2000. The Commission's project, set up by the Runnymede Trust with financial help from the Joseph Rowntree Charitable Trust and the

Nuffield and Paul Hamlyn Foundations, spanned three years, involving consultation with civil servants, academics, government departments, NGOs, community organizations, and members of the public. The report is considered to be the most comprehensive overview of race and ethnic relations in Britain thus far (Vertovec 2001), and its main task was to identify the current state of multiethnic Britain, the newer racisms, in turn, emphasizing ways of countering the latter in order to make Britain a vibrant multicultural society (Modood 2013; Weedon 2004). In particular, it highlighted a stronger sense of belonging to the polity more than the concept of liberal citizenship, which meant that Britishness had to be reimagined.

Of all the questions raised for reconsideration, it was the point on rethinking national identity that evoked the most hostile reception in the conservative press. Media reactions were controversial mainly because of a domino effect after a right-wing newspaper claimed that the report to see "British" as meaning "racist" (Weedon 2004). Modood (2013) argues that such a misrepresentation of the report is an important aspect of multiculturalism. By this he means that a story that a country tells about itself to itself, including the discourse and images in which the national identity is communicated and through which people acquire and redefine their sense of national belonging, had to be revitalized so that the present and future—and not only the past—could be reflected upon. In Britain, the relationship between Muslims and multiculturalism has evoked much debate; there are two explanations of this according to Meer and Modood (2009). The first is that Muslims' claims-making has been especially difficult to accommodate (Joppke 2004), which is illustrated by the issue of veiling, and has been conflated in public discussions with forced marriages, female genital mutilation, and the rejection of current laws and the suggestion of replacing these with Sharia law (Meer and Modood 2013).

Many points in the Parekh report embrace Stuart Hall's arguments about the failure of broadcasters to represent racial and cultural diversity as a positive asset (Davis 2004). The subject of identity and hybridity has taken a central place in Hall's work, and he has argued at length for a position of identity as a way of understanding discontinuities with the past, as opposed to the claim for a search for an authentic Caribbean identity. Hall, for example, pointed out that there is no pure or authentic sense of where people come from, and that diasporic people—in this case Caribbeans—do not simply return "home" because it is an imagined community (Davis 2004). This kind of multiculturalism, instead, delves into the cultural complexities of ethnic identities and, in particular, the processes of formation and change that are produced in-between the local and the global (Hall 1996; Meer and Modood 2009).

Stuart Hall (1997) states that Englishness has been decentred by the dispersal of capital to Washington, Wall Street, and Tokyo, and also by the influx of the migration of peoples. As a result of the weakening of English identity, Thatcherism has strengthened Englishness, and narrows it to a firmer definition than before. The voices of Thatcherism frequently ask questions like, "Are you one of us?" but those who are part of the "us" are marginal and do not include either blacks or women (Hall 1997). These questions continue to be asked, but the answers do not demonstrate the same level of confidence as during the Thatcher-era.

The alienation of Muslim communities in contemporary Britain is considered to be the result of social disconnectedness and the negative consequences of 9/11, the Iraq war, and the London bombings (Karim 2006; Turner 2006). In the aftermath of the more recent terror events in Paris and Sydney, questions of citizenship have come to the fore when homegrown acts of terrorism have been conducted by national citizens. In addition, public attitudes towards migrants have been hardened and become more suspicious, as the discussions of Muslim identity versus Islamist fundamentalism have been coloured by confused arguments about the intentions of refugees in the European press.

Although the arrival of refugees and non-European immigration is a rather new experience in Sweden when contrasted with other Western countries, it is also one of the five countries in the European Union (EU) that receives the most asylum seekers per capita. During the immediate post-war phase, Sweden received large groups of refugees, followed by labour immigration in the late 1950s, to early 1970s when an "immigration stop" was put into effect (Borevi 2014). From then on, immigrants from non-European countries increased. Sweden hosts around 1.5 million foreign-born residents, which equals 15 % of the Swedish population, of which the most substantial part is born outside the EU. After migrants from Finland, the largest groups include Iraqis, Yugoslavs, and Iranians (Borevi 2014).

Sweden and its neighbours are regarded as traditionally homogeneous countries, which, therefore, highlight the migration-related "challenges to citizenship" (Bay et al. 2010). Generally, there are different views on Sweden and its approach to the multicultural society; while on the one hand, it has been considered successful and hailed for its egalitarianism and social welfare system with a generous asylum policy (Eliassi 2013; Dahlström 2004; Schierup and Ålund 2011), there are those who believe that it has led to increased xenophobia followed by more restrictive Swedish immigration policy. By the 1960s, Sweden had incorporated a specific policy to foster healthy immigration and integration into Swedish society. The policy, inspired by the universal welfare state principle, namely, a Social Democratic welfare state regime, characterized comprehensive and generous redistributive benefits and welfare services provided to the whole population, and not only specific groups (Esping-Andersen 1990, in Borevi 2014). It was the aim of the Swedish model for immigrants, in line with T.H. Marshall's influential citizenship theory, that the allocation of citizenship rights, with an emphasis on *social rights*, was an important element in cultivating a sense of belonging and national community (Marshall 1950, in Borevi 2014).

Characteristic of the Scandinavian welfare state overall, but especially so in Sweden, was merging the idea of access to comprehensive and generous welfare services with full employment and economic growth (Sainsbury 2012). From the 1970s, the policies contained more pronounced multicultural goals that attempted to avoid any ethnic "Swedifying" tactics, and were, instead, designed to support ethnic identities. Immigrants and their children were given the possibility to retain their language and other cultural practices and organizations. It was stated that immigrants should "have the opportunity to choose between their own ethnic affiliation and the Swedish majority culture" (Government Bill 1975/1976, p. 26 in Borevi 2014). Sweden's neighbours had a different approach, although there were also similarities. For example, Denmark had an assimilationist, or even anti-multiculturalist policy. Like France, Denmark has never considered itself as a multicultural country despite its ethnic diversity. Cultural diversity has generally been viewed as un-Danish (Jensen 2010; Vertovec and Wessendorf 2010). Denmark maintained its policy to advocate Danish cultural, linguistic, and political homogeneity. The differences between the Swedish and the Danish models have been explained by contrasting perceptions of national identity and active citizenship.

Since the late 1990s, integration policies and citizenship rights have experienced a significant change, which was seen in the introduction of different types of integration tests, including citizenship courses, language tests, and knowledge of cultural norms and values (Hellgren and Hobson 2008; Vertovec and Wessendorf 2010). Banting and Kymlicka (2013) argue that the notion that policy developments entail a backlash against multiculturalism derives from the assumption that civic integration is inherently incompatible with multiculturalism. They debunk this belief by shifting their gaze to Australia and Canada where multicultural policies have been combined with strong integration policies, with a clear focus on employment, speaking the national language, and sharing liberal values (Banting and Kymlicka 2013).

The changing discourse of Swedish immigration policy has similarities with that of other European countries where multiculturalism had been embraced. For instance, in the Netherlands the government had recognized that ethnic communities had the right to set up their own schools and to receive funding from the state. The Dutch retreat from multiculturalism took place to a much greater degree, however, which included a large-scale abandonment of dual-citizenship programmes and withdrawal of national-level funding for minority organizations and activities supporting cultural difference (Meer and Modood 2009; Modood 2013). The new civic integration policy was characterized by a "give and take" relationship, which means that migrants need to meet different requirements in order to gain access to various rights (Borevi 2014). Nevertheless, Sweden diverges from many other countries, as individuals are neither obliged to pass any tests in order to gain benefits nor will they be denied residence permits if they fail to undertake certain programmes. Sweden, unlike, for example, Denmark, does not apply different integration courses (Borevi 2014). Denmark, on the contrary, has gone furthest in employing civic integration policies and demands. In order to gain permanent residence status in Denmark, new arrivals must have taken part in the mandatory introduction programme, passed the language test, and, have a total residence period in Denmark of five years (Adamo 2008). Adding to these restrictions is the age limit of 24 years for marriages with third-country nationals and a required deposit (of approximately €7400) before family reunification (Jønsson and Petersen 2012). Given such comparisons, it is clear to see that Sweden's approach strongly supports the idea that access to civic rights is important for individual integration.

Yet, there are emerging trends in Swedish society that point to a less tolerant social and political climate, particularly with the rise of the anti-migrant Sweden Democrats. Besides the more formal rights of citizenship, it is the attitudes, language, and ideas circulating in the media and the public that are important to bear in mind. Since the 1990s, crimes with racial and xenophobic motives have increased in Sweden (Bunar 2007), while racism and xenophobia have not been considered as political or structural problems in the society, but, rather, as inherent in adolescent behaviours (Bunar 2007). In addition to these crimes, immigrants in Sweden have had to deal with more structural, political, and social questions of exclusion and alienation. Gender linked to multiculturalism issues in Sweden has, for example, included the discourse of "honour-killing." The term "honour-killing" refers to the killing of women in the name of honour, for having supposedly brought "shame" to their families. Honour-based violence takes place in many countries around the world, from South and Central America, to various Eastern European countries, and in places in the Middle East, Africa, and South Asia (Meetoo and Mirza 2007). In Britain and Sweden, the debates on honour-killing have intensified after a few cases became known, which have often led to polarized debates about immigration and gender equality (Meetoo and Mirza 2007). In the British discourse, these acts have been rather invisible because of the private–public division that framed the domestic violence discourse; however, since 9/9, migrant women have become highly visible and ethnicized (Meetoo and Mirza 2007).

In Sweden, media accounts and policy discourses related to honour-killing have mainly talked about the issue through the lens of cultural essentialism. There are obvious contrasting differences between, for instance, minority violence and domestic violence among ethnic Swedes. While the former is culturalized, the latter is individualized and belittled (Narayan 1997; Razack 2008). Razack (2004) explains that the approach to the general problem of honour-killing and forced marriages has not been understood as manifestations of the generic violence against women that both majority and minority cultures fail to condemn. Furthermore, parallels have been made between honour-killing conceived as culture and the gun-related domestic murders of women in the United States (Narayan 1997).

In earlier research on Kurdish diaspora in the context of honour-killing (see Eliassi 2010, 2013; Alinia 2004), young female respondents referred frequently to the question of "honour culture" debate, and how they were stigmatized in the good and the evil narratives often deployed when discussing the topic. Scholars have discussed how practices of forced marriage and honour-killing are not compatible with liberal democratic societies. Kymlicka (1999), for example, has pointed out in his early studies that liberalism had overlooked grave injustices and that intragroup inequalities must be approached with care. However, he has also argued for a restricted form of "cultural rights" and has not demonstrated support for the granting of "special rights" to cultures that oppress their members. It is in relation to this, and in the context of gender and multiculturalism, that Susan Moller Okin (1999) has directed her criticism, which points to the fact that none of the defenders of multicultural group rights have addressed the issue of cultural practices that subordinate women. Okin has addressed Kymlicka and the limited work devoted to solving within-group inequalities, in particular between the genders, as the latter inequalities are not as visible as other issues. In turn, Okin's *Is multiculturalism bad for women?* engages with the granting of group rights that allow some minority cultures to maintain their culture as it is, which may not be in the best interests of girls and women within those cultures.

One expression of "successful" integration is the naturalization of migrants. For example, obtaining Swedish nationality is a prerequisite in the process of integration, while the conception of naturalization dates back to before the construction of the nation-state (Blommaert and Verschueren 1998). However, the naturalization process is positive, as people of foreign descent can more easily gain the right to take part in political activities such as voting, as those who have been "naturalized" cannot be denied this. The problem is that this form of official status does not eradicate resentful attitudes towards ethnic difference (Blommaert and Verschueren 1998). A naturalized Swede, for example, is an easy target of racism and discrimination as a non-naturalized foreigner. By the same token, in the UK, when a Pakistani receives British citizenship, he or she will not, by definition, escape racial antagonism. Naturalization seems intended to strengthen the sense of an imagined community by conflating the naturalized citizen with the naturalized nation, thereby celebrated for becoming part of the fabric of everyday life and reasoning (Billig 1995). The problem is that this rarely matches realities on the ground. Furthermore, in some countries, such as France and Germany, naturalization means abandoning the identity of the old homeland. Some countries are not pleased with their citizens holding multiple identities, and in, for example, Germany and France, naturalization requests state that disproportionate attachment to the migrants' home country or religion can be an expression of refusing naturalization (Banting and Kymlicka 2012; Kivisto 2002). Such a civic-assimilationist approach rejects the idea of citizens holding multiple identities. The rejection is most apparent in dress codes or in the prohibition of dual citizenship. Of course, such statement, as Benhabib (2005) rightly points out, demands first abandoning a false dichotomy between identity and citizenship, and second, the attempt to reject certain identities exceeds the purely legal-universal conception of citizenship.

FEAR AND WORRY IN THE NATION

The discussion on multiculturalism is not new and demonstrates a mainstream opinion in Europe,[4] but it has been exacerbated in recent years. This has been the case particularly since 9/11, and later after the terror attacks in London and Madrid. The most recent terrorist attacks in France and Australia have exacerbated the situation further. Based on evidence from "Multiculturalism Policy Index," which traces the development of multiculturalism policies in 21 OECD countries, scholars like Banting and Kymlicka (2013) state that the retreat from multiculturalism has been witnessed on the level of discourse rather than of policy. They mention that although there has been a retreat in a few countries, it is not the pattern in general.

Earlier research (i.e. Asad 2003; Radhakrishnan 2003; Eliassi 2010) on European discourse argues that post-colonial subjects are generally portrayed as threats to European national identities. We can see this most evidently in the aftermath of each event and terrorist attack that resulted in calls for an increasing worrying-ness. "Those who are not with us, are against us" became a well-known slogan with a substantial currency: it is "us" against the threats. What, or who, those threats are, is unclear. What is clearer, however, is that the notion of the Other keeps coming up in these debates. By way of alluding to a "common blood," debates on migrants have been implicated in creating and substantiating the idea of an authentic Europe.

The migrant debates about the failure of multiculturalism have not necessarily been racist per se, but the tone set in the debates by some specific concepts conveys a number of distinctive characters of an otherwise intertwined net of descriptions of culture, which are dangerously close to post-colonial views. The description explicitly brings forward a growing demarcation of "us and them," which, in turn, produces ideas of the Self and the Other. Running alongside this has been the portrayal of the West being enlightened and the East being backward, noticeable in what Cameron implied that "they" (referring to young Muslim men and migrant families) have countered "Western values." The other characteristic relates to essentialist views of cultures as static and unchangeable. This suggests that cultures have definite boundaries, which have become almost tangible territories within a single society. Some of these characteristics have been expressed more explicitly, such as in distinctions between different ethnic or religious groups, while others have been more implicit, such as in the case of the UK riots, conveyed through essentialist notions of belongingness and home. The riots in 2010 demonstrated, although subtly, how identity is deeply interwoven into what we expect from cultures' performativities and actions. Deeply engraved notions of the imagined community became more apparent when the question arose of how these young individuals could do these things to their *own* community.[5] Anthony Cohen has addressed this phenomenon and argued that "ethnicity has come to be regarded as a mode of action and of representation: it refers to a decision people make to depict themselves or others symbolically as the bearers of a certain cultural identity" (Cohen 1994, p. 119). In turn, these characteristics demonstrate that it is not the strategies that have been criticized, but rather it is diversity that has come under attack, which, for those with racist views, can often provide further motivation or legitimacy (Karim 2006). What is striking is the ease with which extreme far-right parties have hijacked the "migrant problem," exaggerated through tabloid newspapers and other media, to reinforce views on non-Western minority communities as unwilling to integrate into Western societies (Rattansi 2011).

Beyond problems with integration, there are assertive problematic ideas about questions of ethnicity and belonging. Ethnic categories are frequently employed to explain events and phenomenon, whether it is to protect or to marginalize identities. The key issues, as identified here, are the risks we run when we consider that ethnicity is an organic condition (Cardus 2010). Although the racial category has been replaced with the idea of cultural ethnicity, theories in Europe harbour the notion that people who move carry their ethnic traits from one society to another as if they are static and genetically coded and isolated from social relations (Cardus 2010).

Some observers (i.e. Joppke 2004) suggest that debates on migrants should not be conflated with actual changes of opinions among the general public, and should not be seen as a real reflection of people's opinions about migrants. This may be the case, but then we need to ask how it is that the political far-right has gained more popular support in a number of countries in Europe recently. In Sweden, Sweden Democrats, an anti-immigrant party, secured 5.7% seats in the 2010 election. While their success came as a surprise in what has been viewed as a traditionally tolerant liberal society, it is indeed part of a new European development. Sweden became the third EU member in June 2010, only to find itself without a governing majority after elections marked by the rise of far-right, anti-migration parties. Other countries in similar position were Belgium and the Netherlands. The Sweden Democrats held 14% of parliamentary seats after it became the third largest party in the 2014 general election.

We need to further inquire why it is that in the early twenty-first century, refugee centres in Sweden are being burnt in a series of attacks. The attacks have paralleled rising tensions, as refugees from the worst affected places in the world, Syria and Iraq, arrive into the country. Do attacks on multiculturalism spawn attacks on refugees and migrants on the ground? It is difficult not to assume that the language used by politicians and other pundits when addressing migration does not find its way into people's everyday lives. Having said that, according to polls (Vertovec and Wessendorf 2010), attitudes towards multicultural society and minority cultures have not been dramatically affected, despite public disputes. Other researchers claim the opposite. Popular perceptions of immigration and integration policies are understood to be closely linked to current policy changes. For example, the rapid increase in anti-immigrant sentiments, mostly concerned with migrants associated with Islam, was one of the key reasons why at the beginning of 2000, the Netherlands adopted one of the most aggressive assimilation policies in Europe (Entzinger 2003).

It is difficult to draw any distinct links between the public debates and the rise of an anti-immigrant wave without further in-depth research. Perhaps, the changes are linked to foreign political dynamics, media portrayal, and security questions in global conflict zones, or, perhaps, the culturalist explanations assumed by feminists, journalists, and political officials about family violence, honour-killing, and forced marriage that have charged the radical right-wing with a wealth of problems with which to fight immigration (Akkerman and Hagelund 2007). The concept of honour-killing has i.e. become much more prevalent in right-wing and racist repertoires (Alinia 2013). What is clear is that most Western countries ended the state-sponsored subjugation of ethnic, racial, or religious minorities by the 1960s and 1970s under the influence of human rights movements, yet ethnic and cultural hierarchies have remained in place and are even reinforced in many Western societies (Kymlicka 2010).

NOTES

1. New York Times, "Sarkozy Backs Drive to Eliminate the Burqa," June 22, 2009.
2. The central criterion for the acknowledgement of citizenship in Germany is the principle of *jus sanguinis* (descent). Not long ago, it became easier for adult immigrants to apply for German citizenship after fulfilling the criteria of eight years of residence. Though it became possible for children to have double citizenship in 1999, they must choose to become German citizens exclusively before they turn 23, or they lose their German citizenship (Kondo 2001).
3. There have been six cases of honour-killings in Sweden between 1986 and 2012. One of the reasons why this particular case has been debated so extensively is that many times Fadime herself brought the matter into the public domain and appeared in the media discussing these issues.
4. Earlier mediated events like the Salman Rushdie fatwa in 1989 and Danish cartoon crisis of 2005 had led to conservatives questioning multiculturalism.
5. This can be compared to the Brixton riots of 1981. While both events took place when a Conservative prime minister was wrestling with the effects of a global economic downturn and unemployment, the debates on the 1981 riots had a particular racial focus. Although both sets of riots ultimately were about feelings of social alienation and exclusion, the different discourses of segregation versus "How children of Britain could do this to their own community," are more evident. The Guardian, "A new kind of riot? From Brixton 1981 to Tottenham 2011," December 9, 2011.

CHAPTER 3

Nations, Diaspora, Identity, and Alternative Explorations

INTRODUCTION

This chapter is loosely divided into two parts. The first part discusses the key concepts that the debates on multiculturalism have generated. What has been striking is that these debates seem to rest on an idea that societies are, or should be, homogeneous, with as few differences as possible. When differences appeared, it was not the policy of the given state that was questioned, but the whole idea of multiculturalism (Karim 2006). This is best explored through the tone, and the vocabulary used as the focus is largely placed on perceptions of the Self and Other. Whether honour-killing, forced marriage, and the veil are cultural or religious issues is an entirely different discussion. Furthermore, questions of inequality and ontology also belong to another discourse. Here, it is rather the methods, rhetoric, and purpose surrounding each of these events that have been identified as problematic, as they have marginalized migrants.

Scholars assert that migrants have been targets of racial profiling (Eid and Karim 2014). The "war on terror" has been interpreted by Muslims as a "war on Islam" (Masud 2008). Other related concepts that I will unpack in this first part include the concepts of nation, nationalism, and identity. The idea of the nation-state has implied that ethnicity and territory implicate a natural relationship, particularly as reflected in culture and language.

© The Author(s) 2016
J. Mahmod, *Kurdish Diaspora Online*, The Palgrave
Macmillan Series in International Political Communication,
DOI 10.1057/978-1-137-51347-2_3

Specific focus will be devoted to the "imagined community" that has been implied throughout migration debates.

Following this is a thorough exploration of diaspora. Although the most powerful feature of diaspora and transnationalism has been to confront the singular notion of the nation, the popular use of both of these terms has cost them much value and significance. Bauböck and Faist (2010) explain that while the value of a concept in the social sciences can be measured by its penetration into academic publications, multiple disciplines, mass media, and other public discourses, the concepts of diaspora and transnationalism may have diminished their academic value through their successful proliferation. By providing a detailed exploration of the empirical case study presented later in this book, it is part of this book's intention to regain some of that power. The purpose here is naturally not to offer "better" concepts, but rather to demonstrate how diasporic transnational practices through the use of multidisciplinary lenses and multiple qualitative methods can trigger new perspectives and insights into the fluid, sometimes contradictory, and increasingly multiconscious diasporas. By way of engaging in post-colonial and post-modern theories, the debates and tone within them can more easily be understood, including how and why the rhetoric used can morph into augmented tensions and diverge communities.

The second part introduces alternative concepts that serve as "methodological nodes," with which to discover and analyse the different perspectives that the online–offline nexus presents. As will become clear in the discussion outlined shortly, the concept of identity has been particularly tricky, and while it is always in motion, it has remained fixed and essentialized. Thinking through scripts in this context, how people are ascribed certain "texts" to behave in certain ways that make them who they are, namely, Kurdish, woman, homosexual, and so on (Appiah 2005), the attempt is to grasp how people change identity and self-perception, particularly in new locations after years of living. Connected to this is Judith Butler's (1988, 1993, 1997) concept of performativity that will, and in a similar vein, help to visualize how identities and scripts are done and undone. The chapter ends with a section on the Internet and online spaces. I propose to view the Internet and online space as the "online scene." The reason for this metaphorical description is simply because the scene describes aptly how the online environment works and how it diverges from the traditional media, not only in terms of technicalities such as two-way/multiple, synchronic communication, but rather the kind of *sociality* it creates and how it changes relations between people.

NATIONS, BELONGING, AND THE OTHER

> The two most significant factors generating nationalism and ethnicity are both linked closely to the rise of capitalism. They can be described summarily as mass communications and mass migrations. (Anderson 1992, p. 7)

Drawing from the debates on multiculturalism and the latest discussions of the refugee crisis, one major entity against which the Self is conceptualized is the nation (Eid and Karim 2014). Such imagining is not a trivial or an innocent act, but selective and deeply encoded historically, culturally, and politically (Karim 2006). Michael Billig (1995) calls this "banal nationalism," referring to the small ways in which citizens are told of their national place. The reminders are so familiar, repetitive, and subtle that they are not consciously registered by citizens. Thus, the banality lies in these mundane representations, and not in the flag being waved during a national crisis. It is the flag hanging quietly outside a building and the historical figures on the banknotes, looking at you and reminding you of your national place. Nations are "not only constructions, but also continually in the making" (Hage 1996, p. 465). National identity comprises all these unconscious reminders that become a habit of the social life. These habits include those of thinking and communicating; through language, we convey nationalism when we talk about nationhood. A national identity is situated within a homeland, physically, legally, socially, and emotionally, which is, in turn, situated within a world of nations (Billig 1995).

Billig (1995) refers to Henri Tajfel to explain how the modernist world of the nation-state, psychologically speaking, resembles the state of mind in which differences between members of categories are minimized and differences between categories are exaggerated. The question is, therefore, not what national identity is, but what it means to have a national identity (Billig 1995). This includes ways of imagining "us, the nation" that are different from "them, the foreigners." The national category is theoretical, but it is also concrete. It is concrete in terms of juridical and social citizenship and in how these strategies manage people living in the community (Anderson 1983; Banton 1994). Nationalism as a political doctrine is the belief that people are divided into nations and that nations have the right to self-determination (Ignatieff 1994). The cultural idea of nationalism is that the nation provides them with a principal form of belonging, and the moral ideal is that nationalism justifies the use of violence to protect the nation against enemies, internal or external. Ignatieff (1994) distinguishes between civic and ethnic nationalisms. The former considers the nation as a community of equals regardless of colour, roots, gender, language, or ethnicity, while the latter asserts that individuals' attachments are inborn, not chosen. Ethnic nationalism may have a stronger hold than the former, but the realities that seem to follow do not match well with the ideas. Two Serbs may share the Serbian ethnic identity that unites them against Croats, but it does not hinder them from internal conflicts or different worldviews. Ignatieff explains that ethnicity does not in itself create social cohesion or a community, and when it fails to do so, which it cannot, it leads to unity by force and violence (Ignatieff 1994). This explains why ethnic nationalist states are more authoritarian than democratic societies. Killing in the name of the nation is legitimized by an appeal to blood and loyalty, a sacrifice that persuades people that it is better to die for the nation instead of appealing to their worst instincts regarding killing (Anderson 2006; Billig 1995; Ignatieff 1994).

The Imagined Community

The mass media, in particular, has played a key role in the formation of the nation-state as a coherent and natural entity (Anderson 2006). Benedict Anderson has described nations as imagined communities given that most people who believe they belong together will never meet and know each other. Other scholars (i.e. Morley 1992) have also underlined that the emergence of national identities cannot be properly understood without reference to the role of communication technology. Although homogeneous societies have rarely existed due to continuous episodes of migration, tools of modernity contributed to people a shared belief that they belonged together in the same homogeneous community based on their ethnic background. In the same nation, mass media encouraged individuals to freely participate in political projects, emphasizing national symbols, such as the portrayal of national leaders or the frequent retelling of national myths.

Scholars have examined how print in particular has emphasized national stereotypes, positive connotations and images of the nation, and reproduction of the national interest and boundaries prevailed in the press (Schlesinger 1991). Through the different symbols produced by the nation-state that foster a national unity, it is easy to fall into the pattern of drawing differences between oneself and other people. This essentialist-primordialist notion of culture and identities is embedded in the migrant debates, while historical allusions are present throughout. Sometimes it is unambiguously expressed, for example, in the discourse on the Islamic threats and fear of Muslims. Sometimes it is implied by words in subtle phrases, such as in the discussions about the London riots in 2011, mentioned in the previous chapter. The terminology connotes identity as deeply interwoven into what we expect from its performativities and acts, and how belongingness is viewed. The discussions around the London riots reveal how the imagined community still prevails within the frames of multiculturalism when some "authentic" citizens are viewed as belonging to the community while others are not.

Anderson has stressed how everyday rituals of newspaper reading and the imagining of other people doing the same thing created a concept of the nation. However, "An American will never meet, or even know the names of more than a handful of his fellow Americans. He has no idea what they are up to at any one time. But he has complete confidence in their steady, anonymous, simultaneous activity" (Anderson 1983, p. 31). This means that people are believed to share a strong sense of unity and common belonging based on nationality and ethnicity. An example to illustrate the meaning of television within the Kurdish context is the satellite television station Med TV. For Kurds, this transnational television channel, launched in 1995, had a significant effect on Kurdish national identity. Med TV, based in London and Belgium, demonstrated the crucial link between technology and a sense of belonging and shared culture; the television station has paved the way for activities promoting "Kurdishness." In the Middle Eastern context, Med TV has been talked about as one of the most interesting uses of DBS (Direct Broadcasting Satellites) technology, bringing news, documentaries, and entertainment to a population of 30 million Kurds living inside and outside the homeland to sustain itself against forceful suppression (Karim 1998).

Med TV was such a powerful national channel for the Kurds that it even threatened the Turkish state's single coherent sovereign presence in politically and culturally important ways. As Ankara used diplomatic power to prevent Kurdish education outside Turkish borders, in Denmark and elsewhere, Med TV was an imperative educational resource for millions of viewers on a daily basis. The logo "Med TV" had the colours of the Kurdish flag, and in the upper corner of the screen was a statement of Kurdishness and the right to independence (Hassanpour 2003). The Kurdish flag itself reappeared on the screen, and each day the channel's programming began with the Kurdish national anthem *Ey Reqîb* (O Enemy). The channel established relations with Kurdish viewers, not as audience members but as citizens of a Kurdish state, and thus employed a rather de-territorialized power. Its viewers could experience citizenship of a borderless state with its national anthem and flag through its national television and news agency. Med TV viewers considered the medium as the realization of one of their dreams, of independence: "Indeed, every day Med-TV raised the Kurdish flag in about two million homes. It was obvious that Turkey would treat each satellite dish as a Kurdish flag hoisted on the rooftops of every building in the south-east" (Hassanpour 2003, pp. 84–85).[1] Against this background, it is understandable that television generally, and Med TV in particular, has played a significant role for the notion of nationhood and Kurdishness for those Kurds residing outside their country of origin, resonating with Anderson's type of the imagined community (although there is no nation-state in this case).

Television has, thus, produced the community, which strongly influences thinking about identity, belonging, and attachment. Needless to say, Kurdish nationalism differs from state nationalism. Diaspora communities in this case are the result of a divergent nationalism; "state nation building is almost always connected to minority nation-destroying" (Kymlicka and Straehle 2000, p. 70). Nevertheless, television and its power to infuse national feeling also reflect Anderson's conception of the imagined community.

Europe and Its Other

While the EU qualifies as the most enlightened political formation in the post-colonial world, there has been an increase of fear of the Other, the exclusion of migrants, and a growing xenophobia. Arjun Appadurai (2006) explains that behind the idea of a modern nation is an integral and dangerous idea of "national ethnos," no matter how kind its political system and public voices are concerning multiculturalism and inclusion. This is why globalization is a Janus-faced process that benefits economies and has made capitalism technically more sophisticated and movable, simultaneously facilitating migrant flows and mobility. While global economic factors have had an impact, the state-led discourse is based on fear and insecurity. It is consequently this discourse that hinders an essential reform that aims at a greater inclusion (Sater 2013).

But why is it that minorities evoke so much fear? Why does the identity of others cause so much terror and uncertainty? Who belongs to the nation-state and on what ground is that determined? In his work *Fear of Small Numbers*, Appadurai argues that the idea of modern national sovereignty presumes some kind of "ethnic genius," and that ethnic violence is likely when the national majority views the ethnic minority as an obstacle to "a pure and untainted national ethnos" (p. 56). By removing the minority, the nation would be coherent. At the same time, minorities, in such cases, become the physical representation of the failed national project. "Minorities" are novel constructions and a geographical category that have gradually absorbed concerns about the nation, citizenship, and belonging. The first groups to be viewed as insufficient are those who normally become the target of marginalization or cleansing (e.g. migrants, the disabled, the aged, and the sick) (Appadurai 2006). This was the case in the Nazi Germany where these categories were subject to extermination attempts, with Jews as a prime example. But, neither minorities nor majorities come pre-formed; they are constructed within specific circumstances in national narratives (Appadurai 2006; Appiah 1994). They are also the result of memories of the violence that produced existing states. Appadurai states this well when he says that "Minorities, in a word, are metaphors and reminders of the betrayal national project," real or imagined (p. 43). The minority—the disabled, the religiously divergent, the migrant, the illegal, and the unwelcome—"blur the lines between 'us' and 'them,' here and there, in and out, healthy and unhealthy, loyal and disloyal, needed but unwelcome" (Appadurai 2006, p. 44). The double bind in the age of globalization is that the "minor" is both necessary and unwelcome. It is the Other that is in need of a defining Self (Said 1978), but it can never be "us" (we can exclude it, reject it, maintain it, deny it, or eliminate it) (Appadurai 2006).

In global events such as war or terrorist attacks, these categories are enhanced. Consider the terror attacks in Lebanon, Syria, and France that took place in late 2015. Paris received a global outpouring of sympathy; monuments around the world were lit up in the colours of the French flag, while political leaders gave speeches about "shared values." Waves of social media outrage soon appeared, which declared that "Arab lives matter less."[2] Morley and Robins (1995) have argued that "many of us in the West have only to sit on a couch and press a button to behold the exotic Other; the global news media have made us all into armchair anthropologists or ethnographers, nightly witnesses to the strange customs of Others" (p. 7). Meanwhile, Euro-identity gives little space to the large numbers of migrant and diasporic populations that now live in the continent. What does the idea of Europe add up to when so many within feel that they are excluded (Morley and Robins 1995)?

Culture becomes synonymous with borders (Blommaert and Verschueren 1998), and the culture gap widens, in an inconsistent way—the further away geographically, the more different they are. The differences become unbridgeable because they are thought to be innate. Cultural traits that widen this gap between cultures include differences in language, religion, dress, traditions, and so on. Blommaert and Verschueren (1998) explain this phenomenon in the following way: Mediterranean people (i.e. Spaniards, Italians, Greeks)—and, to a reduced extent, Eastern European immigrants—are less likely to encounter "cultural shock" and dissonance. Due to the growing flow of immigrants from Eastern Europe, their position has changed to their disadvantage in terms of attitudes towards the latter group. Still, they remain less different than, for instance, Afghans. Yet, in a comparison between Poles and Congolese (formerly Zaireans), such a conception can easily be questioned. Belgians had more interaction with Congolese than with Poles. Hence, following the aforementioned logic, Belgians should, in fact, be more affiliated with Congolese due to the country's historical background. Moreover, one of their official languages is French, and a significant portion of the population has converted to Christianity. So, why do Belgians look at Congolese culture as exotic despite their shared history, while categorically tie up with other groups that may differ in terms of language and history? Even further away from "our culture" are those North African communities that, alongside "Arab cultures," generate raw generalizations. Furthermore, their culture is frequently reduced to religion and its related traditions, despite the vast diversity of people coming from different countries, doctrines, and socio-economic contexts.

A tour around the world shows who everyone else is; you are what they are not (Hall 1997). To be English, for instance, is to know yourself in relation to the hot-blooded or traumatized people (Hall 1997). Identity is structured around representation producing a set of opposites

(Hall 1997). When identifications are made, they stem from history, economic relations, cultural discourses, as well as sexuality.

The binary of the Orient and the West has been an auxiliary in contrasting the "image, idea, personality and experience" that has identified the former as backward and the latter as enlightened and an advanced form of human civilization (Said 1978). Eid and Karim (2014) explain that it is the common tendency among humans to divide the world into the Self and the Other and that this opposition works as an organizing notion that shapes our discourse about relationships. This conceptualization can be made by people, but is also evident in institutions. Furthermore, the relationship between the Self and the Other is not necessarily essentialized, yet it also occurs in accordance with the ways it is imagined by the Self. While monolithic images of Muslims in the West portray them as violent and barbaric on the one hand, Muslim narratives about Westerners as immoral and driven by imperial power dominate on the other (Eid and Karim 2014). Thereby, human life is filled with tensions, and the same entities or people that are recognized as part of the Self can be considered as part of the Other in a different context. The circumstances of a specific discourse or a culture effectuate different views (Eid and Karim 2014). The dynamics and vigour of the minority are just as real as within the West–East binary, although they seem to lack the kind of implicit derogation of attributes of the Other that so sharply distinguished the orientalist discourse (Schein 1997). Looking at diaspora individuals, such intervention is facilitated as the changing identity produces, not one *other* against the nation, but multiple contrasting others (Schein 2000). What the diaspora does is to bring to the state a consciousness in which both the Self and the Other are situated "in an impossible quest for identity amidst the endless play of differences" (Day 2000, p. 225).

From a different perspective, some scholars have examined the orientalizing discourse *within* a group of people. Observing the framework of internal orientalism (Schein 1997), it can be helpful in taking into account how minorities themselves are active players in presenting and differentiating themselves among each other. Such shift, from the West–East dichotomy to *internal othering* can weaken the homogenization of people from the East.

In her work, *Gender and Internal Orientalism in China*, Louisa Schein (1997, 2000) coined the expression "internal orientalism," which is a modification of Said's original formulation. Said (1978) has outlined the discourse of European colonial relation with the East, especially Muslims, which were viewed as a declining civilization. Said has therefore described the "strength" of Western cultural discourse and how it represented the Muslim world (Schein 2000). Schein has argued that by accepting Said's Orientalism, one risks rendering the East mute and passive. Furthermore, the West–East dichotomy suggests that difference can only exist between these meta-categories of white and the Other, which enhances the homogenization of people from the East.

Instead, Schein (1997, 2000) describes the internal others within China, involved in a complex mimesis that echoed the European Self and the Oriental Other. She demonstrates a set of practices that take place within China, using the example of more cosmopolitan Chinese contrasting themselves with "exotic" minority cultures. The concept displays the relationship between imagining and cultural/political domination that takes place interethnically within China. In this process, she shows how the "orientalist" agent of dominant representation is used within a sector of the Chinese elite, which engages in a domestic othering. Schein (1997) also discusses the view of China as representing the West. An "internal other" (or others) positioned at the geographic/cognitive periphery of the Chinese state has represented the aim for a remedy of a Self, weakened and threatened at the centre by the alteration during previous decades of radical change. In what seems to be a contradiction, minorities were represented by way of contrast at the same time that their customs were (selectively) employed as elements of Chinese culture. The approach taken here is akin to that of other researchers, such as Ong (1993) on "petty orientalism," Pyke and Dang (2003), Abelmann (2009) on "intra-ethnic othering," and Eliassi (2013) on "internal otherization."

Defining Diaspora

The most powerful challenge to the imagined community comes from diaspora and transnational practices (Karim 2006). Diaspora confronts the coherence of a nation and people with its fluid character and brings along alternative ways to think about identity, belonging, and homeland. The notion of the national constructions and the national economy, possibly represented via a national cultural identity, is under pressure (Hall 1997). According to Hall, the weak arrangements are not bearable for much longer owing to different processes within the globalization development that concerns economy and capitalism, and also the local labour and other type of migration. These migration movements produce new types of identities as they develop commitment to multiple locations. Yet, like nations, academic research has overwhelmingly grown towards the idea of an "imagined diaspora" (see i.e. Fazal and Tsagarousianou 2002; de Santis 2003; Tsaliki 2003; Tsagarousianou 2004; Georgiou 2006). For example, Roza Tsagarousianou (2004) says that diaspora should not be considered as "given communities," but rather as "imagined communities," that continually reinvent themselves. The term is an extension of Anderson's concept, which proposes that people have created an imagined landscape where they produce myths and dreams of the homeland to which they belong and will one day return.

In a discussion of the Armenian diasporic experience, it is evident that diasporic relationships to the past refuse to remain in the past (Kazanjian and Nichanian 2003). Here, diasporic loss is constituted in relation to the future, which is defined by "a past event that is still to happen" (Kazanjian and Nichanian 2003, p. 128). This understanding of loss takes diaspora out of its relationship to physical territory and into that which is bound to the problem of history and memory. In thinking about diaspora and loss, it might be tempting to understand the substance of diasporic loss as being equivalent to the loss of homeland, and diaspora transnational links back to the homeland through new technologies not only confirms this but also facilitates reconnecting them. Diasporas became "long-distance nationalists" (Anderson 1992), because of their consistent involvement in homeland affairs (Sheffer 1986). Vertovec has also defined diaspora as "an imagined connection" between a post-migration people and a place of origin and with people of similar cultural origins in other places (2000, p. 12).

Old and New Diasporas

The term diaspora originally referred to scattered communities that were forcefully displaced from their native homeland through migration (Braziel and Mannur 2003; Brubaker 2005; Cohen 1996; Safran 1991). The concept initially encompassed particular groups of victims who were historically displaced, such as Jews and Armenians (Tölölyan 1996; Bauböck and Faist 2010). Many typologies have been developed seeking to define diasporic formations, and we find ourselves interfacing several strata of displacement that have been named "classical diaspora" (Sheffer 1986), "old and new diaspora" (Spivak et al. 1996; Mishra 2006), "victim" or "cultural diaspora" (Cohen 2001), as well as religious or other ethnic minorities in Europe (Bauböck and Faist 2010). These definitions can all be summed up in three characteristics as per Bauböck and Faist's description (2010). The first characteristic concerns the reasons of dispersal and movement. Old notions of diaspora suggest forced dispersal to be the root of diasporic formations, as in the Jewish or Armenian cases mentioned earlier, while newer notions refer to any kind of movement and migration, such as trade diaspora like that of Chinese, or labour as in the case of Turkish and Mexican migration (Cohen 1997, in Bauböck and Faist 2010). The second characteristic links the settlement country with the homeland. Older ideas of diaspora imply that there is a wish for a return to an imagined homeland, and projects that imply that there are such intentions (Safran 1991). More recent ideas speak of continuous linkages across borders such as in transnational practices, or, as Faist (2008) calls it, "migration-development nexus," which emphasizes lateral ties and the current structural transformation of politics, economics, and culture globally. The third characteristic relates to the integration of migrants and minorities into the countries of settlement. Previous views of diaspora indicate that the members are not fully integrated into the "host societies," politically, culturally, or economically, while contemporary views emphasize hybridity (Bhabha 1994). These characteristics overlapping old and new ideas of diaspora have all contributed useful and applicable insights, and from the perspective of the empirical dialogues and activities of this book, these trajectories appear to overlap.

However, one problem within diaspora studies concerns the background stories that have been overlooked. Cohen (2001) states that some scholars find it difficult to separate the compelling from the voluntary elements in the motivation to move. It is such intermingling that creates confusion, as people who are forced to move from the homeland due to catastrophes, war, and oppression are equated with people who move with a passport and do so safely by plane or in a train, all with the knowledge that there is a secure return. This is why the concept has lost a certain power (Tölölyan 1996) when it is not reserved for particular experiences but makes everyone diasporic, which, in turn, leaves no one distinctively so (Brubaker 2005). This is best illustrated by citing the case of Turkish-speaking diaspora. In their work on these diasporas, Asu Aksoy and Kevin Robins (2000, 2003) propose that transnational Turkish television has implications for the Turkish-speaking community and that there are many ways of being Turkish. They elaborate on how transnationalism is a process of de-mythologization of the homeland, and suggest a move away from longing and nostalgia to, instead, include the idea of a decreased sense of belonging through transnational media experiences.

While the critique by Robins and Aksoy concerning the blind spots of diaspora and the tendency to essentialize communities are valuable, we need to be cautious how we talk of diaspora. They have problematically gathered diverse communities and people into one "Turkish-speaking diaspora," consisting of Turks, Kurds, and Turkish-Cypriots (see also Hepp 2009; Christensen 2011a, b). Their emphasis on migration and movement from one country to another as an experience of separation does not offer an explanatory value and an interest in background experiences. James Clifford (1994), a key thinker on diasporas, has stressed that we need to think about what diaspora defines itself against, especially those who were pulled out of their homeland. While I will describe the violent relationship between Turkey and its Kurdish minority in the next chapter, it is enough here to say that oppressive policies against the Kurds go back 40 years. The Kurds in Turkey have had a difficult history marked by inequalities, linguicide, subordination, and violence, and have labelled Kurds as "Mountain Turks," in addition to the activities of other authoritarian states (Iraq, Iran, Syria). Kurds have, for decades, been engaged in nation-building and developing citizenship rights in all authoritarian states, where their mere existence has been subject to eradication. This is a legitimate argument to make when we see that Kurdish activists in diaspora have managed to tactically reshape the community's relationship with European nation-states, intergovernmental organizations, as well as non-governmental organizations. This has resulted in, for instance, a strengthened Kurdish community by way of claiming an identity distinct from that of Turkish immigrants (Eccarius-Kelly 2008). Clause Leggewie, a German political scientist, has addressed the work mobilization among Kurds, and in his article titled "Why Turks in Germany have become Kurds, not Germans" (1996), he stated that due to the denial of earlier identity politics in Turkey, Kurds in their new environment identified themselves as Kurds.

Theoretical questions are therefore at stake, not only regarding adequate methods to use for collecting and analysing empirical experiences, but also concerning the understanding of the reality status that a researcher ascribes to these experiences. Given how diaspora has emerged in relation to power, and in both turning to and turning away from power (Cho

2007), it is easier to understand criticism by Tölölyan (1996), Schnapper (1999), and Butler (2001) of how the term has been used. In the same way, Indo-Caribbean people have been included in the Indian diaspora group (Lynnebakke 2007). Gajjala and Gajjala (2008) have made a comment on this in their work on South Asian diaspora, particularly regarding how phrasings such as "Indian diasporas," "Pakistani diasporas," or "Bangladeshi diasporas" change the picture in ways that might not be productive in order to understand how people from these locations have travelled.

What I attempt here is to underline the danger in essentializing migrants by identifying them exclusively according to their diasporic status. Without any interest in their stories and in their socio-economic and political background, we run the risk of producing a counterproductive narrative, one that operates against their own stories. Conflating Kurds with the wider categories of "Turkish-speaking" or "Iraqi/Arab" migrants belittles the root cause of why Kurds left their states and became diasporas in different Western countries.[3]

As a point of departure, I locate the Kurdish diaspora within the context of *old diaspora* drawn from descriptions by Spivak et al. (1996) and Mishra (2007). Old diaspora is connected to histories of various forms of oppression that—as opposed to new transnational forms of diaspora—do not emerge out of the security of moving through the world with the knowledge of a return. The existential difference "forces us to face up to the scars and fractures, to the blisters and sores, to the psychic traumas of bodies on the move" (Mishra 2007, p. 212). Kurdish migration is understood as involuntary dispersal, both within the Middle East and beyond (Bruneau 2010; Chatty 2010). Having said that, even this argument faces challenges, as it implies that Kurdish diaspora is homogeneous. It is therefore not enough to merely identify displacement reasons; we also need to follow diasporic individuals' experiences, transnational practices, and their new relationship to the settlement country. The task here goes beyond describing the reasons why people become a diaspora, and also includes how their transnational practices impact their identity remaking and, in turn, their double consciousness.

Transnationalism and Double Consciousness

Although it has become commonplace to use diaspora and transnationalism interchangeably as they both refer to cross-border movements, there is a distinct difference between them. While diaspora refers to what was described earlier—national or religious groups living outside their homeland—transnationalism can be defined more narrowly; it refers to the links that different groups maintain across state borders, or by way of different conducts, be they networks, organizations, activities, or technologies (Bauböck and Faist 2010). Sometimes these activities are described as mirroring the globalization of capital, and in other instances they are viewed as grassroots reactions to this process (Glick Schiller et al. 1992; Smith 1999). Central to Glick Schiller et al.'s (1992) argument on transnationalism is that migrants and their networks comprise social relations that create processes of transnational change through a variety of activities and interactions across state borders. The migrants themselves are said to develop dual or multiple identities, and they are simultaneously involved in more than one society. Although earlier migrants also frequently took an active interest in their homeland (the word "transnationalism" was first used by Bourne in 1916 to refer to migrants who maintained ties to their home countries), the discourse on transnationalism suggests that contemporary immigration is, in some sense, different from earlier ones (Ang 2003). At least, in part, this difference between past and present is a reflection of the relative ease of travel today and a consequence of improved communication technologies (Glick Schiller et al. 1992). Moreover, there is an intensification of the social processes that comprise cultural intersection and mobility across space (Ong 1999).[4]

I am concerned here with the cultural potential that may be inherent in these transnational developments, and we need to be attentive to the possibilities that these new connections may be creating, in turn moving beyond identity and imagined community. Examining the spatialization of the nation through cultural "flows" between borders and the production of transnational "hybrid" subjects have proved to be an influential and exciting field that cross-cuts the social sciences and humanities. Studies in transnationalism have challenged the boundaries of the nation-state and the stability of its borders and criticized policy-oriented research aimed at better managing and assimilating migrant populations (Alonso and Oiarzabal 2010; Karim 2006; Ignacio 2005). What is worth noting here is that the evolving nature of technology, transport, and globalized movements across borders—whether voluntary or forced—appears to confirm that transnational activities have gone through different phases and transformed their character.

In order to avoid the "global babble" (Abu-Lughod 1991) and not viewing everyone as transnational, thus with no special significance for research, I identify specific set of experiences of diasporas that may differ from other types of engagements that transcend borders and state of mind. Firstly, the activities that fall within the framework of transnationalism are considered here as including, for example, engagement in election voting, consistent and organized practices, and regular and sustained social agreements over time across nations—and not only between the settlement country and the homeland, but also laterally between different countries where diasporas are settled.

Following on from Aihwa Ong's definition of transnationalism, I place an emphasis on the *intensification* of the social processes constituting "condition of cultural interconnectedness and mobility across space" (1999, p. 4). This allows us to not only view diaspora and migrants as national or ethnic projects, but also as new forms of shaping identity and practicing citizenship (Soysal 2001; Østergaard-Nielsen 2003a). Insights into the practices of transnationalism are theoretically interesting to understand how diasporic people reconnect with their homeland and reinvigorate their sense of national identity. However, and this is one of the major gaps in academic scholarship and public writing, it may more critically give us the opportunity to understand what we can add in terms of redefinitions, renegotiations, and awareness. What truly can contribute to an original phenomenon and a reasonable fresh topic of investigation are the intense exchanges, new platforms, and new ways of transacting relationships with different nation-states (Portes et al. 1999). Therefore, transnationalism is not only about directing activities towards the origin and maintaining ties, but also about what the diaspora brings back in terms of experiences and the lessons learn about multiple communities and attachments. Cross-border activities, including multiple communities, attachments, and histories, have spawned a *diaspora consciousness* (Clifford 1994; Safran 1991; Vertovec 1999). This state of mind is paradoxical in its nature, comprising both negative experiences of exclusion and discrimination on the one hand, and more positive affinities on the other (Vertovec 1999). Diaspora consciousness is considered to be a "source of resistance" through the engagement and visibility in the public sphere (Vertovec 1999). Therefore, the consciousness encapsulates a variety of experiences, a mind-set, and a sense of identity among diaspora with a paradoxical nature (Oonk 2007).

Gilroy (1993) talks about *double consciousness*, which he reinterprets from the writings of W.E.B. Du Bois. Gilroy uses the term to define the state of mind that was cultivated among African diaspora in a complex cultural and social intermingling between Africa, Europe, and America. Gilroy has explained that striving to be both European and black requires some specific forms of double consciousness, but that racist, nationalist, and ethnically absolutist discourses orchestrate relationships so that these identities live in their singularities and appear to be mutually exclusive. Here, the ideas of nation, nationality, national belonging, and nationalism are paramount (Gilroy 1993). In *There Ain't No Black in the Union Jack* (1987), Gilroy demonstrates how the diaspora culture of black immigrant communities in Britain expresses a certain set of local and global attachments. But, in order for there to be a form of consciousness, there also needs to be a sense of unity to some degree in Atlantic Africa's diasporic culture. It is a complex landscape that Gilroy paints, where self-consciousness is immersed in lateral relationships as opposed to the horizontal emotions that nationalism produces. Therefore, such a dual perspective can be in conflict with nationalist modes of thinking. Acknowledging that there is more than one language or more than one recipe for social interaction means that one can criticize those entities that speak in universalizing terms in relation to civilization or nations and families (Gunew 2004).

In his updated work, Gilroy (2005) questions the concept of double consciousness, and refers to Condoleezza Rice and her ilk, and says, "they don't seem to have been gifted with second sight or disabled by any inner doubleness" (p. 440). While Gilroy considers the idea of leaving the concept of double consciousness where it was found, in the nineteenth century, I am more intrigued to expand the concept in order to reinvigorate the transnational practices within the current framework of technological habits, and to emphasize the multiple consciousness of the twenty-first century. Gilroy mentions Du Bois' complicated life and that he repeatedly changed his ideological commitments and political tactics; towards the end of his days, he had a quarrel with the US government over some international and domestic issues that might have been, in Gilroy's view, a sign of abandoning the idea of double consciousness. Gilroy asks us to consider what the contemporary analogues of Du Bois' uncomfortable gestures may be. It is exactly these complicated and contradictory commitments that I find intriguing to explore further to consider the contemporary analogues.

SCRIPTS, PERFORMATIVITY, AND THE ONLINE SCENE

The intensified debates suggest that a significant change is taking place in recent decades and that it has contributed to a crisis of identity (Hall 1997). The crisis comes because something that is assumed to be coherent and stable is replaced by uncertainties (Mercer 1990). Looking back at the multiculturalism debates, it is clear that it is not the policies and methods that have been criticized, but, rather, it is diversity as an idea that has come under attack (Karim 2006) and, "if you attack my culture, you attack me, in a way that I cannot avoid and which goes to the heart of who I am" (Kelly 2002, p. 7).

It is obvious by now that identities do matter, socially, politically, and academically. It matters for Muslims, Americans, and certainly for Kurds. Identity gives people a compass to locate their place in the world and their surroundings; a link between individuals and collectivities in different ways (Woodward 2004). What may cause many conflicting issues is, however, that identity is regarded as rooted in kinship. Because identity is rooted in differences, it becomes a battle of inclusion and exclusion. It is in relation to difference that identities are constituted, and vice versa, difference is constituted in relation to identities (Campbell 1994; Morley and Robins 1995).

However, if the constructionist view is that identity is fluid and always in process (Hall 1992; Clifford 1997; Gilroy 1997; Woodward 2004), and we know that culture is part of the context in which identities develop, the critical question becomes how identity changes. The pressing question may, therefore, not be what identity is anymore, but rather how identity is redefined. What makes identities undergo changes, and what makes identities reject changes? These are questions that are important to answer in the context of multiculturalism and the policies that are created.

Identity as Scripts and Performativities

The most valuable way to consider identity is as a dialogical character. The sociological conception is that identity is shaped in the interactions between people and the society (Hall 1992). It is for such reasons that identity within post-modern discourse is conceived as having no fixed essence but becomes a "moveable feast" that is continuously transforming (Hall 1992). Hall continues to explain that if we think that we have a cohesive identity throughout life, it is merely because of the narratives that have been created about ourselves. I develop this with one example. "Where are you from? If you hear that question in a normal situation, it is common that you answer that you are a Kurd. The answer is obviously influenced by various factors. Factors such as that you belong to a minority in a multicultural society, you belong to an oppressed group, a group that has not received enough attention in relation to their size, etc. What happens if you ask yourself that question? Is the same response given? Do you see yourself primarily as a Kurd? Can you see yourself as only an individual without any categories?" These are questions that young diasporic Kurds have grappled with in their online communities. The framing of the questions, with pre-supposed accounts of the constitutions of Kurdish identity, indicates that certain acts and strategies are embedded in who is a "real" Kurd. But they are also embedded with the awareness of the contestations that may appear when the dynamics changes. To be a diasporic Kurd has connotations of complexities in terms of what one has to do (and per definition not do) to remain an "authentic" Kurd. Within the delicate Kurdish context, these questions are particularly remarkable as they downplay the cultural, national, and ethnic commonality that Kurds have been struggling with for decades. They have often led to fierce responses including insults, name calling, and flames. Although these kind of questions were embedded in many of the topics and discussions circulating online and offline, the responses varied greatly from essentialist claims to constructionist understandings. To look at the diasporic condition, we must, therefore, follow their dialogues.

From the expressions by the diasporic Kurd, we can see that "the large collective identities that call for recognition come with notions of how a proper person of a kind behaves" (Appiah 2005, p. 108). Collective identities come with what Appiah has coined, *scripts*. Scripts are socially created narratives and ideas about how people of a certain category ought to act (Appiah 2005). There are different ways of "behaving" as straight, a woman, Mexican, European, and so on, but the scripts and the notions they are allotted provide norms and models that play a role in shaping life. Collective identities provide scripts, which are narratives people use in creating their projects and telling their life stories (Appiah 2005). "I am a woman" or "I am homosexual" denotes a kind of pre-conceived understanding of how that person ought to act. Scripts, however, change over time. For instance, the Civil Rights Movements of the 1960s and 1970s helped to establish new and different ways of being black, gay, and female (Appiah 2005). Scripts of how to live life are therefore continuously in the making by individuals and collectivities, which in that sense can "write *against* culture" (Abu-Lughod 1991).

What one person demands may overstep the requirements of another. These tensions may arise between young men and women, generations, different locations, and so on, but they are all based on social and cultural expectations of performativities (Butler 1988, 1993, 1997). Therefore, problematizing these pre-written scripts is a performativity that diverges from them. The theory of performativity, outlined by Judith Butler, declares that identity is an outcome of performance, and not vice versa (Bell 1999).

If multiculturalism is open to new belongings between the nation and its migrants, it means that belonging is not ontologically given but is rather a construction and achievement on different levels. We have, however, witnessed that public speeches implied a more rigid nexus. The crux of the theory of performativity is the critique of the fixed nexus of identity and belonging. The construction, as well as the deconstruction, of belonging should involve a performative dimension (Bell 1999; Fortier 2000). Performativity refers to utterances by people. When individuals express their words, they also perform a certain act rather than merely describing things. The theory is based on the linguistic theories of J.L. Austin (1975) that suggest that people do things with words. The concept assists in understanding the operation of the very abstractions of self-perception that goes beyond the language you speak, the clothes you wear, and the car you drive, but it is also part of "the art of everyday life" (Gilroy 1997). Butler (1988, 1993, 1997) has extended this to demonstrate how gender identity is constructed and deconstructed through repetition of practices and discourses. Butler pointed out how femininity and masculinity are mutually (and also multiply) constructed, rather than being separated from each other. The importance of this statement is that there is de facto no origin or essence a priori the act, and gender is a construction that regularly conceals its genesis (1988). When Butler says gender identity is a performative act, she refers to the repeated regularity in the performativities that create certain social and cultural norms, which gain a form of authority. And although Butler used the theory of performativity on identity construction of gender, the concept has also been used in relation to national, ethnic, sexual, and other collective identities (see Boyarin and Boyarin 1993; Fortier 2000; Bell 1999; Kuntsman 2009). These are studies that represent some of the most inventive courses of thought in the field (Bell 1999). Bell (1999) puts it aptly when she says that the theory of performativity exposes a concern with theoretical and conceptual issues by challenging the "integrity of their theoretical analyses around specific questions or examples" (p. 10). The way in which relations between places and identities, and people and their bodies have been easily sought demands a scholarship that intervenes and confronts such processes (Bell 1999).

The aim here is not to replace identity or render it a futile term. Instead, the concept of performativity helps to more lucidly demonstrate the elasticity of the concept and how sensitive culture and identity are with their many fissures and are not determined by one or two social variables (Morrell 2008).

The act of performativity has a history, and this is where it accords with the concept of scripts as individuals are acting upon certain sanctions and prescriptions that are referred back to the history of collectivity. This is why it is crucial to look at how people are defined and who benefits from these definitions. Practically, this means that we need to go beyond mere activities and interpret what it is around those activities that are *acts* that give meaning to names and notions (Butler 1993). In doing so, it is useful to also look at the negation of acts, which, by definition, mean embracing other counter-acts. Fortier (2000) outlined how the effect of religious performativity worked to sustain community religious belief among the Italian diaspora. In the same way, Boyarin and Boyarin (1993) have discussed how Judaism is not constant with a given "essence," but is performed to a greater or lesser extent, depending on the context within which the Jewish individual finds herself/himself. As will be described in Chaps. 5, 6, and 7, I have analysed the speech-acts, not as banal words, but sprung from pre-scripted norms that are either successful in their enactments or a failure. It is in these moments I have identified the negotiations that young Kurds online make in their definitions of being a Kurd and where they belong. Although I have been interested in the online–offline nexus,[5] it is the online "stage" that I mainly draw from as it has made these everyday abstractions more visible.

If identity performs as a dialogue between people, it is the conversations that I want to capture in order to see how individuals reconstruct the understanding of themselves. Given that new technologies offer more opportunities for new ways of interactions, it is the online exchanges that constitute the focal point in this book, followed by face-to-face interviews. The possession of a rich language, with expressions not only in terms of words and sentences but also in terms of emotions, flames, and passion, in different online channels has been a valuable source for such purpose. I conflate expressions online with performativities, rather than performativities with identities.[6] In particular, the diasporic individuals' use of the Internet carries informative and important effects beyond technologies.

New Technology and the New Information Sphere

> For what is at stake in these technical innovations, I contend, is not simply an increased "efficiency" of interchange, enabling new avenues of investment, increased productivity at work and new domains of leisure and consumption, but a broad and extensive change in the culture, in the way identities are structured. (Poster 1995b, p. 41)

> [W]e stand by our approach and our conclusions: that although it was said, and continues to be said, that the internet was going to virtual single-handedly change the world, this has not been the case. (Curran et al. 2012, p. 181)

These two accounts of the Internet question whether it does, or does not, have an impact on society and people. While early research emphasized the Internet's endless opportunities, recent work has, instead, highlighted the limitations of the Internet and how predictions of its relentlessly changing possibilities were wrong (Curran et al. 2012, p. 179). In contrast to much literature, James Curran and his colleagues give a critical perspective of the digital technology. As the title of their book reveals, the power of the Internet has been misunderstood. There are many different theories about the Internet, and although in this book I emphasize its great possibilities, it is important to also place the technology in a wider context of globalization and other structural changes that play key roles in the transformations we see. New technology has collapsed space and time, and is fundamentally changing our comprehension of this world and incites new ways of self-interpretation (Jones 1999; Morley and Robins 1995; Rheingold 1993).

Until the 1990s, research on the Internet dealt mainly with the then new media as "cyberspace" and discussions focused on the binaries of online versus offline, virtual versus real, and synchronous versus asynchronous (Miller and Slater 2000; Slater 2002; Livingstone 2005; Verschueren 2005; Boellstorff 2008). The shift from Web 1.0 to 2.0 (O'Reilly 2005) has changed one-way, passive communication to active and participatory communication. With the fast development of the Internet and other technologies, different types of networks and platforms are generating new forms of social and cultural interactions. Within the World Wide Web, new and different technologies develop continuously, from more static chat communities to social networks and tailor-made communities with new audio-visual characteristics. You could say that technologies within the technology continues to develop, and users are said to have gained more control, and can create, express, and critique anytime in different ways, and this has created a myriad of options. Excluded communities and other vulnerable groups can enter this platform and increase their chances of being heard. Alonso and Oiarzabal (2010) offer interesting cases where people have used mobile devices in the effort to change regimes as in the Philippines, or change public opinion as in Spain in 2004, or to bypass government control over media censorship such as during the Green Revolution in Iran in June 2009. In the Middle East, digital technology and online activities have played an important role in the developments making people critically aware of how bad the situation was (Seib 2012). A tweet from a local citizen in Egypt can have a profound penetration and outreach that differ in character from the information given in the controlled TV sphere. Social media, such as Twitter, Facebook, LinkedIn, and other types of digital channels, have powered people mobilization (i.e. gender inequality, LGBT, ethnic oppression), providing existence to covered perspectives as well as presenting opportunities for new ties between people.

However, it is noteworthy that satellite TV has also had other important impacts. In the Middle East, satellite TV stations like Al Jazeera, Al Arabiya, and Abu Dhabi TV have been important sources of news coverage. While their information and communication sphere differ from that of the Internet, the channels have served as alternatives to, for example, BBC, CNN, and other Western sources for the Arab populations (Seib 2007). The challenges and the threat the new technology poses to some governments and political entities are mirrored in the crackdown and censorship of the media. These governments have long kept tight reins on both new and traditional media to avoid potential challenges and confrontations. Strict media control through monitoring and surveillance systems, shutdown of publications, websites, and social media, jailing journalists and bloggers, have all been part of their tactics (CFR[7]). Human

Rights Watch (HRW) has reported a number of nations, including Turkey, Iran, China, and Pakistan, for imposing Internet censorship.[8] In particular, Turkey has been in the media frequently for reaching "dangerous levels in limiting freedom of expression," according to CPJ (the Committee to Protect Journalists), and furthermore it declared that Turkey was the "world's worst jailer of journalists" in 2012 and 2013.[9] The images and expressions that circulate online do not always strike a chord with the national narratives of those governments. Therefore, while for many people, the digital technologies seem to have made life easier, other negative notions and limitations are also concomitant of the technologies, which merit its own discussion. Yet, it is enough to say here that it is questions of anonymity, trust, fear, integrity, and power that not only users are concerned about, but that this also concerns scholarship, governments, non-governmental organizations (NGOs), and other organizations.

The lack of access to computers, along with Internet connection and literacy, acts as a barrier to go online. Statistics show that 40% of the world population has an Internet connection today, according to Internet World Stats,[10] which means that the vast majority is "offline." The number is rising steadily however; between 1999 and 2013, the number has increased tenfold. Where inhabitants have access, the use of converging technologies has become quotidian experiences, and most people in the West are increasingly plugged-in on a daily basis. The exchanges take place anytime and anywhere, through text messages, e-mails, social media, video telephones, online communities, and all introduce new dimensions and forms of interactions. Phenomena like YouTube, Wi-Fi, the blogosphere, and convergences of different technologies and mobile telephones have made the online space an integral part of people's lives. The discrepancy between online and offline, which was made in the early phases of the Internet, remains a dead letter. It is clear that the online space does not exist in a void, independent of the offline environment, but is part and parcel of the everyday life and has a place in a wider field of communication flows connected with the private life and work.

Placing the new digital media against traditional media, the nature of communications, speed, and outreach counters earlier national media that was vital in the construction of the imagined national formation. This type of "info-sphere," including newspaper, radio, cinema, and television, has contributed strongly to these articulation of the romantic nationalist discourse (Alonso and Oiarzabal 2010). With the access to new devices such as satellite communications, the Internet, and mobile telephones, this sphere as changed considerably. Apart from following the vertical line such as television, radio, and newspaper, the communication now crossed into lateral lines by more active citizens, complicating the understanding and formation of identities.

Apart from the significant works of James Clifford (1994) shifting gaze from roots to routes and Stuart Hall's (1996) new ethnicities that have had important value for the direction of this book, studies that take a similar approach include Gajjala and Gajjala's (2008) compiling work on South Asian Technospaces (2008), in which they challenge categories such as homeland, diaspora, feminism, and post-colonialism. By weaving in post-colonial theory, media, and diaspora studies, Gajjala and Gajjala develop insights from different angles, arguing that diaspora dispersal and engagement in new cultures should not be understood as a singular process. Gajjala (2013) rightly suggests that the way in which categories of the "third-world" in connection to the Internet and online/offline are talked about needs to be more nuanced than before.

In Alonso and Oiarzabel's edited volume *Diaspora in the New Media Age* (2010), their introduction emphasizes a key point that resonates with the viewpoint here, which is how diaspora individuals bring with them their senses of identity and community before entering the online space, which leads to either reinforcing their prior notions or changing them. Everyone online becomes an "immigrant" because the Internet does not belong to any nation or people (Alonso and Oiarzabel 2010). This brings me to how I define the Internet and online space, metaphorically, as an online scene. Viewed this way, the nexus resembles a theatrical play—the scripts, performativities, and the online scene.

The Online Scene

Internet and its space have been discussed and conceptualized in many different ways, with some scholars propounding the positive, sometimes revolutionary aspects of it (Poster 1995a), while others argue against any exaggerations of the new media (Curran et al. 2012). Perhaps, most of all, the Internet has been celebrated for its distance and time-shrinking features.

However, new technology ought to be seen as more than a tool to communicate with, it being such an integral part of individuals' lives (Poster 1995a). Tim Berners-Lee, founder of the World Wide Web, has described the web as "more a social creation than a technical one" (1999, p. 133). Sherry Turkle, who has studied human–technology interaction for years, stated early on that the Internet is changing the way we think and the very foundation of community, sexuality, and identity. The confrontations online with technology are a confrontation with the sense of human identity, she explains (1995). Although Turkle's later works are less affirmative about the impact technology has on people, in particular, teenagers, the important point here is how the online space is contributing to the growth of post-modern thinking. Identity becomes de-centred that moves away from singular narratives.

The most compelling idea on how to view the online community for this book, I draw from Mishra's view of a theatre scene:

> The scene is where all kinds of statements enter into some form of sociality and it is this sociality—understood as the participatory relationship between diverse actors (statements)—that generates the scene. A scene is not a territory, which suggests enclosures, limits and borders. It is a simulated locus generated by the act of performative *participation* and not by any claims to membership. A scene is *staged* when there is a society of two or more statements acting out a scene. (Mishra 2006, p. 7)

In this way, the online scene, or stage, is free from national, gender, or ethnic borders, and anyone with a computer and Internet connection can enter and travel across borders. The online sphere enables opportunities and de-territorialization of "home" (Gajjala 2002, p. 179), not only for diasporas or a particular group, but for everyone who enters the stage. The point here is not that we need to foist academic vocabulary with new terms and labels, but rather the main point is how to envision the contrasting notions between traditional media (television, radio, newspaper) and new media.

Those who inhabit the social stage are part of the interplay of online communities and networks in different ways, and regardless of where they live, they become global audiences and located producers (Gajjala 2013). The "first world" and "third world" binary becomes less visible and the offline terminology of "minority" and "majority" has less significance. This is not to say that they have disappeared, as the majority of the online inhabitants are located in the Western parts of the world, but the technology power, literacy, hyper-invisibility and visibility, and conversations across and within ethnicities inform of changed practice, agency, and representation. Far from dissipating nationalism or essentialism, there is an erasure of differences as well as similarities, however. A strategically homogeneous and "pure" identity is not as visible as in the offline environment, or as dominantly conveyed through the traditional media.

The characters on the online stage differ in many ways from Anderson's description of the traditional media in which governance is trying to organize citizens in accordance with ethnicities and nationalities in the effort to accentuate such identities. Hence, the information sphere has changed for the past three decades that has a great impact on the formation of national and cultural identities and the notion of belonging. It is of utmost significance that the online stage has invited an array of cultural and social personalities across boundaries of ethnicity, religion, class, age, education, and, perhaps to a lesser degree, gender (see Alonso and Oiarzabal 2010).

NOTES

1. It should be noted that new forms of violence emerged against Med TV; that is, Turkey insisted that Britain and other EU countries take action against the channel and revoke its broadcasting licences, arguing that it threatened Turkey's territorial integrity and that the channel was propagating PKK-led (Kurdish Workers Party) terrorism. However, this attempt failed, as there was no evidence of PKK connection to the TV channel (Hassanpour 2003). This is again a clear demarcation of diasporic experiences when Kurdish and Turkish populations in, for example, Germany, have had many public disputes which concern the very question of ethnic identity and the sense of belongingness. These satellite transnational channels have been significant in enabling individuals and communities to remain in contact. Telephony, the Internet, and satellite television have helped to create a web of connections among ethnic diasporas living in different parts of the world.

2. The New York Times, "Beirut, Also the Site of Deadly Attacks, Feels Forgotten," November 15, 2015.

3. Other issues related to this concerns questions that Dawn Chatty has raised; why some people move during times of war and extreme political coercion and others remain in situ, go underground, or face political imprisonment, torture, or even death (Chatty 2010). In a similar vein, Sara Ahmed (1999) highlights the social conditions that make some movements possible and others impossible. Ahmed cautions regarding the differences evident in definitions of choice and force. As she states, while refugees are considered to have moved forcefully due to extreme persecution and that other migrants make free choices means to assume force only operates in this way. What needs to be highlighted here are the constraints on choice not just imposed on the body from the outside, but are consti-

tutive of subjects in the first place. Given such differentiations, it is also important to take into account how the everyday life among those who have left and those who have remained can impact on notions of identity, nationalism, and citizenship, and further highlight how technology is used in that context.

4. Ong (1999) distinguishes between transnationality and transnationalism; transnationality is used as the "trans" denotes both moving through spaces and across as well as changing the nature of something.

5. In earlier research, I have argued that online interaction and community cannot be divorced from offline social and political contexts (Mahmod 2011).

6. The difference between the statements "the ball is red" and "give me the ball" is evident in the action taking place in the second statement (Mahmod 2005, p. 33). The announcement of attending a Kurdish event, concert, or demonstration, or statements about marriage within the ethnic group can be included in the performativities of ethnic belonging infusing Kurdishness, or vice versa. A performative act is, therefore, to some extent, influenced by its successful achievement (i.e. Habermas includes this aspect in his *Theory of Communicative Action* [1984]). It is not the intention here to police participants in either the online or offline environment, but rather I aim to discover how these are articulated and redefined in interactions online, as well as at the crossroads of the online and offline. The information environment expresses new trends as paywalls and international call charges are removed in a time of crisis.

7. Council of Foreign Relations, http://www.cfr.org/about, accessed September 15, 2015.

8. HRW, "Human Rights Watch Submission: World Development Report on Internet for Development," August 25, 2015.

9. CPJ, "Second worst year on record for jailed journalists," December 18, 2013.

10. Internet Live Stats, accessed November 10, 2015.

CHAPTER 4

State Struggles in the Middle East and the Kurdish Diaspora

Introduction

This chapter briefly explores the development of the relationship between the authoritarian states and Kurdish ethnic and cultural identity, which has produced strong narratives of wounds in the construction of an identity and of belonging among Kurds living outside Kurdistan (Curtis 2005). The political identity of the Kurdish diaspora is embedded in historical and contemporary Kurdish challenges to the national authority in the surrounding Middle Eastern countries of Kurdistan. Kurds, who are the largest stateless nation in the world, are politically divided between four states in the Middle East, namely, Turkey, Iraq, Syria, and Iran, and are scattered around the world, with a growing diaspora in the West. For a thorough account of the history and politics in the different regions of Kurdistan, see, among others, works by Amir Hassanpour (1992, 1994), David McDowall (2004), and Mahmod Mola Ezat (1992, 1995, 1997, 2000).

The crackdown on Kurds and their demands for ethnic rights, recognition, and independence has been one of the bloodiest sources of ethnic conflict in the Modern Middle East. The Kurds belong to the Sunni Muslim, Indo-European-speaking people, and therefore linguistically distinct from both Turkish and Arabic, but related to Farsi. Based on religion, two-thirds of the Kurdish population is Sunni Muslims, with the remaining one-third consisting of Alevi and Yezidi religious minorities,

© The Author(s) 2016   65
J. Mahmod, *Kurdish Diaspora Online*, The Palgrave
Macmillan Series in International Political Communication,
DOI 10.1057/978-1-137-51347-2_4

and a smaller number of Christians and Jews. This implies that Kurds are religiously different from their neighbours; compared to the neighbouring states, Kurds are more secular as religion takes a backseat.

No accurate figure for the Kurdish population exists, but moderate estimations are that there are approximately 30 million Kurds in their "transnational Kurdistan" (Anderson and Anderson 2014; Council of Foreign Relations 2014), 15 million in Turkey (18–23% of the population), 6.5 million in Iran (11%), 3.5–4 million in Iraq (17–20%), and 1 million in Syria (9%) (Gunter 2009; see also Ammann 2005 for similar figures). There are also smaller Kurdish groups settled in Georgia, Azerbaijan, Kyrgyzstan, Israel, Armenia, Russia, and Lebanon. The figures vary considerably in the literature that exists; hence, the actual size of the Kurdish population has remained an "enigma" due to the lack of accurate and systematic empirical research (Ayata 2011).

The Kurdish political outlook is different in all regions of Kurdistan, and these differences have grown in recent years due to the political agenda of the authoritarian states. One could say that Kurdistan, divided between four countries, is a multicultural and transnational region, with intra-Kurdish differentiations including religious, tribal, social class, gender, and political and ideological differences, as well as different political–institutional experiences of national identity and citizenship in Iraq, Iran, Turkey, Syria, and among the European Kurds. It is an exceptionally difficult task to gain a clear idea of the relationship between Kurds and the authoritarian states and the developments within, without taking into account the global and political factors that have had a decisive impact on the processes in each region. Therefore, although the range of questions concerning the "Kurdish question" centers around issues of citizenship rights and identity recognition in all the Kurdish regions, the differences in developments are explained not only by the endogenous politics of the Kurds, but also by the international approach to each of these regions. The asymmetrical nature of nation-state-building processes and national-identity formations is a part of this complexity (Natali 2005).

In the following section, I will briefly describe some of the key issues in the authoritarian states, which, to different degrees, have caused the Kurdish migration to several European countries and beyond. Because the conversations and topics in the empirical material gathered between 2010 and 2011 speak mainly of the events in Iraq and Turkey, the pending discussion will pay more attention to these two countries.

From Turkey's Kemalism to Chemical Ali in Iraq

While Turkey has in many respects been viewed as the more democratic of the authoritarian states in which Kurds live, it has suppressed Kurds the most (Romano 2002). When Turkish nation building started in 1920, it adapted the Kemalist notion of Turkish secularism and modernization; "Turkey did not rise phoenix-like out of the ashes of the Ottoman Empire. It was 'made' in the image of the Kemalist elite which won the national struggle against foreign invaders and the old regime" (Ahmad 1993, ix). Since then, the country's politics has cultivated a complete denial of Kurds (Vali 2006). As part of the Turkification process driven by the new Turkish nation-state, the Kurdish language, schools, publications, and associations were banned a few years later. As compared with Kurds in Iraq, Kurds in Turkey did not have the same possibility to express their "Kurdayeti" (Kurdishness/ethnic identity) and to a greater extent had to deny its existence (Natali 2005). Kurds were forced to become Turks and suppress their Kurdish identity while simultaneously admitting to the pride and happiness over their "Turkish identity" (Zeydanlioglu 2008; Natali 2005). In schools they had to repeat, "I am a Turk, I am honest, I am hard working" (Natali 2005). The mechanism chosen to deliver the diversity ideal that accompanied the Ottoman Empire was homogenization of its citizens (Alinia 2004; Vali 2006). Turkish politics has since then been accused of both ethnocide and linguicide due to its assimilation and oppression practices (Hassanpour 1994). When assimilation tactics did not work, Kurdish men, women, and children were sent to prison. Layla Zana, a Kurdish human rights advocate and the first Kurdish woman to take a seat in the Turkish parliament, was, for instance, sentenced to 15 years in prison for speaking Kurdish in the parliament in 1994. Despite such extreme repercussions, Kurds have maintained a strong resistance against the Turkish authorities, but many have also assimilated and have more or less replaced their Kurdish identity with that of Turkish.

Since the 1980s, Turkish politics has been increasingly coloured by the tension between the universal and the particular, and among those tensions the "Kurdish question" has been considered the most politically taxing and challenging one (Yildiz 2005). The strongest resistance against the Turkish state has been the Kurdistan's Workers Party (PKK) established in the beginning of the 1980s, which earlier demanded independence and, later, autonomy and cultural rights (Khayati 2008). Scholars (i.e. Bozarslan 2014, in Baser 2015) state that the violence and other means employed by PKK gained support because of the authoritarian state's persecution and the limited possibility of pursuing an opposition party through legal means. Bahar Baser (2015) observes in her research that many of the detained Kurds in Diyarbakir became PKK supporters, and sought asylum in Europe or remained in Turkey to continue their activities. Among her interviewees were many Kurdish activists who were held in prison during the 1980s and the beginning of the 1990s. Baser further argues that many of the migrants became internally displaced before applying for asylum in Europe.

Consequently, many of the Kurds who arrived in Europe as asylum seekers, in particular in Germany, pursued activities that were affected by their brutal experiences in the homeland. Germany has therefore become an important platform for Kurds to maintain the struggle for Kurdish rights. The Turkish authorities expected, perhaps, because of Germany's ungenerous citizenship policy, that the Kurdish migrants would be assimilated and gradually the "Kurdish question" would disappear (van Bruinessen 1999). One could argue that Turkey and Germany, apart from the history of immigration that connects them, also have in common the distinction of being the most unlikely models for a peaceful and unified Europe (Hsu 2010). Both have histories coloured by imperial expansionist campaigns and violence. However, the Kurdish diaspora was intensely engaged in transnational activities that had a significant impact on three fields: the linguistic development, media technology, and political organizations. Martin van Bruinessen (2000), an anthropologist who has worked on the Kurdish question, has asserted that the maintenance of the mother tongue by Kurdish diaspora has been an important factor in sustaining Kurdish culture, as Turkey outlawed the scholarly education of the Kurdish language and other cultural expressions. The recovery of a Kurdish consciousness has therefore, to a great extent, taken place in the diaspora as, for example, Newroz (the New Year) and other traditions had been banned for years in Turkey. Information and communication technologies, both the Internet and satellite TV, have been important tools in the articulation of Kurdish cultural and political identity. Med TV broadcasting by diasporic Kurds, as mentioned earlier, has played a significant role not only for Kurds from Turkey but also for Kurds from the other regions. One example cited to display the effectiveness of migrants' transnational networks among Kurdish political mobilization in Europe is when the PKK leader Abdullah Ocalan was captured in Kenya in 1999. Within hours of the incident, protests around the world took place, well organized via TV channels, telephones, and faxes (Fawcett 2001). Embassies were occupied throughout Europe, and in particular Germany, where protests took place in each city (Østergaard-Nielsen 2003b).

In Turkey, the Kurdish question has meant a burgeoning ethnic assertiveness in the form of identity politics, which demands the recognition of difference. In recent years, the Kurds have changed their approach and politics, going from an aim to establish Kurdish autonomy to demanding citizenship rights and recognition. The outcome of the 2007 parliamentary election was a significant moment for Kurds when they reached the 10% hurdle, which provided the opportunity to promote the Kurdish interest. At the same time, Turkey and its modernity have undergone crises and transformation. From 2002, and until the point when Turkey addressed the Kurdish question as a security problem and therefore attempted to approach it militarily, Turkey changed its Kurdish agenda more in line with what was required for EU membership. Nonetheless, it soon became clear that the laws that would allow cultural rights for the Kurds (such as language teaching and broadcasting) did not meet expectations, and, furthermore, were "modest by world standards" (Somer 2005). There were a number of incidents that countered the promises made by Turkish governments, including the jailing of Kurdish children for participating in demonstrations (Cicek 2011) and of Kurdish politicians who were accused of links with PKK affiliates. In 2006, the European Parliament and a number of human rights organizations criticized the Turkish government for its inadequate process of questions of freedom of expression, minority rights, corruption, and violence against women (Eccarius-Kelly 2008). The criticism was enhanced during the 2015 elections in the country when the Turkish public television was considered to be partisan, allocating limited media space to the opposition parties. It is, perhaps, after the Gezi events that Turkey heightened its restrictions on freedom of speech. During the Gezi protests in May 2013 that started in Istanbul's Taksim Square, the Turkish police attacked peaceful protesters, which, in turn, led to even more reactions. Thousands of people took to the streets to protest against the government's increasingly severe attitude (Baser 2015).

The most recent events in Turkey have displayed how the Kurdish question is not solely limited to the Turkish realm of politics, but has become a "European" or even a transnational debate (Baser 2015), with links to its neighbouring countries in the Middle East (van Bruinessen 1999). During the General Election, in June 2015 and then later during the re-election in November 2015, the Justice and Development Party (AKP) and President Recep Tayyip Erdogan were accused of censoring the media and limiting the opposing parties' presence in the media. Under the banner "New Turkey," Erdogan provoked sizeable tensions inside and outside the country. In the government's election campaign, requests from Turkey to block Twitter were more than from any other country, besides Iran and China.[1] In the direct aftermath of the rise of the Islamic State (IS) and their redrawing of the borders between Turkey, Iraq, and Syria, Turkey has attracted global attention and much criticism from governmental and non-governmental sources for its crackdown on its ethnic minorities, journalists, and media (Human Rights Watch 2014).[2]

The People's Democratic Party (HDP), established in 2012 and which largely represents Kurds, successfully gained 13.2% of the votes and became the third largest party in the Turkish parliament in the election of June 2015, thus denying Erdogan's party, AKP, its majority. Erdogan suffered the biggest setback in 13 years; "This is the end of identity politics in Turkey," scholars at Bilgi University in Istanbul stated, meaning that the threshold barrier the HDP overcame symbolically meant that identity barriers had been breached.[3] Analysts stated that the election produced what is equivalent to a cultural revolution in the Turkish political sphere. This would give access to female and LGBT (lesbian, gay, bisexual and transgender) candidates, and the long-oppressed Kurdish minority would be represented in the parliament. However, shortly after the results, Erdogan pressed for new election after the country's Prime Minister, Davutoglu, allegedly failed to form a coalition; it was argued that Erdogan did not want a coalition government and intended to win back the majority in the new election. Amid renewed fighting between Kurds and Turkish authorities, hundreds of people were killed in two major suicide bombings at pro-Kurdish gatherings, carried out by the Islamic State. The Turkish police used tear gas against crowds protesting against the terrorist group. Turkey found itself facing the worst violence in years. HDP was accused of having ties with the PKK, and as a successor party to numerous banned forerunners with the first party established in 1990, this was not the first time. This can explain one of the barriers facing the Kurdish struggle for recognition; the Turkish government consistently portrays Kurdish affiliations as a threat against the nation (Bozarslan 2000, in Eliassi 2013).

As a major neighbour to Iraq, Turkey has been rather pre-occupied with preventing Iraqi-Kurds' statehood, with the United States attempting to balance between the growing conflicts (Somer 2005) in the wake of the most recent events in Syria and a battlefield that contains a number of different factions such as the Kurdish Peshmerga from Iraqi Kurdistan,

People's Protection Units (YPG, Kurdish force in Syria), and the US-led coalition. Therefore, Turkey's primary interest lies in Iraq's political and economic stability (Somer 2005). This means that Turkey does not support an ethnic federation in Iraq, which has been a persistent question since the removal of Saddam Hussein in 2003.

In Iraq, Saddam Hussein devoted considerable efforts and power in trying to create a distinct identity for Iraq that would mould the three major communities—Shia Muslims, Sunni Muslims, and the Kurds—into one polity. His success was not complete, but the notion of a national identity was present. During the 35 years of Ba'ath Party rule in Saddam's Iraq, Kurds and the Kurdish Peshmerga fighters faced increasing suppression for most of these years preceding the US-led removal of Iraq from Kuwait in 1991.

One of the most notable events in the recent history of the Kurds is the Anfal campaign.[4] The cousin of Saddam Hussein, Ali Hassan al-Majid, also called "Chemical Ali," was in charge of the Anfal campaigns and the genocide of the Kurds, and was later convicted and sentenced to death in 2007. According to an audiotape of a meeting of Iraqi officials that took place in 1988, and which was subsequently published by Human Rights Watch (HRW), al-Majid vowed to employ chemical weapons against the Kurds, saying, "I will kill them with chemical weapons! Who is going to say anything? The international community? Fuck them!—The international community and those who listen to them ... I will not attack them with chemicals just one day, but I will continue to attack them with chemicals for fifteen days" (Hardi 2011, p. 107). This was a systematic genocide operation conducted between 1986 and 1989 in which thousands of Kurdish men, women, and children were gassed and executed. The attacks were part of an ongoing campaign and, although statistics vary and may be disputed, it is estimated that approximately 4000 of the 5000 Kurdish villages in northern Iraq were destroyed, and that between 150,000–200,000 civilians were killed (McDowall 2004).[5] The campaign displaced at least one million of the Kurdish population. The peak of the campaign (although not initially part of the operation) was the genocide in Halabja in March 1988, with 5000 civilians killed and another 10,000 injured. Christopher Hitchens said of this crime that it "was for the Kurds what the Warsaw ghetto is to the Jews, or Guernica to the Basques, or Wounded Knee to the Sioux" (Hardi 2011, p. 109). Despite the scale of operation, the systematic genocide and attacks received little media attention. The campaign was overshadowed by the Iran–Iraq war, and by the dramatic events that followed in the wake of the 2003 invasion of Iraq. But one also has to consider the role of new media that plays a significant part in this kind of national crisis. During the Anfal campaign, the Internet did not exist in the shape it does today, and the kind of activities we see online nowadays in relation to the political crises concerning, for example, the Middle East, the Islamic State, and Kurdistan were not evident.

The US-led control of Iraq following the invasion of Kuwait paved the way for substantial Kurdish autonomy.[6] Since 2003, the Kurdish Regional Government (KRG), then consisting of two main political parties—the Kurdistan Democratic Party (KDP) of Massoud Barzani and the Patriotic Union of Kurdistan (PUK) led then by Jalal Talabani—increased its political stability and focused on investments and construction, facilitated by the secular character of Kurds lacking in the rest of the country. However, Baghdad–Erbil relations remained tensed throughout the post-Saddam era, particularly concerning political and economic agreements. One of the most problematic issues have been Article 58 of Iraq, which is adamantly opposed to holding a referendum on the future status of Kirkuk (Anderson and Anderson 2014), an oil-rich city simultaneously claimed by Kurds, Arabs, and Turkmen. Therefore, having suffered greatly under a centralized Ba'ath-dominated government, the Kurds had a special interest in breaking away from the historical pattern of tragedies. The Kurdish region has managed to invest financial and political means to rebuild the society, but Kurdish leaders have been challenged on different occasions for not being able to focus on long-term goals, and internal problems re-emerged as many Kurds became increasingly dissatisfied due to widespread corruption and nepotism. Despite this, the Kurdish region in Iraq has been undergoing an economic boom and has enjoyed full autonomy. Having such a unique position in comparison to the other Kurdish regions, it has gradually demonstrated more potential for democracy in the Middle East, while also attracting foreign investment, labour migrants, as well as tourists.

This changed dramatically on June 10, 2014, and the dynamics and power balance cracked when Mosul, Iraq's second largest city, fell into the hands of the Islamic State (formerly known as "ISIS" or the Arabic acronym "Daesh"), followed by the establishment a self-proclaimed caliphate by Abu Bakr al-Baghdadi. Within one year, the terrorist organization managed to change the geographic borders established by the colonial powers in the Sykes–Picot agreement in the early twentieth century. The group has since then consistently increased their operations by invading

Sunni- and Kurdish-dominated parts of Iraq and Syria at surprisingly high speed. In particular, the fight against IS has been conducted by Kurds on the ground. The Sunni group also demonstrated skilful use of social media in pursuing marketing of its brutal methods and acts against civilians and hostages, aiming at recruiting and shocking its antagonists in the region and beyond (Cockburn 2014). The rise of IS has changed the political agenda in a profound way, and the consequences are being felt and followed across the countries in the Middle East, as well as in Western countries through terror attacks and the subsequent refugee influx to some degree.

The organization has also claimed responsibility for attacks in Algeria, Egypt, Tunisia, and Nigeria where Boko Haram declared an alliance with the IS. In particular, areas with diverse populations have developed into battlegrounds. In Baquba and the Diyala province, both Sunni and Shia have fled the violence. The main targets of the IS atrocities have been Shias, Kurds, and Christians. Patrick Cockburn (2014), a veteran correspondent in the Middle East, has argued that the revolt marks the end of a distinct period in Iraqi history initiated by the overthrow of Saddam Hussein by the US- and British-led invasion of March 2003.

A Line in the Sand

The Sykes–Picot agreement in 1916 between Great Britain and France marked the end of the Ottoman Empire, and a division of Kurdistan between the four states (Barr 2012). Decades of conflict between Kurds and the authorities in Iraq, Iran, Turkey, Syria can be traced back to this era, including the civil wars in Syria and Iraq and the Israeli–Palestinian conflict. Arab states, excluding Egypt, are new creations, which is worth noting in the analysis of the current situation in the Middle East. In the media and debates, we often hear about the Sunni–Shia divide, but we also need to take into account the arbitrary borders that divided nationalities by colonial powers. "A line in the sand" was drawn from A (Acre in Palestine) to K (Kirkuk, in Kurdistan region) (Barr 2012). The region north of this line, including both Syria and Lebanon, was given to France; the region south of the line, incorporating the provinces of Basra, Baghdad, Transjordan, and Palestine, was taken by Great Britain. The secret agreement had its critics: perhaps, most famously, T.E. Lawrence ("Lawrence of Arabia"), who understood the regional religious and national differences. Both Britain and France, and their Arab allies, were fully unaware of the content of both the Treaty of Sèvres (1920) and the Treaty of Lausanne (1923). Apart from failing to reach independence, colonial intervention continued in the 1920s until the 1940s, fuelling nationalist conflicts in North Africa, Syria, and Iraq. This history is important to note because it helps to understand the complex situation with the regional, civil, and sectarian strife ongoing throughout the Middle East. It also shows the haphazard borders created in the region completely ignored the traditional ethnic and religious groups, and the divisions imagined among the different groups.

Although the Kurds still have a vision of an independent state, many of the other objectives have been put aside. This is not merely because of the opposition of countries such as Syria, Iran, and Turkey on which Kurds in Iraq are economically dependent, but also because given the security threats that prevail since IS establishment, the weaknesses of the Kurdish region have been revealed. These, alongside other issues such as economic challenges and the fear of being betrayed again by non-regional powers, have hindered the achievement of such goals. Simultaneously, the shift in geographic borders and politics, however, as opposed to de facto autonomy, may also encourage Kurds in Syria to demand sovereignty and independence, which the Turkish authorities vigorously oppose. Turkey, with more than 20% Kurds, imagines that the establishment of an independent Kurdish state on the Iraqi and Syrian side of the border would have a sweeping effect on their own Kurdish population. Despite this, the Kurdish leadership in Iraq has reached a modus vivendi with the Turkish government, and perhaps, there will be a similar development in Syria with the Kurds there.

KURDS OF SYRIA AND IRAN

Syria has the smallest Kurdish population among the four states, two million, but the Kurds are the largest ethnic minority in the country; discrimination against the Kurds has been ongoing since 1950s (Chatty 2010; Lowe 2006). The governmental discrimination against the Kurds started partly in response to the instability in the neighbouring countries, Iraq and Turkey. This was worsened when Syria joined Egypt to form the United Arab Republic. Kurds have been subject to assimilationist structural policies and Arabization while also stripped off their citizenship rights. However, Christian villages also went through this Arabization process (Tejel 2009). This was part of the incorporation of the "other." To the Kurdish "heroes" in Syria, Saladin Ayyubi has become a national symbol, although he has not made any public claims concerning his Kurdish ethnic identity (Tejel 2009). Saladin was a well-known Kurd, who retook Jerusalem from the Crusaders and used military means to establish an Islamic kingdom, rather than a Kurdish one (Romano 2006).

During the 50 years since the discrimination was enhanced, there has not been much organized Kurdish resistance to ending intolerant policies in Syria, but a significant number of Kurds in Syria have fought in the Kurdish uprisings in Iraq and Turkey (Chatty 2010). This status quo in Syria changed in 2003, with the Anglo-American invasion in Iraq and Kurdish gains in the territory bordering Syria. The ethnic strife was the worst seen in Syria in decades. Dawn Chatty (2010) explains that it was evident that the Syrian Kurdish community experienced a political awakening when the Syrian government decided to end its support to Abdullah Ocalan and the PKK after pressure from Turkey (Savelsberg 2014). This was followed by 10,000 troops crossing the Syrian border to force the PKK leader to be handed over (Chatty 2010; McDowall 2004).

A little Syrian "spring" emerged when a liberal tone prevailed, powered by America for a push towards democracy and human rights (Chatty 2010). Political organizations became more openly active, Kurdish books and music were distributed, and private Kurdish language classes proliferated (Chatty 2010; Tejel 2009). Bashar al-Assad, who had become the new president in 2002, visited the Kurdish province of Hasakah, and became the first president to do so in the country. The same year, young Kurds and supporters emerged, as the Yeketi (or Unity) Party, a pro-KDP group, called for the Syrian government to recognize Kurdish culture and acknowledge the Kurdish nation's existence; this was followed by several arrests of Kurdish activists. As Chatty (2010) argues, like the attempts to promote multiethnic nationhood in the last decades of Ottoman Empire, the Kurds in Syria are struggling to be recognized as Syrians and as Kurds in a nation-state that is unofficially multiethnic but formally Pan-Arab. As in other states, the development is not merely dependent on internal factors, but also on regional and international influences.

Syria is currently in a civil war that broke out as a result of the Arab Spring movement in the Middle East and North Africa but which was brutally hindered by the Syrian regime. Even before that, the Kurdish population in Syria has been involved in a series of long-term problems that they share with Iraq, Turkey, and Iran, and have attempted to secure their Kurdish rights from those in power, either Bashar al-Assad or the French High Commissioner (Savelsberg 2014).

There has not been a serious armed struggle against the government, and in the early years of Syria, the relationship between both Kurds and Arabs was relatively stable. After implementing a Pan-Arabist ideology (being strongly suspicious of Kurdish national consciousness challenging national unity), Kurds and other groups were denied recognition. From 1961 onwards, a policy of Arabization of Kurdish areas and Kurds was initiated. Moreover, when the Ba'ath party was in power, Kurds lost many rights, including education and employment, were deprived of their Syrian citizenship, and Kurdish towns were renamed (Lowe 2006), for example, Kobani became Ayn al-Arab.

Although the situation has been difficult, since 1976 the pressure has decreased after president Bashar al-Assad officially renounced from follow-up of the Arabization plan (McDowall 1992). The situation has changed even more with the advent of the Arab Spring and, in particular more recently, the Democratic Union Party (PYD) as the largest opposition group, which has supported the revolution against the Assad government as well as the fight against the Islamic State. The consequences of the Arab Spring have perhaps been felt more in Syria than in any other Middle Eastern country (Anderson and Anderson 2014). Despite the long-running conflict, the regime in Syria— unlike those in Tunisia, Egypt, Libya, and Yemen—has thus far survived. A number of factors can explain this status quo, namely the opposition's lack of coordination, the Islamic State's influence, and international politics.

Iran differs from both Turkey and Iraq on the basis that the country has a longer history as a nation-state, but the systematic homogenization of its citizens has also been an issue. Non-Persians, such as Baluchis, Lurs, Turkmens, and Kurds, have been subject to politics of exclusion and othering. The socio-economic, political, and cultural outcomes of the Islamic revolution in 1979 have had a major impact on everyday life of Kurds. After the establishment of the Islamic republic, a "holy war" was declared against Kurds through military attacks against the population and its political leaders (Chaliand 1993; Mola Ezat 1992). The result of this campaign was thousands of dead civilians between 1979 and 1992.

The dream of a Kurdish independent Kurdistan, the Republic of Mahabad, was briefly realized in Iran from December 1945 to December 1946, with Qazi Mohammad as its president (Chaliand 1993; Mola Ezat 1992, 1995, 1997). In the early 1940s, Mahabad enjoyed freedoms that allowed intellectual groups to explore ideas of nationalism that had the potential to ease towards a more united Kurdish thinking. However, the republic lasted less than a year, and the President and several other Kurdish officials were assassinated in 1947 (O'Shea 2004; Wahlbeck 1999; Mola Ezat 1992, 1995).

Years of oppression of the Kurds in Iran provided strong incentives for the Kurds to join the Iranian Revolution of 1979. It was obvious that Ayatollah Khomeini's aim to establish a centralized Islamic republic would decrease the Kurds' goal of Kurdish autonomy, that is, minorities such as Kurds, Baluchis, and Lurks were advised to not be called minorities as it implied differences between them and Persians. Khomeini's rejection of ethnic and cultural pluralism meant that Kurds were, again, subject to forced inclusion, but not exclusion, if they admitted their Persian identity.

Since President Hassan Rouhani came to power in August and until the close of 2013, Iran has reportedly executed more than 200 people, a substantial number being Kurdish activists (Stansfield 2014). Other minority groups lacking basic rights include the Baluchis, Turmens, and Armenians. Scholars view Kurdish nationalism in Iran as a modern phenomenon derived from socio-economic and cultural dislocations that have left marks among Kurds in Iran, which in turn have been manifested in some of their reactions to events near them (Stansfield 2014; Vali 2014). For the almost seven million Kurds in Iran, composing almost 10% of the total population, the Arab Spring, the creation of the Kurdish autonomous region of Iraq, the ongoing peace-process in Turkey, and even the attempts to establish a Kurdish region in the war zone Syria could be tantalizing cases of what Kurds in other parts of the separated Kurdistan can accomplish (Stansfield 2014).

KURDS AS THE OTHER IN THE MIDDLE EAST

The political, cultural, social, and economic narratives of each nation-state where Kurds are settled are testament to extreme forms of oppression and assimilationist policies. Ignatieff (1994, p. 137) defined it as meaning that Kurdistan is "the meeting point of four of the most aggressive and expansionary nationalisms in the modern world," and Romano and Gurses (2014, p. 5) have stated that, "Turkey, Iran, and Iraq do not really suffer from a 'Kurdish problem' or 'issue' but rather a 'democracy problem.'"

Kurdish nationalism has been shaped by the politics of affirmation of Kurdish national identity. It has its roots in the political and cultural processes and practices of the construction of modern nation-states and national identities in the multiethnic and multicultural societies of Iran, Iraq, Syria, and Turkey during the interwar period (Vali 1998). The emergent nationalism in these countries, and the nationalist discourse constructed to legitimize their authoritarian rule and hegemonic political culture, have varied substantially in form and character. Their structural dynamics charted diverse paths of modernization and development, with varying effects on the general political and cultural processes of denial and exclusion of Kurdish identity in their respective national territories (Vali 1998). The rules in these nation-states are close to what could be called "internal post-colonialism," or what some call "poor peoples' colonialism" on the part of those third-world states created within artificial frontiers derived from imperialism (Vanly 1992). Internal post-colonialism is concentrated against often sizable minorities, and it has been suggested that it may be both more brutal and more harmful than the classical type of colonialism (Vanly 1992; Entessar 2010). The effects of economic exploitation are aggravated by an absence of local development and by the extent to which minority oppression is stimulated by chauvinism under democratic traditions that generally restricted the more extreme forms of injustice under the old colonialism. In the Middle East, the Kurds are one of its victims (cf. Sidaway 2000), and the explanation for this points to the early stages of state-building processes that post-colonial states have reached (Rear 2008). Accordingly, the leaders of these nominal states are pre-occupied with the question of how to strengthen their power, or rather how to strengthen the state itself, against rival leaders from other groups placed within the state. These are a diverse set of examples of the precarious relationship between the Kurds and their states. Both cultural and socio-political discriminations against the Kurds have consequently led to a sustained quality of Kurdish ethnic consciousness (Entessar 2010). In particular, Kurdish diaspora activities have served as an important site for the renaissance of a Kurdish identity.

THE KURDISH DIASPORA IN EUROPE

During the course of a century-long battle for Kurdish independence, almost two million Kurds have fled their authoritarian states, and many more have been internally displaced. In the search for safety, the Kurdish exodus has taken various routes to cities like Damascus, Beirut, Tehran, Istanbul, and Jerusalem, or further afield to Western Europe and beyond. Minority status has been a continuous reality for all Kurds in the four authoritarian states, and it has persisted after migration to Sweden, the UK, Germany, France, and other Western countries, as they are assigned a minority status not only as an ethnic collectivity, but also with regard to religious and gender categories (Eliassi 2010). However, it is also equally clear that the Kurdish diaspora has been one of the most active and productive diasporas in terms of political mobilization.

There are no precise nor updated census of the Kurdish diaspora in Europe, as statistics generally register the countries from which migrants emigrate and not by their ethnicity. One of the most recent and accurate estimations of the number of Kurds in Europe was published in a report to the Parliamentary Assembly of the Council of Europe in 2006 there are around 1,3 million Kurds in Western Europe (Russell-Johnston 2006). The largest Kurdish diaspora can be found in Germany with around 800,000 Kurds (see Baser 2015; Russell-Johnston 2006). The overwhelming part of those—70–75%—live in Germany due to the country's *Gastarbeiter* labour recruitment programme that attracted migrants from Turkey, while Kurds from Iraq form the largest part of the Kurdish communities in Great Britain, Sweden, and the Netherlands (Emanuelsson 2005). Approximately 150,000 Kurds inhabit France, 100,000 the UK, 100,000 Sweden, 80,000 the Netherlands, and 60,000 Switzerland and Austria (Russell-Johnston 2006). Along with Kurds in Germany, the Kurdish population in Sweden appears to be one of the most active diasporic groups. Many settled in Sweden are politicized Kurds who arrived in Sweden as political refugees. Many intellectuals, artists, writers and political activists reached Sweden from the 1960s onwards and have played a significant role in placing the Kurdish stateless nation on the map.

There are also around 15,000–20,000 Kurds in the USA, and more than 6000 in Canada (Council of Europe). One of the explanations behind the lack of adequate statistics about Kurds is that many of them have been registered according to the sending country's nationality and rarely with regard to ethnicity. Although Kurds constitute one of the largest groups of refugees worldwide, it is not possible to assess the total number of Kurdish refugees using UNHCR figures, as they are documented only as Iranian, Iraqi, or Turkish asylum seekers (Ayata 2011). This is the case for especially Kurds from Turkey who were registered with Turks as labour migrants although swelling number of Turkish citizens (ethnic Kurds mainly) arrived as refugees and asylum seekers in Germany (Østergaard-Nielsen 2003b). This does not de facto mean that those who did leave for economic reasons and not as refugees do not take part in political activities (Østergaard-Nielsen 2003b).

Despite the lack of accuracy in these estimations, figures continue to be reproduced without problematizing their genesis. For instance, different organizations provide numbers without updating them. Furthermore, birth rates and other factors are disregarded in various estimations. Displacement, which is the essential factor in Kurdish history, makes the Kurdish population even higher than suggested. The significance of this lies, therefore, not in the attempt to find the most accurate numbers (as they are absent), but in the reasons behind the difficulties in doing so. The problem with extrapolation is that it omits the unequal and distinct factors that *push* Kurds, as opposed to, for instance, migrant Turks to move to Europe and elsewhere (Ayata 2011), which, in turn, has implications for how diasporic groups of people are talked *about* in absence of the histories that have made them a diaspora in the first place. In this case, it is perhaps more interesting to look at the different *waves* of migration and the character of each event. Although Kurdish migration in Europe dates back to the nineteenth century (Hassanpour and Mojab 2005), more recent waves are more commonly referred due to the transnationalization of the Kurdish cause. Kurdish migration to Europe can be divided into three waves (Ayata 2011; Gill et al. 2014): (a) students and intellectuals from the mid-1950s, (b) labour migration during 1960s and 1970s, and (c) asylum seekers during 1980s and 1990s.

Within the Kurdish migration from Iraqi Kurdistan starting from the 1970s, four main characteristics are noticeable. The first three exoduses took place during the struggle against the Iraqi state (Akkaya 2011). Hundreds of thousands fled through Iran and Turkey to seek protections. A minor number of them were able to migrate to Europe. The chief migration occurred during the 1990s, the fourth wave, due to the economic embargo that grew during the endogenous fighting between Kurdish groups between 1994 and 1998 (Akkaya 2011). The Kurdish exiles in 1960–1975 and post-1975 have a different character, with the former being characterized by single young men, often from the urban middle or upper middle class and highly educated sections (Sheikhmous 1990). Political activity was strong, and the level of religious commitment was low. Other groups were from rural areas, with a low level of education. Kurdish migrants, post-1975 were, on the contrary, more mixed because of the large amount of refugees and more varied reasons for migration. The Kurdish armed resistance in Turkey, Iran, and Iraq during the 1980s pushed many refugees out in diaspora. In contrast to earlier migration, these were families, groups with different levels of education, and people with varied social backgrounds and political and religious engagements (Sheikhmous 1990; Alinia 2004). These descriptions show that there are different migratory experiences also within what can be classified as "victim diaspora" (Cohen 1996).

One important aspect of the Kurdish diaspora, among other political diasporas, is that the political and cultural activities among them from a de-territorialized space did not only have important implications for their own positions and maintenance of their culture in diaspora, but also provided the Kurds in their homelands with support. Concurrent developments in Turkey and Iraq reinforce the important role members of the Kurdish diaspora play (Eccarius-Kelly 2008) while also strengthening the notion of the Kurdistan homeland. Different concrete strategies are apparent, especially among young Kurds when conversing about Kurdistan. There are several contributing factors that drove the Kurdish diaspora through a transnational success in forming a distinct Kurdish question that involved the issues they had struggled with for years in the authoritarian states that all relate to identity and belonging: the EU's persistent interest in maintaining peace in the Middle East, in particular in Iraq and Turkey; a noticeable Kurdish intelligentsia, consisting of politicians, academics, students, and other activists; frequent creation and use of mass media channels, such as satellite television and digital media; and a new democratic space within the societies of Europe that allowed Kurds to lobby for political and cultural rights, which stand in stark contrast to the environments in Iraq, Syria, Turkey, and Iran. Therefore, despite being a relatively small and newly developed diaspora, Kurds have managed to gain allies within existent nation-states and global organizations as compared to, for instance, Somali and Hmong communities in the USA, Pakistani immigrants in Britain, and Maghreb immigrants in France (Eccarius-Kelly 2008).

Generally speaking, immigrants lack the expertize to effectively promote their interests in Brussels, yet, the transnational Kurdish diaspora displays a remarkable case due to both their resilience and the circumstances, as the political interests also conflate with that of EU members. The Kurdish diasporas have been of importance to Kurdish political parties for the following reasons: they have provided financial as well as human resources, allowed the parties to educate their cadres and develop communications in various media, established useful networks of contacts with governments and non-government organizations and persons, and assembled the human critical mass needed to put pressure on governments and public opinion (van Bruinessen 1999). On the basis of these reasons, the Kurdish diaspora began to play an increasingly important role in the internationalization of the "Kurdish Question," and placed it on the European agenda (van Bruinessen 1999; Hassanpour 2003; Romano 2006) as well as on national agendas. Kurdish diaspora contributed to the renaissance of Kurdish culture and stimulated a renewal within Kurdistan itself, and created a consciousness around the nation Kurdistan.

Powerful instruments in diaspora, such as a dynamic Kurdish media landscape, have created immense possibilities. The Med TV channel was licensed to a group of Kurdish citizens in Britain after years of demands, in particular from Kurds in Europe, to have a television station of their own. The TV's office was in London, but the main production work took place in studios in Brussels and Stockholm (because of lack of political freedom, the channel could not report directly from Kurdistan). The shutdown of the TV channel did not stop other satellite channels emerging, such as KurdSat, Kurdistan TV, Gali Kurdistan, Komala, Newroz TV, Rojava TV, Speda Channel, Rojhalat TV, Payam, Ronhai TV, Kurd Channel, Aso Sat, and more, which are all connected to political parties from the four Kurdish regions (Eliassi 2013). Furthermore, social media have seen an explosion of online Kurdish groups linked to themes of Kurdish independence and Kurdish diaspora. YouTube, Twitter, websites, and Facebook activities inform of an intense presence by a younger generation of Kurds, but also among the first generation living in diaspora.

Consequently, this has also steered the Kurds to no longer be a voiceless immigrant community, but besides this their political activism and interests also show entrepreneurial achievements (Eccarius-Kelly 2008). The progress has been traced to the skilful use of different political channels and transnational activism that were directed towards European institutions (Eccarius-Kelly 2008; Blätte 2006). In part, the success in these stories can also be linked to the interests of Western nation-states. The EU's confirmation that Turkey follows the directions before joining the EU and the US long-term political engagement in Iraq are indeed contributing factors that have enhanced the status of the Kurdish diaspora. Within the countries of settlement, the Kurdish diasporas have achieved cultural, political, and social recognition in terms of the right to study their language, radio and TV broadcasting, publications, and access to the political and cultural public sphere (Eccarius-Kelly 2008).

Perhaps, this has become even more enhanced considering the political situation in Syria and Iraq, where Kurdish forces have played a significant role in the battle against IS. Kurdish forces (YPG and Peshmerga) have been on the front lines against the group, and their bravery has made them, men and women, well known in the international media, in particular in each city and town—including Kobane and Sinjar—that have been liberated by them and the US-led coalition. It is notable that a large part of the international community has raised their voices in support of Kurds, their rights, and even independence in the near future.

There is furthermore a growing academic literature on Kurdish refugee migration and the Kurdish diaspora (see van Bruinessen 1999, 2000; Hassanpour 2003; Hassanpour and Mojab 2005; Sheikhmous 2000; Wahlbeck 1999, 2010) drawing on different disciplinary approaches, with the crux of investigation being the relationship between Kurdish migration (both involuntary and labour) and the geopolitical position of Kurdistan that has involved a sustained struggle within and outside to achieve full political, cultural, and social rights. A large part of Kurdish studies has, until recently, focused on the Kurdish struggle, perhaps with a significant focus on the Kurdish–Turkish context (see Baser 2013; Eccarius-Kelly 2008; Keles 2015; van Bruinessen 1999, 2000; Leggewie 1996; Østergaard-Nielsen 2003b). Increasingly more research has been devoted to the scientific study of diaspora formation vis-à-vis hostland policies, particularly in a transnational context, for instance, Alinia (2004), Baser (2015), Eccarius-Kelly (2008), Eliassi (2013) Eriksen (2006), Khayati (2008), Sheyholislami (2008).

However, studies of Kurdish diaspora and new media and online communication have been extremely limited, even more so regarding ethnographic online studies. Furthermore, there is a greater need for studies with a distinctive focal point on younger generations of Kurds in Europe. As Eliassi (2013) has noted, much of the work about Kurds has centred around the first generation, refugees, and nationalism, with an explicit attention to homeland transnational activities and hostland experiences of exclusion. In works on the information and communication technologies, researchers have concluded that Kurds have displayed their online activities on websites, online communities, blogs, and other channels, which have served as important platforms for the strengthening of a national and cultural identity (Candan and Hunger 2008; Eriksen 2007; Romano 2002; Sheyholislami 2010).

Notes

1. Transparency Report: Removal Requests, January 1–June 30, 2015.
2. Human Rights Watch (HRW), "Turkey: Internet Freedom, Rights in Sharp Decline," September 2, 2014.
3. Guardian, "Turkey election ruling party loses majority as pro-Kurdish HDP gains seats," June 7, 2015b.
4. The term "Anfal" means "spoils" in Arabic and is evocative of one of the worst human rights violations ever committed by Saddam Hussein. Those who were killed in the Anfal Campaign are said to have been "Anfalized" (Hardi 2011).
5. Even today, new mass graves are being found, which makes statistics unreliable. Final figures may prove even higher than stated in different reports and research.
6. After Iraqi forces suppressed an initial post-war Kurdish uprising, the USA and its allies instituted a "no-fly zone" over the Kurdish areas, protecting the Kurds from Iraqi Ba'ath forces.

PART II

Arriving on the Scene

CHAPTER 5

"Is it OK?"–Challenging Gender Roles

Introduction

The conversations in the Kurdish transnational community have covered a gamut of questions and topics, from personal interests like marriage and relationships, to more public concerns like political developments in the homeland and the settlement country. The following reconstruction of the discussion threads[1] in this and the following chapter uses particular sites, events, or examples in order to display the complex terrain of diasporic contemplations. Owing to the richness and multisited (online–offline) empirical data, parts of the theoretical discussion are woven into these chapters. The intention is to provide a theoretical layer that offers analytical tools to understand crucial concepts embedded in the dialogues and exchanges presented.

First, a word needs to be said about the structure of these chapters. In the following two chapters, the online conversations are presented in the first part, while the offline interviews constitute the latter part. The rationale behind such a partition is, firstly, that the main corpus of the material consists of the online texts. Secondly, the methodological procedure went from online to offline, which explains specific references and parallels to the online interactions made during the interviews. The dynamic here, and for the sections that follow, is that the online–offline entrances provide some interesting discrepancies, whereas the offline encounters help to grasp cross-cultural dialectics, the socio-political expectations, and how young

© The Author(s) 2016
J. Mahmod, *Kurdish Diaspora Online*, The Palgrave
Macmillan Series in International Political Communication,
DOI 10.1057/978-1-137-51347-2_5

Kurds have changed perceptions through these experiences. In such a way, the face-to-face interviews should not merely be understood in terms of how the online space differs from that on the ground, but also how offline performativities have changed post-online encounters. This methodological approach, to move from online activities to offline meetings with the online participants, is rather unusual in diaspora studies and media, in particular in Kurdish studies. This is one of the significant contributions of this book. Adding to this unique approach the supplementary in-depth interviews with Kurdish repatriates in their homeland, Kurdistan (Iraq), which I conducted during 2015, is presented in Chap. 7. The changing political scene in Kurdistan in the post-Saddam era has created new opportunities for Kurds to return to this region of Kurdistan. In the chapter, I present Kurdish returnees' highly challenging experiences in their origin country that have changed the Kurdish consciousness to a great degree.

This first chapter starts with delineating how young diasporic individuals respond to the Western stereotypical discussion on honour-related crimes in Sweden and the UK, which has evoked strong reactions because of the way in which authorities in these settings deal with the problem. This is followed by the homeland tragedies and traditions that involve Kurds in diaspora and the different ways that connect them to their origin and a sense of Kurdishness. They include historical tragedies, such as genocide, as well as cultural events such as Newroz and other Kurdish traditional celebrations. The following section is a walk-through of interrelated issues that disclose how female and male participants challenge norms that are engraved within gender roles. They concern personal ponderings of relationships, marriage, and sex questions, what is acceptable and what is taboo. Women have visibly been more active in these discussions and initiated more discussions, but male members were also present and have responded to many of these issues, in particular in the Swedish forum. The section also includes a passage on the religious-ethnic tensions that interrelated with questions on the Kurdish ethnic culture on the one hand, and gender roles and sexuality on the other. In the particular extract reconstructed in this chapter, the burqa ban is discussed among the members in light of the burqa debates that were ongoing in several European nations at the time. Related to this are discussions about marital obligation as strategies to reproduce the Kurdish nation. The offline interviews will finally shed light on online–offline nuances and contradictions. I will start with brief description of the online community, Viva Kurdistan.

Transnational Viva Kurdistan

Viva Kurdistan, created in 2004, is a transnational online community consisting of eight independent forums: Danish, Dutch, French, German, Norwegian, Swedish, British, and the Kurdish. Each of these forums is restricted to their own national language. Until now, there has been no similar transnational community like Viva Kurdistan; the community was, therefore, a unique moment for Kurds in diaspora, as well as for homeland-based Kurds, to connect in this way. My participant observation took place during 2009–2011, but the collection of the material (conversation) was conducted overwhelmingly during 2010. Most of the members belong to second- and third-generation Kurds (aged 18–30 years). The online community is text-based, but the Web 2.0 site has developed a number of audiovisual features such as blogs, video sharing, and web applications, which have widened the ways of interacting. Each forum has different categories, such as politics, relationships, culture and art, and Internet; in these, different discussion threads are produced that can turn into several pages of long discussions. The methods ranged from observation to immersion in the examination of online interactions to understand how and why certain views emerge from their dialogues. In a second step, I interviewed 18 participants from three different locations, namely Sweden, Britain, and Kurdistan, half of whom were female participants.

TACKLING HONOUR DEBATE IN EUROPE

Much of the academic scholarship has detailed how the political and social responses to domestic violence against minority women in the West have been exclusively culturalist. In other words, violence among minority people is understood as deriving from culture solely, which has consequently stigmatized ethnic and religious communities. These tendencies are also discussed among young Kurds living in Europe. This first section demonstrates how young Kurds explore and confront questions relating to minority and gender issues and to stereotypes. The members found themselves battling with disturbing images of them as a culture of potential honour-killers. Media representations of how ethnic minority women are positioned in relation to white women in Western equal and liberal societies were intensified some years ago as the question of multiculturalism was questioned in the public sphere in European societies. Minority women became visible arguments against the idea of a multicultural society in a number of listed respects such as the burqa, forced marriage, female genital mutilation, and honour-killing. These debates have addressed the ways in which cultural meanings of ethnicity influence the construction of male violence against women in, mainly, Muslim cases (although the question of honour violence has been connected to culture rather than to religion, in scholarship) and non-Muslim cases. Whereas the former is culturalized, the latter falls under the rubric of "domestic violence."

In Sweden, debates of honour-killing were evoked in 2002 when Fadime Sahindal, a young woman of Kurdish origin, was killed by her father. Although there had been similar cases in Sweden earlier, it was not until this particular case was known that a flame of debates took off in the media.[2] In the Swedish public sphere, honour-killing has led to discussions on "honour culture," addressing Kurdish culture in particular (see also Eliassi 2010; Alinia 2004). It was contended that the honour-related violence and gender oppression are collective and cultural acts, taking place mainly in the Middle East. The control of women's sexuality through surveillance and punishment has been placed at the center of the honour discourse (Schlytter and Linell 2009). Intense debates on different occasions led to social policies funded by the Swedish government in order to contest what has become known as "vulnerable girls in strongly patriarchal families" (Hedström 2004 cited in Eliassi 2010, p. 19). Moreover, mainstream political parties in Sweden have used the racial-ethnic card on honour-killing that, according to Zenia Hellgren and Barbara Hobson (2008), gives "legitimacy for proposals to limit immigration or introduce new conditions for citizenship, such as language requirements or tests of values" (cited in Khayati 2008, p. 225). In the aftermath of the Fadime case, Kurds particularly became hyper-visible in the Swedish society, and especially young female Kurds felt stigmatized, as expressed during the interviews I conducted with them. The victimization of Muslim women by patriarchal constructions of Islam and Middle Eastern people has consequently served to invite a "rescue mission" (Jiwani 2014). These notions were reflected in both online conversation and offline interviews among Kurdish female and male participants. Consider the following quote taken from an advert created by the Swedish authority, placed on the forum of Viva Kurdistan by its founders, against which many online participants reacted strongly.

"If you think that your family can choose who you fall in love with…
If you think it is normal to be locked in after school…
If you think you must accept to be married against your will…
Then you should absolutely come to us: http://www.polisen.se/
komtilloss/
The Police"

The reaction among young Kurds is mainly against the cynical implications that Kurds in Sweden belong to a culture that is abusive. Although the question of honour has been raised among the participants on numerous occasions and has been something of a hot topic, the police's objective regarding the advert backfired in the forum. Most responses to the advert expressed opposing arguments against an interrogating approach by the authority.

"[I]f a person has knowledge in how honor is functioning among certain families with certain traditions, they should also know that the person cannot leave the family just like that. The aim cannot be to divide families, but to change views and values that are not in accordance with a democratic and human model. These are Western cosmetic solutions. (*Police advert on Viva Kurdistan*, Swedish Forum, January 24, 2010)

To live in loneliness and avoid other Kurds, to constantly look over the shoulder, to always have to think about what you say at work since someone might know your family. These cases are horrible. (*To all girls who are victims of honor-related violence*, Swedish Forum, May 8, 2010)

Online participants did not question the debates per se but questioned how Swedish authorities applied the methods of a "quick fix" to a deeply imprinted patriarchal problem, as reflected in the aforementioned extracts. The concern among young Kurds was mainly that the Swedish authorities' approach is not dealing with the issues from the perspective of gender and patriarchal structures, but from an ethnocentric view. Kurds voiced dissatisfaction with Swedish multiculturalism policies that did not show any sensitivity to the real problems. They felt that what had been absent in the public concern about honour-killing was a dialogue between authorities and the affected minority, on equal terms. Such dialogue would, in turn, not render the Kurdish population to honour culture, but, instead, show the very diverse and heterogeneous people, which is incredibly important in the representation of different views in the context of gender and multiculturalism. This became clearer when Kurdish participants initiated numerous discussions against the site owners and their decision to place the advert on the Kurdish community's default page. They contended that the image conveyed through the advert was not merely negative for the Kurdish population but also part of the rise of xenophobia in Sweden.

If these are acts that have been repeated and named as the result of the expressions in Judith Butler's (1993) explanation, how is it that the acts of those who do *not* commit honour-killing do not eclipse all other and name, in this case, the Kurdish culture as a non-violent culture? Instead, Kurds feel that the acts of a few people have made all fathers with Kurdish backgrounds potential killers and each betrayed individual would consider killing another person. Yasmin Jiwani (2014) has in her work illustrated how the media coverage of the killings of Muslim women by Muslim men is reported within the frame of culture clashes and not domestic violence. She refers to Stuart Hall and his colleagues who explain that labels are important when applied within the context of big and dramatic incidents, as they identify and assign the incidents and give them associations and connotations that are mobilized as a referential point with each similar event. Hall et al. (1982), for example, say that the term "mugging" was not used to simply describe a crime, but had become a "central symbol" for the tensions and problems in America involving black ghettos. In similar ways, the crime of honour as a label is associated with specific geographies, cultures, and religious systems, for instance, Islam in certain Middle Eastern societies. These are sensational labels that "stick."

But what are the consequences when minority groups are being culturalized and collectivized by the acts of a few people? The intention here is not to discuss the act of honour-killing itself, but the stickiness of the label in relation to honour-killing (Jiwani 2014) and to disclose the ideologies behind such discussions where not only minority women are portrayed as the Other but also an entire culture. Therefore, the pressing questions relate to what the consequences are when conflating post-colonial stereotypes with real problems that need to be dealt with objectively. What associations are being produced? Who are the stakeholders? Which are the powers behind this economy of demarcating, referencing, and circulating notions of identities of this kind? These questions seem legitimate to ask if we consider the media coverage of women with Canadian backgrounds, who were similarly killed like minority women, tended to individualize the crime by focusing solely on the spouse committing the murder. In these cases, culture or ethnic backgrounds are not mentioned (Jiwani 2014). In contrast to the European/white Canadian cases, victims of femicide from immigrant groups were identified easily through the references to culture or religion. Other scholars (i.e. Baker, Gregware, and Cassidy 1999 in Jiwani [2014]) have argued that particular elements of crime of honour are current within both the East and the West, but in the latter it has become individualized as opposed to familial or tribal.

The discussions on honour-killing among the Kurds in Sweden highlight exactly these questions as to why different explanations are provided for different cultural backgrounds; individual versus collective. Masoud Kamali (2004), a Swedish Professor of Social Work, has, in his work on honour-killing, demonstrated that cultural explanation is usually offered when speaking of honour-related violence, while culture is never mentioned in relation to Swedish ethnic male-on-female violence. The same observations were made in the UK where there were a few cases, but within the Pakistani community. It was overwhelmingly the Kurds in the Swedish forum that discussed the honor topic in a comparison with both the Kurds in the British forum and the Kurds settled in their homeland. I will explain this further in the offline section, where Kurds settled in the UK explained why they did not engage in such discussions, but the note made here is that the comparative methodological approach resulted in discovering the absence of some discussions, which is an important aspect and could add to the analysis.

The UK has certainly not been short of these heated discussions in the public sphere. Organizations like Southall Black Sisters identified honour-related violence as a form of domestic violence since "singling out honour killings risks promoting a racist agenda rather than gender equality" (Gupta and Hutchinson 2005, p. 8). The difference between the definitions here is how violence is placed outside and inside the domestic milieus. While all domestic murders of women take place within a "cultural context," culture is the prism through which only the actions of minorities are viewed.[3] While some women rights organizations have argued that honour-killing should not be defined as domestic violence because of certain of their characteristics (such as deliberate and premeditated killing), the most persuasive approach is to understand honour-killings as violence against women, stressing that these acts committed in the name of honour are not different from other acts of violence against

women (Kelly and Lovett 2005, p. 199). This approach does not assume a
difference between violence committed against women in black minority
and ethnic communities and in dominant white communities, as differentiations could strengthen power relations between women and men of
different ethnic backgrounds (Meetoo and Mirza 2007, p. 59; cf. Thapar-
Björkert 2011, p. 184).

> There are more Swedes that hit their women and daughters and molest
> them sexually. But the focus is always on us that create more hatred. (*The
> family's honor is between the woman's legs*, Swedish Forum, July 5, 2010)

The words echo the abstractions put forward by scholars who have
researched the question on honour for years. Kurds feel stigmatized, and
much of the questions were directed towards media and why the interest
was specifically in them when the act is more common among other ethnic groups, they contended. Simultaneously, young men talked about the
portrayal of them as criminals and backward, and women felt victimized
and harassed by the rhetoric of the media. Razack (2004) states that the
approach to the general problem of honour-killing and forced marriages
is not understood as manifestations of the generic violence against women
that both majority and minority fail to condemn. However, the Internet
seems to have paved a way for a space where young women and men
can contest the Western ideologies as well as norms and ideas within the
Kurdish culture. There is a greater appetite to confront customary notions
of honour and shame that frame the right to control the sexuality and the
reproductive powers of young people, particularly those of women's bodies, by men, but also by young people with traditional views and by older
generation of migrants. Therefore, the reactions to contemporary gender
issues are not necessarily driven by ethnic or national notions of what
it means to be a Kurd, but are also social and political markers of their
diverse backgrounds within the community itself.

It is here noteworthy to refer back to Butler (1988) who explains that
even if there are individual ways of "doing" identity, the individual is still
regarded in accordance with certain prescriptions, which proclaim that
they are not completely individual but referred back to the collectivity.
It is in these definitions and ascriptions that the importance of exploring who benefits and who does not is made clear. When in the Western
contexts, the acts are individualized or referred to domestic or patriarchal
structures, and serve to display the societal issues that are being dealt with

in a formalized way. This can be contrasted by "crimes of passion," which was a valid defence in France and other European countries until the 1970s (Jiwani 2014).

The relevant point made here is the different coverage that convicted killers and honour-killers receive. Razack (2008) emphasizes the honour/passion dichotomy symbolizing Muslims stuck in pre-modernity, while Westerners are enlightened subjects who act upon individualistic and rational choices, "even if the choice is a bad one" (p. 128). In Sweden, the reporting of murders committed by Swedish men has been named "family tragedies," which is a stark contrast to the depiction of Fadime's case, where the entire Kurdish community has been implicitly accused of honour-killing (Runsten 2006), which is also resonating in the responses by the Kurdish youth online. Participants felt as if Swedish authorities depicted Kurds as the other, with the main aim being to portray themselves as modernized Westerners.

> The police say, "if you think this and that, you should come to us". Well, if a girl THINKS that she must accept to be married against her will, why would she go to the police? She'd obviously not go anywhere. This add doesn't make any sense and is just discriminating and it assumes Kurds are stupid, although obviously they are the ones that are imbeciles." (*Police advert on Viva Kurdistan*, Swedish Forum, January 24, 2010)

The participant aims at ridiculing the rhetoric mind-set of the police by scrutinizing the phrasings used. Given the many follow-ups and inclining replies, the poster had made a valid point. It is important to mention here that there were members who conversely agreed with the advert and applauded the punitive tactic. They would argue that the "100-year-old problem" would not go away without modest meddling. Therefore, the aforementioned post also served to discuss against these voices.

Earlier researchers on honour-killing have tried to identify why these incidents have created such intense and recurrent debates in Sweden. One of the explanations put forward is that the country's gender equality discourse has been the core of the political agenda for a long time (Hellgren and Hobson 2008). Hellgren and Hobson, for example, say that one has to acknowledge how gender equality has become a marker of Swedish state identity in order to understand the ways in which national identities are being reflected and magnified through multiculturalist politics,[4] as became particularly visible during Sweden's presidency of the Council of

Ministries of the European Union. Honour-killing has thus been a significant site for the identification of Swedishness, but also, in opposing terms,
what kind of cultural identities are *not* Swedish. It is perhaps not unex-
pected that compared to the recurrent news about domestic violence, the
subject of honour overshadows all other. Many critics have highlighted the
problems with police and other intervening agencies, raising the issue that
if honour crimes are isolated from other kinds of domestic violence and
are referred to culture, then the risk of stereotyping minorities as more
accepting of these crimes increases.

These gender issues have also been used by far-right groups to support
their campaigns against immigration. For example, in the Netherlands,
social researchers (Baukje and Saharso 2006) state that although the public discourse has in essence regarded women of minority groups, in particular Muslims, as passive victims and as planning with these activities,
there is a greater awareness that gender issues are not merely seen within
the cultural framework but rather have other socio-economic factors to
it. However, in a wider multiculturalism context, the Fadime case became
a national drama in Sweden as one of the threat points needed in multicultural societies (Hellgren and Hobson 2008). This can be compared to
Norway, where religion and Islam have been the matter of focus, while in
Sweden the ethnocultural difference had been the core matter (Hellgren
and Hobson 2008; Wikan 2003).

In the Swedish-Kurdish online community, the honour-killing question
divided the community into two camps: those opposing the condescending rhetoric used by the police and those in full agreement with them.
However, many of these discussions also morphed into the question of
the female body and sexuality, which created many more heated debates
online. The Fadime topic was not only interesting to discuss online in
relation to the advert, but also as it set in motion numerous, otherwise
sensitive, themes about gender roles, sexuality, and the body, which I will
revert to in the section *Contesting Gender Norms*. But first, the next section presents a couple of key sources for a strong unity among the Kurds
online that include yearly events that were much talked about frequently
and passionately.

CULTURAL ARTEFACTS AND POST-MEMORIES
OF TRAGEDIES

Collective Memories of Halabja

Every year, Kurds in Kurdistan and in diaspora commemorate the genocide in Halabja on March 16, which is one of the most specific events of historical significance that took place in 1988. While participants talk about the loss of a piece of history, it is also a loss of a territory, or indeed a part of the losing the homeland, long before they even became a diasporic group. On the other hand, the commonality that is strongly created in this context is mostly standing on the "space" of history rather than the place. Therefore, what is significant here is the constant nostalgic reference, not to the physical nation or a state, but to the space that occupies their *minds* in a profound way.

> I myself have a close friend who lost his uncle, these are my compatriots, how can I turn a blind eye to such things? If I don't mourn, if I don't remember that history, if I don't show myself as a part of the Kurdish people, then I shall never even say I am a Kurd. (*Halabja Martyrs*!!!! Swedish Forum, June 16, 2010)

> Canada has just acknowledged Halabja as genocide! Hope the rest of the world follows their path! The happiness in my mother's eyes, the pride of my father who has just participated in a debate at Newroz TV live and tried to raise the voices of the Halabja population, and the hope that my parents, relatives and friends will on a beautiful day, slowly but surely, perhaps can gain some peace in their minds when the surrounding world actually starts to react. (*Halabja*, British Forum, March 18, 2010)

> A day like this (March 16, 1988) is the important day for us Kurds to remember, the day of Helebce.[5] 5000 people were killed by chemical weapons. We need to give this attention and never forget the cruelties of this day that changed the rest of our lives. (*T6: HELEBCE*, Kurdish Forum, March 16, 2010)

In these accounts, Kurdish participants in the forums show how collective memory and mourning convey a people's history and culture, and consequently its identity, and how this plays an important role for diasporic Kurds. This collective memory serves as a shared awareness of the presence of the past. The statements illustrate how historical memories coloured by tragedies constitute a key element in cultivating a sense of belonging today, in this case strongly expressed by the declaration that "then I shall never say I am a Kurd." Although this significant event took place in the Kurdish region of Iraq and there is no universal and mono-lithic Kurdish collective memory, the memories of suffering have spanned geographies and the commonality of this victimhood has created a wide-spread shared consciousness that the participants relate to. The posts demonstrate the involvement of the wider Kurdish diaspora and how it embodies a profound political and cultural weight, as well as suggest certain uniqueness in the Kurdish experience.

The understanding of the process of collective memory also discloses much about the contemporary sense of identity and its dependence on the past (Stier 1996). Memory in that sense is about the present or, rather, the particular way of imagining and representing the present by turning attention towards the past. The production of this kind of cultural memory is important in developing and sustaining links for the second and third generations. The younger generations, whether they have witnessed the incidents themselves or not, can provide "testimonies" as an effective way of making the past public and transmitting a particular Kurdish history that has been silent. Telling this story and the cruelty of the oppression is necessary for these participants as a political act because it reveals both the injustice committed against the people and, implicitly, the reasons under-lying the formation of the diaspora.

The second aspect of these posts, taken from the British and Kurdish forums, relates to the politics of the genocide and the lack of response from the international community. The memorialization of the genocide has, in recent years, accelerated and generated political debate internation-ally, from initiating petitions for its recognition as genocide to providing accurate information about its scale and cruelty. Offline events, therefore, had strong influences on the online practices.

Members of the online site changed their avatars to symbolize Kurdish national days, for example, Newroz during the celebration, or Halabja during the yearly memorial of "Never forget Halabja." Offline, people took part in the commemoration of Halabja in cities across Sweden and thousands of candles were lit for the victims in the gas attack on March 16, 2008. Among the people were numerous prominent Swedish politicians, with Sven Otto Littorin, from the ruling party *Moderaterna*, saying, "Kurds are an important asset to Sweden and they are often good example of very successful integration" (Eliassi 2013, p. 10).

Marianne Hirsch has in her work on the children of Holocaust survivors introduced the concept of "postmemory," referring to those who have a generational and historical distance from the Holocaust. Postmemory can be a powerful form of memory, as the link to the source is mediated memory, but with a considerable imaginative investment and production. Postmemory can be applied to those individuals growing up with these kinds of narratives that preceded their birth, and whose own stories are being delayed by those of previous generations that are characterized by a kind of trauma never fully reproduced (Hirsch 1997). In the present context, I refer to postmemory not on the basis that the children of immigrant parents did not experience this, as some Kurds among second-generation migrants did indeed experience these incidents, even if many of them were children at the time and perhaps have no vivid memories of them. I refer to this concept, as it shows the production of a history through memories that are mediated though different means and which have proved to be an important subject in retaining the Kurdish identity and also in spreading the knowledge in the country and worldwide.

The role of the Internet and the various technologies as a transnational communicative tool in informing about the tragic history can be used as an example of how young Kurds highlight this event. Many Kurds state that the genocide of Halabja was not given sufficient attention at the time it was carried out, and therefore they now wish to draw the attention of the world to the Anfal Campaigns. The Halabja episode explains the degree to which cultural meanings are embodied in Kurdishness, where memories are integral as an effect of repeated discussions and actions. The disturbing feeling of injustices and the sense of loss, as shown earlier, are present among these young Kurds, which is evident from the discussions on the online forums. These histories also engender a diasporic consciousness among young generations, which explains more clearly why the experience of what has been called "unhoming," with all the resonance of a haunting loss, depends less on moving from one national space to another than it does on the experience and memory of becoming unhomely (Bhabha 1994; Cho 2007). While different diasporas may go through the process of being unhomed, to be unhomely is a state of diasporic consciousness, often haunted by histories which leave one feeling "a small tingle on the skin at the back of your neck and know that something is not quite right" (Cho 2007, p. 19).

The role of historical memories in sustaining belongingness in diaspora is not understood just in terms of historical memories but also in terms of present memories. The references to the genocide of Halabja as the landmark of Kurdish suffering are not only about a memory serving as politics of belonging, but as the "archaeological feature of the future" (Kazanjian and Nichanian 2003, p. 128). Moreover, in relation to the delineation on diasporic creations, the conceptual discussions and understanding of old and new diasporas, voluntary and involuntary, are not simply about immigration from one country to another but also about the implications for the daily lives of diasporic collectivities and individuals.

Newroz

One of the most important days for Kurds is Newroz.[6] Newroz symbolizes the start of the new year (also celebrated by Iranians and other ethnic groups), and it is an important cultural expression that embraces the Kurdish narrative of history, folklore music, dancing, and social gathering. In the diaspora, Kurdish Newroz celebrations are publicly organized by different organizations and draw large crowds of Kurdish youth. Celebrating this day has become one of the most important means of ethnic reaffirmation and has an enormous social meaning even for second and third generations.

The legendary Kawa, a kind of national hero and namesake to many Kurdish children, has also acquired a highly symbolic meaning. The festivity has been highly politicized in, for instance, Turkey and Syria, and, in the case of Turkey, celebrations have repeatedly ended in violent clashes between Kurdish civilians and the Turkish police. Turkish authorities ensure that the festivity is held outside city centers because of its strong expressive national symbolism; millions of Kurds gather to celebrate. What has happened in recent years is that Turks have even started to appropriate this celebration in their own name to diminish its cultural meaning for Kurds in Turkey.

Over the years, the Kurdish populations in diasporas have also encountered difficulties connected to the celebration of Newroz. Each political party or association holds their own Newroz celebration, and the celebration has become increasingly political (van Bruinessen 2000). On Viva Kurdistan, members promoted Newroz events in specific countries or cities well in advance, and participants could follow where events were taking place, while others would travel to attend physically. This symbolic day is important to young Kurds, but there is a serious and long-lived discussion alongside the salutes, excitement, and expectations.

> Hey now I've really had enough of Kurds behavior! Seriously, do Kurds know what Newroz means? Should we really mix politics into Newroz celebrations? Each year, we Kurds have party here in Sweden to celebrate our Newroz. Instead of all the various political parties having their own celebration, all of us should have a large Newroz so that all Kurds from all parts can come to celebrate the dancing and have fun. (*Kurds and their behavior*, Swedish Forum, March 9, 2010)

Just like in previous discussions on sustaining a common language and common history, it is also important to create common festivities. The existence of separate celebrations is a reflection of the political division between Kurds and is seen as a troublesome obstacle for the Kurdish people, thus making the national struggle more difficult. The aforementioned post is extracted from a thread consisting of more than 126 follow-ups, the majority with quite exhaustive replies, with hundreds of readers. The problem that the participants have identified is the priorities that are made, and are said to be either dividing Kurds or uniting them. If, for instance, Newroz celebration is organized by a particular political party, it will be at the expense of Kurdish unity. This is how the discourse in these discussions has been outlined.

> I hate that Kurds constantly try to de-politicize and instead commercialize Newroz! It goes hand in hand with the recurring demand of "unity", which in some linguistic usages, in fact, means "ideology-less", or the need for us to yell "Biji Kurd û Kurdistan,"[7] which just does not mean anything specifically. We Kurds are oppressed, downtrodden, hated, naked, laughed at, mocked, degraded, we need politics more than beer and partying! (*Kurds and their behavior*, Swedish Forum, March 9, 2010)

What this member emphasizes is how the constant demand for commonality, which time and again denotes a non-ideological approach in his view, does not mean anything without politics. Traditional expressions, including music, names, signs, symbols, performances, and narratives, are not merely cultural expressions, but political acts; they play an influential role in conflict contexts. What is argued for in this post retains the same intention of commonality, but without denying the political dimension of cultural expressions. Particular aspects of cultural expressions, in broader dimensions, may create perceptions and values that inform political beliefs and actions among Kurds or other "conflict-related" groups. When a cultural value is seemingly being mobilized for the purposes of politicization, this is a sensitive argument among participants. This approach caused other participants to protest, as urging for *unity,* not division, was the original aim of the topic-maker's thread. In this sense, the failure to achieve a nation-state is exclusively and consistently based on the lack of unity among younger generations of Kurds. Further explanation followed, clarifying the perspective of the participant:

> A politicized human being lives in their reality in a completely different way than a mystified one. For instance, we can imagine that in a country that is miserable for poor people to live in, they have nothing to eat, even though their country is full of riches. A small class consisting of corrupt politicians and financiers, grabbing everything. The politicized poor say in such a case: "I am poor. My children have nothing to eat. I have to do something about it. I know one crowd, where they stored food. Let us organize ourselves and one night hit back and grab the food. This gives us food for our children. In this way, we let the rich know that we are not to play with!" This, the politicized one says. The mystified poor man says: "We are poor. It is capitalism's fault. We need to make the world revolution." See, the mystified does nothing! He relies on his big words and slogans. He escapes reality into the mysterious circumstances he did not understand. (*Kurds and their behavior,* Swedish Forum, March 9, 2010)

This account is a call for still greater politicization of Kurds and their cultural performativities. The de-mystification of the Kurdish call is what will lead to political realism and results. In the same rhetoric, that commonality can only be created and displayed by de-politicization: Kurds online want to make sure that they give a correct image of themselves to the world. Whether it has been a demonstration against Kurds being executed in Iran, or against Turkey when it closed down the democratically elected Democratic Society Party (DTP), there have been arguments on how to put forward their case. A diverse group of young Kurds is fighting for their rights, not just with two different sides, but with several different approaches as to how to generate sympathy. These approaches are negotiated with consideration for the most effective form of representation of themselves. But, when different groups identify themselves in different ways for the same cause, then distinctions appear. The feeling of belonging and of doing something important in the struggle for Kurdish rights comes to the foreground.

> You're just assuming that everyone who criticize your organization is in some mystic way allergic against PKK. Thats not the case, I must say that is pretty tragic that Kurds is more allergic and criticizing the organization of PKK then turks, i guess you as representer of this organization never ask yourself why is that so? Maybe i want to go and celebrate with my brothers sisters from north but not sympathizing with PKK make all Kurds included with the flyer and choice of artist music etc. After all we are all Kurds struggling for same things. (*Newroz celebration in Sweden* [Solnahallen] *20 March*, British Forum, March 9, 2010)

One reason for not accepting any political symbolism during Newroz is based on it dividing people, leading to different celebrations, but the other is that individuals want to associate with the celebration, the history, the suffering, and all that the *cultural* event stands for. Hence, when they see emblems of a political party, in this case the PKK, that they do not support, it disturbs their attachment to the event and involuntarily circumscribes what they are sympathizing with. It has by now become a question of representation. Although different Kurdish political parties in Kurdistan region of Iraq, Turkey, and Iran may share the same ideology, the agenda for Kurdistan differs according to what kind of political outcome they seek. This plays a vital role for Kurdish individuals in how they want to be represented in the international arena. "We are all Kurds struggling for the same thing" is therefore not as unambiguous as the sentence promises.

> Greetings to all Kurds on this day!! It is an important day because it symbolises the day when Kurds were rescued from powerful sources and became more independent. It is nice because it is the first day of spring, and people's approaches are warm and happy. The first day of spring bears so much more than just a simple day for us. (*T7: NEWROZ*, Kurdish Forum, March 20, 2010)

The symbolism of this cultural day is important for all Kurds, but the *reasons* for its importance differ, and how the individual meaning of the day is understood informs us of the political character of diasporic Kurds. Newroz has become a way of promoting the cause for each Kurdish political group and its own partisan interests, of which the Newroz in Trafalgar Square is an example.[8] For Kurdistan-based Kurds, it is promoted as an overall Kurdish event without any intent to address external others and with no party-political influences. Considering the situation on the ground and developments in Iraqi Kurdistan, it is highly doubtful that it will remain this way, as political division has already taken hold. The discussion of the flag in relation to Newroz is also a contested one within the context of different demonstrations that were discussed online.

Another cultural component of existential and politico-cultural importance that is intimately related to identity is the Kurdish language, which has been a common premise discussed throughout the research from online to offline. This is not surprising considering that the ban of the Kurdish language in their homelands has been an integral part of the structural discrimination and oppression of Kurds. In the thread, titled, "It's not 'just', it is more important than the armed struggle," Kurd expressed their concern about how their culture was colonized by oppressive dominant states even outside the borders of Kurdistan, as Kurds were speaking Turkish, Arabic, or Persian. These endeavours can be seen as obligations that Kurdish youth must fulfil, being regarded as the strongest link between culture and homeland, which is conveyed through the words by a Sweden-based Kurd, "You are not Kurds, if you do not know your language, understand your music, cannot communicate with your people and barely know your history and traditions!" (*It's not "just", it is more important than the armed struggle*, Swedish Forum, March 20, 2010).

One way of looking at culture is through those artefacts that are used to form a culture, where individuals become "authentic" members of the ethnic community when those artefacts are applied in daily life (Ignacio 2005, p. 53). The extracts quoted later in the text show how continuation of culture and ethnic belongings can sometimes express itself in stricter and furious manner, and considered to be even more important than the armed fights as the title suggests.

CONTESTING GENDER NORMS

While the Kurdish woman is trying to liberate herself from the dominant Western discourses of the established stereotypes of how the Kurdish woman *is*—a victim of patriarchal structures of backwardness that needs to be rescued—there is also the ongoing challenge within her own culture of liberating herself from established norms of how a woman *should* be. In this section, I delve into the issues of how young women and men talk about themselves as subjects disputing the supranational norms, thus opposing the established traditions that take place both within the Western framework of "freedom" and individualism and the frames of Kurdish culture and collective scripts. The stories here are told by Kurdish diasporic youth living in Sweden, the UK, and in their origin country (majority settled within the Kurdish region of Iraq). They talk about expectations, attitudes, and revolutions of sexuality, gender roles, and cultural codes.

As seen in the discussions, they speak from the perspective of the Western liberal society, cultural traditions, as well as familial expectations, placing them in between expectations and obligations, none of them undisputable or easy to live with and adapt to. As these extracts will show, the notions of a nation-state are never far away, even when deliberating personal and private matters. We need to bear in mind that these delicate topics are not ventilated in the offline environment in the way they are online. It is a significant moment to observe how such, otherwise taboo, questions are talked about and confronted by younger generations of Kurdish diaspora.

Online anonymity and confidentiality have allowed Kurdish women and men to test ideas and confront what commonly is surrounded by perceptions of discomfort and shame. The concerns linked to these topics are reputations and rumours that Kurds expressed in different ways; to demand, in these closed online spaces, the recognition of the female sexuality, while admitting to lies outside the online sphere. Research dealing with questions of sex, gender roles, and other private matters among Kurds is essentially non-existent. Gender and sex talks are important to explore; they are informative processes of diaspora identities, as they may include swift interruptions and resistance when more than one culture is part of the everyday life, and also because they bring the dimension of gender equality and lead to a more direct confrontation by different groups. In the earlier section, we saw an implicit confrontation with Swedish authorities, while in this section Kurds raise the issues of Kurdish gender relationship. Young diasporic Kurds growing up in Western European societies are at a particularly complex juncture engaged in delicate negotiations of gender roles.

The exchanges call for a sophisticated understanding of cross-cultural disputations and socio-political dimensions of Otherness that haunt them within both cultures they live in, deeply embedded in the cultural notions, scripts, of how to act as male, or, in particular, female Kurd. The discussion threads reconstructed in this section manifest the very content of these cultural texts they are trying to negotiate and rewrite. They reflect changing discourses of Kurdish femininity, Kurdish masculinity, and sexuality. The following initial post, made by a female member, illustrates well the lively exchange such topics lead to. They are considered as unconventional discussion topics that are attempted to awake a kind of Kurdish sexual revolution alike "Western individualism and sexuality."

> I am a Kurdish girl and a proud one. But I have biological needs, just like anyone else, I have sexual needs. Just like men, I also have, as a Kurdish girl, been passed by Western individualism. I'm open about this here, but of course when I marry my future Kurdish husband, I won't tell him about my experiences. (*Western individualism and sexuality*, Swedish Forum, April 24, 2010)

> It's completely a wonderful affirmation of the self. To all who criticize her for showing double moral standards she is not to blame, but it is the system's mentality that permeates Kurdish culture. The culture hinders people's freedom to pursue individual ambitions. It's not her fault that she cannot be honest about her sex life (it should not be a dilemma whatsoever—but Kurds have obviously not yet reached the sexual renaissance). (*Western individualism and sexuality*, Swedish Forum, April 26, 2010)

> You are not feeling bad because obviously you live a double life. You say you are ok with lying to your future husband, which just shows that you are not prepared to stand by your actions. Why make it so difficult for yourself? (*Western individualism and sexuality*, Swedish forum, April 25, 2010)

Several aspects are interesting to look at here. While this kind of topic became increasingly more common, they were almost revolutionizing online, and ended in many and lengthy debates about gender roles. First of all, the Swedish forum produced similar topics far more than any other forums in the community. And, within those other forums where participants started discussions, female participants mostly initiated them, while in the Swedish forum, Kurdish men would bring up the gender inequality. Reading these posts, it is obvious that Kurds turn to the online community to discuss issues that matter to them, which otherwise would not be possible or desirable to discuss in other public forums, face-to-face. This becomes more evident as the participant declares that she has to lie to her future partner as, according to her, cultural boundaries prevent her from being honest about her experiences.

The first extract produced at the intersection of private and public spheres (writing anonymously in an online forum where anyone with an account can access it) disputes old and new scripts on multiple levels, through the question she raises, the way she expresses herself, and the reactions from other members of the ethnic community. Reactions belong to both "sides" of the crossroad, which either encourage these interruptions of cultural traditions, "wonderful affirmation," or question why a Kurdish girl has to "make it so difficult" for herself. The other part of the responses which address her "double life"—living a confidential life, offline, of which her future partner cannot know of—shows the dynamic between the online and offline interactions.

In their responses, these women, and men to some extent, think aloud about how they want to lead their lives, not to expose their private affairs but to, seek recognition. This requirement for recognition makes it, in the way Appiah (1994) has outlined, difficult for people who want to treat their body as personal dimensions of the self. Personal here means not secret, but not "too tightly scripted" (p. 163). Appiah argues the problem we should worry about is that collective identities—the way in which people identify themselves as members of a certain nationality, ethnicity, gender, sexuality, and religion—carry with them norms of how an authentic person of that community should behave. These scripts thus hinder people to live or to be treated as equals by other members of the society.

So, why does someone who resists collective norms within a certain culture have the need at the same time to seek recognition from other people within the group? The irony lies in that the authenticity of an identity, which requires us to also reject much of what is conventional in community, has been twisted so that it has become the basis of a "politics of recognition." On that basis, Appiah discards that this involves ultimately looking for a group's recognition as an archetype. This is where it creates problems also within the multicultural society, as the politics of recognition places centre stage, people's skin, colour, sexuality, religion, and so on, instead of personal dimension and performativities. Appiah (1994) rightly asks if politics of recognition can embrace the multiple multicultural identities without abiding them to fixed scripts. To that end, it is interesting to see how these diasporic female and male online participants are affected by being from *there* but living here, which makes the context and temporally gendered identities more specific.

> You should be ashamed of yourself, to talk and behave like that. Do you know what people call girls like you? Are you even a Kurd? Don't come here and ruin the Kurdish reputation. (*Western individualism and sexuality*, Swedish Forum, April 25, 2010)

Participants could also be offended by the openness and the wish to talk about sexuality and the needs by Kurdish women. While most of the members know of how people would react to some sensitive topics, it does not hinder them from posting their views, knowing that they are anonymous. Notwithstanding the security of anonymous identities online, the post illustrates what other studies have observed about women often being harassed and insulted (hostile messages) by male counterparts (Herring 1994; Ferris 1996). The post is written by a male participant, suggesting that the young woman is acting promiscuously, un-Kurdish, and makes insinuations of inappropriate sex business by adding, "Do you know what people call girls like you?" They are harsh words that sometimes mobilize others to follow suit in their condemnations, but often invoke stronger reactions against such insults and flaming from both male and female discussants.

While female participants have usually been more apologetic and displayed a more tolerant tone in the discussions, the topic on sexuality, however, at times, evoked heated discussion among female members also. Although the male members have outnumbered female counterparts in numbers on the online community, Kurdish women have still been in the forefront to test boundaries online. With that said, we need not to carry the idea that the woman, or man, constitute a homogeneous category of understanding identity making. Gender scripts have been revisited, contested, and revised. This is why conceptual ambiguities around the concept diaspora also include the diversity within the diasporic groups scattered in different geographical locations as they start presenting a great deal of internal diversity among themselves.

The catch with the typologies reviewed in Chap. 2 is that the search for a model is not only that they become schematic but also possibly ignore the range within the diasporic group, and the way in which diasporic performativities and scripts and their boundaries change over time, within their own geographical setting in the West. In the context of redefined gender concepts and sexual boundaries, this is perhaps best captured in the articulations between online members themselves, with narratives that travelled across transnational virtual borders as well. In the British forum, where Kurds living in London talked about similar topics, they most often had a different take on these questions. It has been argued from different directions—in the selected forums, but also the other forums, as well as during the interviews—that Sweden-Kurds differentiate on one particular point, which relates to questions of sexuality and gender roles. Sweden-Kurds have been perceived as more liberal and more secular, both positively and negatively expressed by other participants.

But important to note here is that while the character of utterances differs from country to country, sometimes views and arguments conflate across borders, which can be referred to socio-political backgrounds as well.[9] That said, one outstanding exchange in the threads did display a typical view where both female and male participants held a unanimous line about how Kurdish women should behave and cover their body.

> Kurdish girls are very special. Most of them respect our traditions and are proud of being Kurds. But then again, there are some Kurdish boys and girls who are just out of control. (*Kurdish girls think they are special!* British Forum, June 20, 2010)

> Why are you happy to show ur beauty to everyone i mean people who not allowed to see all the parts of ur body. does that make u happy? if ur answers yes then i say no cos u are girls. (*this question for the girls who show her beauty to everyone*, British Forum, June 5, 2010)

This view of women as "cultural symbols" of Kurdishness was not only held by men in these exchanges, but also by young Kurdish women. The quotes tell us that Kurdish women have "failed" to act upon Kurdish representative traditions, and are "out of control." Such perceptions of women accord with memories of home and associations to the cultural economy. The point on the exposure of the body is assuming that female identities are actually charged with the responsibility of physical reproduction of the nationality. Just like the nation can be glorified, so is the woman glorified here. Not only are women talked about in metonymic terms, but also her body must represent purity by covering up and representing the nation.

Collective identities, which Kurds in different context try to reproduce—how they identify themselves as members of a particular ethnicity, gender, sexuality, religion—brought notions of how an "authentic" Kurdish female, more recurrently than men in these context, should behave. This is where Appiah (1994) says that scripts oblige people on how they should act, although there are no fixed ways of behaving if you are gay, woman, or belong to an ethnic group, but the scripts hinder people to live or be treated as equals. He further says that the politics of recognition demands that people's sexuality, skin, and so on, should be recognized politically rather than be treated as a personal dimension.

I noticed a considerable distinction between the different forums in the context of especially gender and religion, which were among the most popular topics in the Swedish forum. Most of the time, Sweden-Kurds were considered to be more open-minded, liberal, or too "Swedified," depending on whom you ask. Perhaps, this was also one of the reasons why Kurds in the Swedish forum would contribute posts in the British forum that would stir up the debates. For instance, in response to these posts with rather expressive rubrics, a Sweden-based young man posted the following:

> As a Kurdish man I hate the Kurdish tradition that prohibits and judges girls but the guys can carry on as pimps and that's okay. (*Kurdish girls think they are special*, British Forum June 20, 2010)

While the impact of sociogender changes have been experienced by, especially, female Kurds, the locations have produced discrapencies between the diaspora Kurds. The poster directs his criticism against the male participants who, he thinks, have objectified Kurdish females. It is plausible to assume that gender difference and the topics discussed online are, to varying degrees, influenced by the offline dynamics (Herring 1994; Stone 2001). With a strong gender agenda in Sweden, young Kurds are replicating these debates online in the Swedish forum.

Discussion on femininity and masculinity has also been subject of conversations among the homeland-based Kurds, but the nature of the exchanges has been wholly different with no interrogating or critical voices. The posts would often be descriptive, for example, about feelings conveyed by love or how many times the fellow participants had been in love. Despite that all members can choose to be anonymous online, and most of them are, the forum has kept a much more conventional line in terms of topics discussed.

Ethnic-Religious Tensions

Closely connected to many of the talks about the female-ethnic body are the discussions about religion. Generally, the more traditional views of the woman's body conflated with religious convictions. There were often tensions between the notions of ethnic identity and religious identity, and participants would create threads encouraging people to prioritize either their religious or their ethnic identity; most of the participants advocated for ethnic importance, while religion took a back seat.

The majority of Kurds are Muslims, but it is fair to say that the Islamic factor in the Middle East politics has had an impact on the Kurdish question. For example, in Iran, in late 1970s, Ayatollah Khomeini ruined the Kurdish dream of a democratic revolution by declaring that Kurds, as Muslims, must obey the Islamic authorities in the country (Zubaida 1992). The situation worsened the conflicts between Sunni and Shia Muslims. In Turkey, the Kurdish struggle, like elsewhere in the 1960s and 1970s, was promoted by secular ideologies. Kurds have continued to support secular and nationalist, and even leftist, politics, in Iraq. The current situation makes it difficult to predict how Kurdish ideologies will be shaped in a rapidly changing political arena, but in comparison with the surrounding countries, the Kurdish regions are more secular.

A remarkable distinction in this context is how fiercely religion was debated, in particular the question of burqa ban, in the Swedish forum, while only a few discussion threads were produced during my ethnographic work in the British forum. This, however, does not reflect an absence of debates in the British public sphere, but can possibly be explained by a more conservative community.

The thought of a Kurd who wants to be Muslim voluntarily makes me shiver. What has Islam given us but death and persecution? (*Kurdistan and Islam*, Swedish Forum July 25, 2010)

I see myself first and foremost as a Muslim, then a Kurd. It's important that we keep our religious values in Europe. We also need to stay connected with other Muslims. (*Nationalism or Religion?* British Forum, February 26, 2011)

It is difficult to pinpoint the reasons behind the diverging views of religion among Kurds, as it is such a heterogeneous population within different religious groups, different geographic locations, and different diasporic settings. But overriding these differences, there is a reoccurring dichotomy between on the one hand religion and Europeanness, and on the other hand religion and Kurdishness. In the latter case, Kurds in Sweden often took the opportunity to differentiate themselves from the Middle Eastern autocratic countries on the basis of religion. They argued that while the neighbouring countries were interested in religious wars and Shia–Sunni domination, Kurds were striving for a democratic secular nation. Making distinct choices to lead a life as either a Muslim or a European Kurd seemed to take up much of all the Kurdish diasporans' lives.

The extract also touches upon later issues I discuss, whereby citizens and members of a community are constantly urged to make a choice between life scripts, whether with respect to gender roles, ethnic or national identities, or religious beliefs. This push for a "default" identity has been made apparent, both by politicians across Europe and by Kurdish participants in the online community. But the overwhelming competing ideas were not found between religion and Europeanness, but rather between Islam and Kurdish ethnicity. Owing to the historical background as well as the current conflicts in the Middle East, it may come as a little surprise that Kurds, in general, are more keen to emphasize their ethnic, rather than Muslim, backgrounds.

"The Burqa is Nasty"

On July 13, 2010, France's lower house of parliament, the National Assembly, approved a bill outlawing the wearing of "clothing intended to hide the face" in public spaces, and imposing a fine or even a jail sentence for offenders. Although the bill was silent on religious identities and communities, it was commonly understood and read to be directed primarily at the Muslim full-body and face-concealing garments, the niqab and the burqa. The former French President Sarkozy declared that "The burqa is not welcome in France because it is contrary to our values and contrary to the ideals we have of a woman's dignity." The bill put France at the centre of states within the EU taking proactive steps against the burqa, together with Belgium that had passed a similar law on April 29, 2010. The bill went into effect in April 2011.[10]

Britain, on the other hand, has avoided such decisions, but the Immigration Minister, Damian Green, called it "rather un-British."[11] In Swedish public debates on the subject, former Prime Minister Fredrik Reinfeldt declared his view on the open society and stated that he does not want to see women wearing the burqa.[12] While I will retell the online dialogues here, I do not intend to engage in any discussions about the burqa belonging to the religious or the cultural discourse. Moreover, the section will not delve into the topic of religion, even if it constituted a substantial part of the discussion threads online.

> "I would choose religion if there was a choice between nationality and religion. The current UK leader is calling multiculturalism a failure because people live different lives, in particular he openly attacks Muslims for not integrating but they are, but they uphold their values as Muslims and for them being a Muslim is beyond nationality i.e. Britishness." (*Nationalism or religion?* British Forum, February 26, 2011)

The quote articulately features the problem in the debates on multiculturalism as a failed concept, based on people living lives that are different and go beyond what is perceived as constituting "Britishness." The extract also touches upon later issues I discuss, whereby citizens and members of a community are constantly urged to make a choice between national ways of living, whether with respect to gender roles, ethnic identities, or religious beliefs. This push for a "default" identity has been made apparent both by politicians across Europe, and by Kurdish participants in the online community.

Muslims trying to preserve their culture and religious values have been seen as a threat to notions of Britishness and what are considered as British values. This is what Paul Gilroy (1987) alludes to when he states that blacks are everlasting strangers in their European homelands and always the enemy within the British domestic environment, a space that, as he argues, has never been pure. Gilroy discusses how manifestations of racism usually articulate a British nationalism constructed as whiteness, and which excludes immigrants, and in particular Muslims and their practices, from any possibility of being included within Britishness. This may be even more palpable in society today, 25 years on from Gilroy, where terrorism, and specifically Islamic fundamentalism, has become the strongest threat to notions of civilization, modernity, and Europeanness. This is noticeable in both foreign and domestic policies and provides a rationalization for military mobilization as well.

Among Kurds, the issue of the burqa has been discussed from a number of different perspectives related to aspects of gender, religion versus culture, veiling by force or choice, and the legal ban versus the free and liberal society. Although the garment is not worn by Kurds, religion has often been pitted against ethnicity in the discussions and therefore made the topic especially interesting for the Kurdish community as well.

> "That disgusting piece of material should be burned and banned throughout the world. So right! The Burqa is nasty. It's created by some uneducated and stupid people. It stands for things that are not compatible with human rights. I hope that Sweden will replicate [other countries] and do exactly the same!" (*The last obstacle for Burqa ban removed*, Swedish Forum, October 9, 2010)

> "Of course you are a racist if you categorically are against the burqa as garment. What do you care about how people dress? This is not about women's right and equality, but about your prejudices against Muslims that is based on ignorance against a religion. You are acting like kids building you reality on Aftonbladet [Sweden's leading tabloid], low, ignorant." (*First France and now Sweden*, Swedish Forum, January 27, 2010)

It is unquestionable that the overwhelming view of the burqa in the forum was in favour of the proposed ban in France, Belgium, Sweden, and elsewhere in Europe. On the basis of the content online, Kurds in the UK took traditionally a more modest stance towards the burqa; they were not quite as opposing as Sweden-Kurds proved to be. The most common argument for such views was based on the burqa being inconsistent with a democratic and free society that should support free-life choices. It is noteworthy that in this particular thread, with 80 follow-ups, 70% of the participation was by female members.

Most of these female participants were against the burqa and in favour of a ban. Within these discussions, *how*[13] participants talk about these issues and how they describe the burqa and people who wear the burqa were outstanding features, although longer and more analytical discussions occurred between participants as well. There were diverging views that argued for the incompatibility of the democratic and free society that claims human rights, and regulation that accepts a ban. While there are many other topics discussed within this category, such as "virginity," "homosexuality," "forced marriage," and other changing patterns related to sex-gender roles, this particular discussion shows the spirit of the struggles and contestations that young diasporic Kurds are engaged in. In the next section, the question of forced marriage takes a different turn.

Marital Obligations

In the framework of marriage, men and women talk about different features that they look for in a future partner, such as education, class, ethnicity, religion, and so on. Most participants online weave in narratives of the reproduction of the nation together with intra-ethnic marriage. The national project, discussed exhaustively throughout the forums and different themes, becomes a gender project. The question of marriage within the own ethnic groups was often a popular discussion.

The discussions allude to the intimate politics of preserving the nation through intra-ethnic marriages. They encouraged a nationalistic agenda, which puts the nation and its reproduction in the first room, and not personal aspirations, as the following quote illustrates. The nation is, however, mainly conflated with the Kurdish woman as the reproducer, inciting a moral obligation among them to strengthen the Kurdish ethnicity. The relation between manhood, womanhood, and nationhood is expressively different among Kurds. Nationalism becomes gendered and sexualized as a strategy to maintain the nation, infusing guilt and even shame. These sentiments evoked and felt are intimately related to the history of the Kurds and the struggles to remain as a distinctive ethnic group as well as building a nation-state. Many times, these discussions lead to provocation and fierce arguments when women especially consider potential life partners outside the ethnic community. Embedded in the discussions is a hierarchy of acceptance in terms of which ethnic backgrounds are "better" or "worse."

> I want to be able to speak Kurdish with my partner and my children to learn Kurdish. This is particularly important as I lack a country, but if I had one, it would have been with a Swedish guy. (*Western individualism and sexuality*, Swedish Forum, April 25, 2010)

> What can be hotter than a Swedish guy learning Kurdish ;-) His nationality does not have to exclude any speaking of Kurdish at home. (*Western individualism and sexuality*, Swedish Forum, April 25, 2010)

> Sure, it is a shame that we mix ourselves with other people and that the Kurdish nation dies. Kurds should be with Kurds, how can girls be with other nationalities? (*Kurdish girl and black guy*, British Forum, May 9, 2010)

Components that are highlighted as important for the reproduction of the nation and the Kurdish identity include a lingua franca, common history, and the future of a nation-state. This is not an uncommon argument among young Kurds in any country. The first post by a young woman declares a view that in the absent Kurdish nation-state dictates her marriage choice exclusively. The ideas embedded in the argument expose a belief that the nation's survival is dependent on the reproduction of culture and national identity. She speaks of herself as the "bearer of the collectivities" (Yuval-Davis 1993). While bureaucracy has been identified as the producer of the nation, Yuval-Davis (1997) highlights the important role of the woman as the reproducer of the nation, biologically, symbolically, and culturally. Such moral obligations outweigh reproductive rights (Yuval-Davis 1996). Her explanation, the reason to why women now are seen as the reproducers, is that women and the family have been located within the private sphere and therefore have not been viewed as politically significant.

Although these views have changed over the years and the boundaries between public and private have become blurred, as we have seen in earlier sections, these perceptions are still embedded in the position of a woman linked to the family and the private sphere, which in turn have consequences for citizenship. When these private matters are brought into the public domain, they cease to be merely a private concern, and convert into a public question. This does not mean that the issue was not of public concern then, but, rather, that it has become more visible, and consequently more challenged, as the young participants are increasingly "thinking aloud" and so breach the public–private identity spheres, and increasingly more with the digitally mediated communication. But ofttimes in the discussions about marriage, Kurds also like to convince other fellow Kurds of the right decision. They refer to intra-ethnic marriage as a collective responsibility.

In her ethnographic online work, M.I. Franklin (2001, 2003, 2004) shows how women living in Samoa, Tonga, and elsewhere, openly, at the junction of public and private sphere, talk about sex-gender roles, sexuality, and femininity and masculinity, and stresses the strains of familial relationships and historical–cultural obligations (2004). In similar ways, Kurdish women in Sweden and the UK (and elsewhere) have expressed personal concerns and responded to the complex private experiences and public expectations. New conventions are being considered in relation to established social conventions and sex-gender roles (Franklin 2004), which can be viewed in light of the second-wave feminist phrase "the personal is political" (meaning that "there is no private domain of a person's life that is not political and there is no political issue that is not personal") (Charlotte Bunch quoted in Franklin 2004, p. 77, with reference to Sargent 1981).

The third post, by a Kurd settled in Britain, confirms that the woman carries this responsibility for the reproduction of the nation and the culture. Not only does this evoke "embarrassment," but the woman would also be a "traitor" if the circle of woman, nation, and family would be broken. The Kurdish woman is identified as the symbolic indicator of the failure of the Kurdish struggle. Marriage and the woman's role are indeed intimately connected to the (imagi)nation, and the struggle for this is tied to family, gender, and sexuality. Any marriage outside the Kurdish sphere is a divorce from the homeland. On the other hand, while views of the survival of the nation were also common among Kurdish men, they were rarely charged with the same duties.

Blended with these serious arguments is the joke-cum-satire presented by the second female poster about how to creatively find a way between these old cultural structures and new hybrid, cosmopolitan, perspectives in which one can loosen the boundaries between nationality and ethnic belonging. The prevalence of the joke also displays how women humouristically allude to gender conventions (Franklin 2004) and make themselves active players in what usually have been heavily gendered discussions, where they have been made passive in questions that indeed include them as women. Jokes serve as methods of communicating what is and what is not appropriate behaviour for members of one's social group and cultural identity.

Linking back to the politics of recognition, Appiah (1994) argues that by seeking to express ourselves we seek recognition of, in this case, a Kurdish identity. To be recognized means social acknowledgement of that collective identity, which demands not only recognizing it, but also demonstrating respect for it. Within these exchanges emerges a hierarchy of ethnicities, a sort of grading of acceptance. As a starting point, endogamy, marriage within the own collective group, is an overwhelming strand that is based mainly on experiences of oppression and the promise to build a united nation. While there are voices that diverge from these notions and aim to break away from these, there is, at the same time, a notion of what is passable and what is unacceptable. The term "enemy" was recurrent and is referred to the surrounding countries or nationalities of Arabs, Persians, and Turks. The terms were frequently used within different contexts, from political to more personal issues.

> I don't go near turks, arabs, and Persians. But if another nationality I don't mind. (*Western individualism and sexuality*, Swedish Forum, April 25, 2010)

> Kurds should be with Kurds, how can girls be with other nationalities? Embarrassing. (*Kurds and Albanians, Female*, Swedish forum, May 19, 2010)

> That girl would be a traitor if she would marry him. This also includes Kurdish guys who marry Turks, Arabs or Iranians. (Love and enemy, Male, English forum, July 9, 2010, in reply to above question from British forum)

The most common reason for advocating endogamy is "cultural practices." The home is where much of the culture is practised and transferred to the children (Okin 1999), but, on the other hand, the aforementioned accounts show that it is also a matter of not intermingling with the "enemies." The hierarchy of relationships becomes more obvious here as especially three ethnic groups are forbidden. It is therefore a smaller problem for women to have a Swedish or British partner than a Turk, Arab, or Persian. These discussions are not projected to introduce a dichotomy, but to capture their hybrid lives as they envision their lives as ethnic Kurds and Swedish citizens. These dynamic and online particularities will be contrasted against offline dialogues that are qualitatively distinctive notwithstanding some interlinked strands.

Offline Delineations

In the following, we move from the online to the offline interviews with members of the online forums. The purpose here is to show how offline and online can overlap and digress on issues that relate to key questions in this book. The reconstruction of the discussions takes places on the basis of those excerpts that "best" illustrate the relationship between online and offline, and what implications this have in relation to the themes covered. The offline nuanced and contradicting passages will add light on three particular aspects. One aspect relates to the different geographic locations in which Kurdish diasporas are settled. For instance, in the context of honor-killing, the participants elucidate how and why the public debates in Sweden affect the young Kurds' everyday life, while the absence of the discussions in the UK, as well as in the homeland, has not created the same kind of momentum among the Kurdish populations. The explanations are directly impacted by the public discourse in their locations.

The other point that derives from the online–offline intersection is how different methods used to collected data, online versus offline, can generate different results. By way of combining online ethnographic work and offline interviews, the different data have been mutually contextualizing (Orgad 2009). Most often, as Slater explains (2002), there is a tendency to treat online and offline environments as context and phenomenon. The offline is explained as that which makes sense of the online experiences (Slater 2002). In other words, it is assumed that a researcher should use offline data to make sense of online data (Orgad 2009). By structuring the online–offline nexus in the way I have here, it becomes more evident how these spaces interconnect. These different sites are neither mirroring nor opposing each other, but they do display contradictions, revisions, and influences of each other. It is this interrelation, the journey of the participants—from offline to online and back to offline—that exposes the implications for their identification and understanding of being a Kurd in Sweden or the UK. It is, therefore, not a comparative analysis between online and offline communications, but rather, it is a continuation of experiences that participants undergo, of which the nuances and contradictions are more explained here.

The conversations about gender roles and female and male sexuality have played out completely differently from those of offline. These anonymous online conversations have been both playful and serious at times. The discrepancies between the unconventional forms of talking about private and confidential concerns online, and the more restricted dialogues offline, will be more evident here. The section will, however, start by explaining why the UK Kurds, and homeland-based Kurds, were not engaged in any discussions on honour-killing, while the topic captured a considerable amount of space in the Swedish forum, as well as here during the interviews. While interviewing the Kurdish individuals in Sweden, they would bring up the honour topic and their personal stories about marginalization. On a few occasions, the female respondents would refer to issues of the honour debates in Sweden. During my conversations with London-based Kurds, I had to specifically ask about the subject and how they relate to it.

> After the thing with Fadime, it's been really strange. Swedes [...] I always have to defend myself ... "Oh, can you have a boyfriend?" "Yes, I can." "Yeah but would they beat you up? Would they kill you?" I'm like "no, it's not like that," and then you explain to them. [...] "Yeah, but are you a Muslim?" It's like that; you get a label. (Interview, female, 19, Sweden)

> Honor killing? It's nothing that I think about really. Here it's been debates about it, but mostly concerns people from Pakistan or India I think. I know that there are issues back home, but that's ... well, I never really talk about with my friends or on Viva. Not sure I've seen any threads on it either. (Interview, female, 26, UK)

This is an interesting insight into the experiences of Kurds in their settlement countries and how the ground events and public debates influence diasporic people, settled in different locations, in different ways. We often talk about the different histories of diasporic formations, in particular, a comprehensive portion of the literature elaborates on voluntary and involuntary dispersion. However, there is limited research on how differences evolve after the relocation of diasporas. Are there underlying assumptions that diaspora deal with the same issues in all the different places they reside in because they are all diasporic people?

Current studies of diaspora bring into light and accentuate the distinctiveness of movements and the interruption, resulting in hybrid identities. Kalra et al. (2005) have singled out one particular theme emerging from the study of diaspora, which is the multilocational qualities or interactions between the homes and abroad, which cannot be reduced to one place or another. Taking another direction to explore diasporic people laterally—whose members are located around the world—we could learn how experiences among a Kurdish diaspora have different meanings and significance for their self-identification. When Kurds are being stigmatized in Sweden and have been strongly portrayed as the other, they are viewed as coming from a backward culture and as tribal people. The Kurdish young woman in Sweden explains in the first excerpt how she has been forced to defend herself against patronizing articulations. Her Kurdish background seemed to lead to specific associations among her Swedish friends, who asked probing question about her family situation related to honour. When we state that intricate social and cultural dynamics in specific groups have formed identities within diasporas, it is not only the historical references that explain this, but also the current and future experiences that shape the characteristics of diasporas.

By contrast, the female and male participants I talked with, both in the UK and in Kurdistan, did not reflect over the questions or face prejudice in this context. The frequent and lengthy online discussions in the Swedish forum and the absence of the discussion in the UK forum inform of the different discourses they are affected by in their everyday lives. None of the British citizens were actually very interested in the topic despite the several cases that traverse through the mass media channels in the country. In the Kurdish regions, there have been even more cases reported in the media, but, again, during the interviews, I had to bring up the question and ask the interviewees of their relation to the topic.

> Yes, it does happen here, but no one is really talking about it. I think Kurds in diaspora discuss the issues more than Kurds here. Kurds in Europe try to bring these issues to the fore and make them known to politicians in order to be dealt with. But on Viva, no one is really discussing it. I can think it's a bit sensitive and maybe girls feel they will be labeled for having opinions about it. (Interview, male, 20, Kurdistan/Iraq)

Participants living in their homeland, in this case Kurdish region in Iraq, are aware of the incidents, and although they are reported in the media, there are no ongoing institutionalized and formal discussions that deal with the real issues. The participants explained that people in general are aware of the cases as they are reported briefly, and many have a firm opinion against this patriarchal system, but the involvement is usually not more than that. Furthermore, the note on girls' position and the discomfort of publicizing views on the matter seem to make it a sensitive task. This leads to the question of how participants in the online forums act differently to topics that are considered taboo and sensitive. While the Swedish forum was overwhelmingly forward in their approach towards these topics, the Kurdish forum was rather restricted. The UK and the rest of the forums such as Danish Norwegian and German could be found somewhere in between.

Online Confidentiality and Offline Restrictions

One of the most popular and dense discussions online was related to gender, sexuality, femininity, and masculinity questions. Opposing this popularity are the interview statements, which declared no interest in taking part in such threads. Simultaneously, all interviewees acknowledged that they were the most popular in terms of volume, participation, and number of views and clicks.

> It can be a post about, for instance, Kurdish values, "is it OK if I do this," and so on ... For them maybe it's not a clear answer, or a question ... they want to test boundaries and see what Kurds can do and can't do without being labeled. (Interview, male 23, Sweden)

> The most popular threads are often the most useless threads, meaning those about "Kurdish girls are like this", "can we do this", "they have been Swedified" and so on. (Interview, female 19, UK)

The excerpts explain the popularity of the theme and how "testing boundaries" without being "public" played a major role in this. The interviewees explained that Viva Kurdistan allows participants to give voice to their concerns and to test boundaries without subjecting to categorization and labels. In contrast to the political discussion threads, the themes linked to gender roles and sexuality involved young females in the forums to a higher degree. One of the factors associated with an online community like Viva Kurdistan is the possibility to raise questions that are considered taboo, not only within the Kurdish context but also more generally. Questions of homosexuality, virginity, and online relationships are questions that young people can approach in a different way online as opposed to in a face-to-face environment. It is evident that anonymity and privacy are decisive factors to what kind of topics find their place online, but were reluctantly talked about during the interviews, perhaps because of how they want to portray themselves to the interviewer. Is it the case that all respondents are genuinely not interested in these questions, or could there be other reasons behind such claims? The multisited approach in my research has allowed such explorations and routes around such questions. As I have had access to both online and offline settings, I came to know that those interviewees, who during the interviews expressed their lack of interest in such banal subjects, did actually take part in online discussions on these topics. Marginalizing this particular topic was a common phenomenon among all participants I met in the different locations. In the instances I asked to reflect the gender and sexuality questions online, they were depicted popular, but insignificant.

The more accurate description of these popular topics can be related back to the respondents explaining how onlineness opens up the testing of confines of norms and traditions, which, however, seems to have been restricted during the offline interviews. It is necessary to consider, therefore, how many online participants vis-à-vis offline respondents are giving uncensored responses, which relate to questions of authenticity rather than anonymity, and which I consider to be one of the main factors in the distinction between online and offline. The aim with this observation is not to evaluate the truthfulness of participants, but rather to improve the understanding of how some topics that may not have been elaborated enough, better suit the online structure. The most important point emerging from the contradictions between offline and online, and the fact that such sensitive topics evoked massive response while they were not attractive to discuss offline, is probably the discrepancies between methodologies when collecting material. As Orgad (2009) argues, researchers should use different types of data in their analytical work as they mutually contextualize each other.

Mixed Marriages Between the Kurds of Diaspora and the Homeland

Drawing from the online discussion, women were often talked about as the reproducers of the nation. There are multiple layers to the question of marriage among Kurds: firstly, different Kurdish regions in the authoritarian states, secondly, different cities within the regions, and thirdly, the observation proposes a changing notion of mixed marriages that also includes a distinction between European Kurds and homeland Kurds. As explained, the avoidance of endogamy lies in the conviction of preserving the ethnic group and the nation, especially as there is no state in this case. Kurdish diaspora sees this as a serious and critical strategy for the survival of a future Kurdistan. This is in particular an issue that diaspora Kurds discuss, as opposed to homeland Kurds who do not face the same kind of encounters and challenges that diaspora Kurds do. When I talked with the interview participants, they opened up for a new insight into the question of mixed marriage.

I would feel more comfortable marrying a Kurdish guy in the future. When we have kids, I don't want the kids to grow up and have two different backgrounds, you know one Kurdish and another for example English. (Interview, female, 20, UK)

But, we've been brought up with two cultures, so don't forget that. We've been brought up with the British culture and the Kurdish culture. It hasn't caused any clash; it has made us more open-minded. So in a sense, even if we don't end up marrying a Kurdish guy, but marry a say … an English guy, it won't be a bad thing, we can still make them Kurdish. (Interview, female 25, UK, *in reply to the above*)

While the first respondent replicates many of the online viewpoints, that it is important to keep the culture Kurdish, it is useful to look more closely at the second interview excerpt, as it challenges the general notion of mixed marriage and what different backgrounds imply. Although diasporic Kurds may wish to retain their culture through marriage to a partner from the same ethnic background, they themselves have grown up with two different backgrounds—different locations, different languages, cultures—as children of immigrant parents. The extract adds an interesting new dimension to how a mixed background is commonly referred to as a *biological* aspect, being "mixed raced," when in fact diasporic individuals also go adopt this hybridity in their socialization processes in the settlement countries, when on the one hand sustaining their original culture, and on the other hand adapting and adopting the new culture. Moreover, a third new aspect, or criteria, is included in the delineation of marital obligation:

I wouldn't like to marry anyone that doesn't live in the UK, because, in that way they would understand the cultures that I've been brought up with. I mean, having a relationship with somebody, you need to have your own space too, to go out with friends, and still enjoy life. Not get married and have him know your whereabouts 24/7. (Interview, female, 25, UK)

My parents don't mind what he does as long as he is educated, but they would prefer somebody in Europe, not in Kurdistan. It has to be a European Kurd. Because we have different mentalities, and there would be a clash. (Interview, female, 19, UK)

It has now been more narrowed down to a European Kurd. The desiderata includes, on the one hand someone who can understand Kurdish history, culture, and language, but on the other hand someone who can also understand European Kurds and their culture, which allows space for independence and individuality. This is also the case in Sweden, where most diasporic Kurds prefer to marry a "Euro-Kurd."[14] I will revert to this point in Chap. 6, where I outline how Kurds in both these locations distinguish themselves both from Kurds "back home" and from new diasporic Kurds in different European countries, creating tensions online and offline in the definition of Kurdishness.

Notes

1. A discussion thread starts with an initial post and as participants respond in the thread, the messages are grouped into a discussion thread, and each thread is differentiated by a topic.
2. There have been six cases of honour-killings in Sweden between 1986 and 2012. One of the reasons why this particular case has been debated frequently could be the many times that Fadime herself brought the matter into the public domain and appeared in the media discussing these issues.
3. The Guardian "A Veil Drawn over Brutal Crimes," 3 October, 2003.
4. Gender equality has recently been pushed even further in Sweden, as activists advocate "gender-neutrality" and propose that society should accept people who do not identify themselves either as female or male. Activists also propose that traditional gender roles should be erased, the use of unisex names (currently, there are 170 legally recognized unisex names), and the use of a new personal pronoun "hen" (a mix of "han" [he] and "hon" [she]), which is completely gender neutral.
5. Halabja may be spelt in different ways in the different Kurdish dialects.
6. The term literally means "New Day" and comes with an etiological legend about a tyrant named Zohak, from whose shoulders grew two snakes that demanded two little children to eat each day. One of these children was saved each time; together they made up a hidden army and are believed to be ancestors of the Kurds. Along with Kawa, a blacksmith, who had lost his sons to the snakes, they eventually besieged and killed the tyrant (Hassanpour and Mojab 2005).
7. This expression is a salute to the Kurd and her/his Kurdish land, and is frequently used among young Kurds in the Forum.
8. In March 2009, the first ever Newroz celebrated at Trafalgar Square in London was partially organized by PKK-related organizations (Halkevi, Fed-Bir) and therefore had many PKK supporters attending the celebrations.
9. Different ways of writing, that is, level of knowledge and language kills, were helpful in identifying members in terms of class, gender, education, new or old diasporas, and so forth. *Slate*, "Sweden's Gender-Neutral Pronoun: Hen," April 11, 2012.
10. Furthermore, Spain has intended to present a law on freedom of religion that will restrict their use in public spaces, while Germany has had heated debates on the burqa garment. Denmark has prohibited wearing the burqa

and niqab in public places since January 2010, while, at the time of writing, the Netherlands was drafting bills that would prohibit the garment in areas of the public sector, notably education.

11. BBC News, "Damian Green says burqa ban would be 'un-British,'" July 18, 2010.
12. Svenska Dagbladet, "Reinfeldt och Sahlin i debattduell," January 27, 2010.
13. Using a data tool such as Nvivo, it is possible not just to look for "big" words and meta-themes but also to identify how "small" words can convey feelings (strength or weakness) and the character (question or a statement) of a post. While online behaviour is often explained by the nature of its environment such as anonymity, it is important to analyse the context in which some words are expressed as the technique itself is not the catalyst behind some actions online.
14. I am using this word in connection to respondents' own terms such as "European-Kurd." The term is also closely connected to what Ayata (2011, p. 4) has termed "Euro-Kurdistan," referring to Kurdish transnational activities in diaspora that are directed towards the "Kurdish homeland."

CHAPTER 6

"Am I a Real Kurd?": Deconstructing Kurdish Identity

INTRODUCTION

One of the pronounced articulations within the diaspora study is how diaspora emerge as new, hybrid constructions. The expression of cultural hybridity is a recurrent idea in the work of British theorists Stuart Hall (1992), Paul Gilroy (1993), and Homi Bhabha (1994). Bhabha calls this a "third place," Hall refers to it as "new ethnicities," and Gilroy as "double consciousness." This third place emerges from the migratory troubles of not feeling at home anywhere, which Mishra (2006) explains by using a "sign of rupture," and that diaspora is the cultural periphery between the settlement country and the country of origin. It is a multiplex and contested space where performativities of diasporic individuals shift and are manifold. As the following sections will display, young Kurds growing up in Western European societies are at a particularly complex juncture, engaged in uneasy, but determined, negotiations of their Kurdish identity.

These online exchanges call for a close-up examination of cross-cultural disputations and socio-political dimensions of otherness that haunt them within both cultures they grow up in. We need to pay careful attention to their words, which ultimately reflect their state of mind, and place them in relevant theoretical discourse so that we do not neglect what they are trying to tell us. If young Kurdish members of the diaspora diverge from imagined notions of how to be a Kurd, if they break away from a romanticized longing for a return to the homeland, or if they feel more at home

© The Author(s) 2016

J. Mahmod, *Kurdish Diaspora Online*, The Palgrave
Macmillan Series in International Political Communication,
DOI 10.1057/978-1-137-51347-2_6

among Swedes or Brits, what does this mean theoretically? It is time to come to terms with older academic patois and to describe more articulately the empirical realities that these younger generations are displaying, and treat such experiences with nuances. This is not to imply that studies on (Kurdish) diaspora have not covered important aspects and experiences, but, rather, that the articulations in the new digital age requires us to expose, what may seem as an uncomfortable task, what traditional media concealed. By delving deeply into what may sometimes seem to be banal words expressed within an online community, and placing these in a broader theoretical framework, new insights challenge some of the traditional notions of diasporis identity. For children of immigrants in Europe, the notion of how to be a Kurd, or what it requires to be a Swede, is not always constructed in accordance with nationalistic projects or victimized sentiments. Instead, as will emerge through the extracts here, Kurds have been very vocal and upfront about what they think of rigid notions of Kurdishness or their place as "guests" in the European societies. Taken together, these new positions of identifications from which they speak, give fresh and crucial insights into the formations they are experiencing.

The dynamics appearing in the dialogues between diasporas are significant in terms of analysing these in a close-up manner through online communication, as they inculcate these theoretical deliberations by postmodern theorists, such as those of Gilroy (1997) when he says that the concept of diaspora "puts emphasis on contingency, indeterminacy, and conflict" (p. 334). To follow diaspora and their everyday communication and activities through transnational lenses, allows us to grasp the lived experiences between homeland and settlement countries, which confront our (often static) perceptions that conflate social and cultural identity with a geographic space (Karim 2006). Looking at diasporic transnational practices and communication, we will see through the conversations held between online participants, how this affects both the nation-state and the diasporic individuals. In this chapter, I examine the different positions from which Kurdish diaspora speak that cut across different geographic nodes of belonging. An individual's identity may change over time and consequently alter the hierarchy of attachments that are regulated by ethnicity, religion, nation, and other forms of belonging that dictate. The discussions within the frame of what I have named "politics" were among the lengthiest, heated, and most in depth and academically written. An overwhelming part of the posts was composed of accounts of the different political parties, histories, elections, citizenship, and identity issues. The concerns being raised here are not only politically sensitive, but also touch upon a personal chord among diasporic Kurds. While online participants were involved in a de-construction of a strict sense of Kurdishness, they were at once visibly affected by it taking into account the emotional and fierce responses evoked.

This chapter is organized around four main sections. The first section presents how participants have dealt with homeland politics and histories of identity politics. They make frequent references to the authoritarian states and how they have been marginalized as the Other by post-colonial regimes. Rather than reconstructing these long-winded descriptions and explanations, one, in particular, interesting contour emerged, which has significant relevance for self-identification, the Self, and the Other. I have named this mechanism as *internal othering*. Because studies have offered in-depth and well-developed descriptions of how Kurds have been the exogenous Other (Hassanpour 1992; Izady 1992; Chaliand 1993; Romano 2002; Alinia 2004; Khayati 2008; Sheyholislami 2008; Ayata 2011), I will only briefly touch upon this issue. More space will be devoted to internal othering in the second section. If the Self and the Other refer to meta-identifications of "us" and "them," internal othering is shifting the gaze and blurring these margins. This has been a useful concept as it disturbs the overarching binaries between the "West and the Rest" that overlooks the diversity within different ethnic groups themselves. Here, I identify different layers of internal othering that the Kurdish online participants were engaged in, and in which they expressed an operation of multiplex identification and contours of commonality and divergences.

In the third section, they shift their discussions to more specifically address issues relating to their settlement countries, such as the rise of far-right movements, racism, and citizenship. In these exchanges, two camps loosely emerged among the Kurdish participants. The first belongs to diasporic Kurds whose families migrated to Europe in the 1980s and the 1990s and who vented strong senses of belongingness, while the second group consisted of Kurds who migrated post-1990s who instead placed themselves in the position of a guest–host relationship. The chapter ends with the interviews with the online participants in three different locations, which shed light on the offline–online journeys and how online interactions have shaped their understanding of the multiple interpretations of Kurdishness. Overlapping all these strands is the increasing uncertainty about "who we are" in the contemporary lives of diaspora Kurds growing up in Europe and in the age of digital media.

Rewinding to Circa 2010

Historical experiences of suppression and inequality and the politics of identity are significant points of references for Kurdish diasporic victims and their attempts of sustaining culture and identity, even among younger generations of Kurds who have not directly experienced the tragedies in the homelands. Most of these participants belong to the second, third, and fourth generations, who grew up outside their homeland(s). The following discussions took place between 2010 and 2011. However, the essential question has remained until today, namely Kurdish independence, while the political scene in the Middle East is continuously changing as described in Chap. 3. During the ethnographic work I conducted (early 2009–2011), the General Election took place in the three different locations (UK, Sweden, and Kurdistan/Iraq), which unexpectedly conflated with my ethnographic case studies. This concurrence of the elections displays both the content related to these events and the different ways in which participants dealt with key questions.

The Iraqi election was manifestly important for young Kurds in diaspora as they engaged not only in terms of the lengthy threads online, but also in terms of time devoted to campaigns and lobbying activities. Discussions related to Turkey were also intense, focusing mainly on human rights questions and the Turkish–Kurdish relationship. Against the backdrop of earlier descriptions of the political events, this chapter recreates the set of intense political discussions that took place in the Swedish and British forums as well as in the Kurdistan setting. These posts capture years of debates and struggles about the fate of the Kurdish identity, the question of Kurdish independence, and other existential questions in both homelands and diaspora.

Kurds as the Other in the Middle East

Everyone who has read a little Kurdish history understands that history re-repeats itself like all other times. When I was younger and read about major events in Kurdish history which the various political parties could have succeeded if they acted in a certain way, but they took stupid decisions and no one won, except Turks, Persians and Arabs.

Now you happen to have the privilege of being in a critical time in modern Kurdish history in which a lot happens, and what you know now will affect the future. Sure, we may all have different ideologies and everyone find them to be the right one, but no one should forget that there are no "us and them" among the Kurds. There is only one Kurdistan and one Kurdish nation.

A home will never hold if everyone under the same roof pull into different directions and disregard the common interests we have." (*Gorran vs. KDP/PUK*, Swedish Forum, February 27, 2010)

The extract belongs to one of the many extensive discussions from the Swedish forum during the 2010 general election in Kurdistan/Iraq. The statement needs to be placed in the context of the historical election period, and how Kurds as a minority within the borders of Iraq, including the Kurdish populations within European borders, could take part in this critical moment. The key point at this stage is the remark that "there are no "us and them" among Kurds," as expressed by the poster, and how it is assumed to be the cornerstone of the reconstruction of one nation and one people. It is with such views that many Kurds created their accounts on Viva Kurdistan to join and discuss Kurdish issues. There are also other online (Facebook) groups and communities, but this one differs based mainly on its transnational characters, and the majority of the members being originally from Kurdistan. In some ways, this echoes the rhetoric used in debates about multiculturalism and how differences are deemed to be obstacles and therefore homogenized through regulations and debates underlying the reproduction of the imagined, Western community. The perspective of "us and them" has been an important element in the conversations when referring to the authoritarian states.

While the discourse of (post-)colonialism has principally been about Western colonization of third-world countries, another important frame for newer states derives from inside the states themselves; *internal post-colonialism* (Vanly 1992). The consequences are still felt among diaspora Kurds, which also explain their persistence to hold on to cultural expression. As explained by Vanly, this kind of chauvinism will make an important point to return to when delineating Kurds' efforts to become complete Swedish citizens.

[I]t is because Kurds have been enslaved and controlled and denied by Arabs and Turks and Persians. [...] calling us "Arabs of Yemen, Turks mountains and relatives of Persian," hence Kurdish identity was totally denied. (*War and Peace in Kurdistan by Ocalan*, British Forum, June 18, 2010)

> Turkey has conducted a psychological war against Kurds for years, which in the first place is about humiliating Kurds to the extent that they don't acknowledge themselves as Kurds. (*Belgian police assault Kurdish TV-channel*, Swedish Forum, March 5, 2010)

The violence in Kurdistan, one of the oldest nationalist conflicts worldwide, is not based on the politics of ethnic exclusion, but on a forced marriage between one national minority and another dominant national group. This repertoire and the fact that Kurds are the largest minority without a state have served as immensely important sources of momentum to which strong attachment is expressed in various ways. The Kurdish resistance in the homelands has been strong, but this has also led them to becoming subject to different policies of oppression and genocide, and the deliberate de-construction of their ethnic identity. In Turkey (late 1920s) and Iraq (1980s), they have encountered policies of systematic oppression and assimilation.

Diasporic participants elaborated on these post-colonial experiences in the origin countries (mainly Iraq and Turkey at the time) and stayed updated with the current affairs in the homelands, which was indeed part of their everyday life. Some scholars argue that these experiences and the rejection in the origin countries constitute the basis of the Kurdish construction of an identity. Such commitment, to keep developing Kurdish culture and politics, is evident in their activities in Sweden and the UK, which have echoed widely in the international community. Connecting back to Chap. 5 and the importance of language that Kurds recognized in order to remain Kurds, it has, in the context of the Self and the Other—or Kurdistan and the authoritarian states—been even more emphasized and fiercely discussed.

> What I see as tragic is the Kurds who live in Sweden, speaks Turkish, Arabic or Persian at home, listening to Turkish, Persian and Arabic music on a daily basis. But it is not 'just' and it is no coincidence, it is their victory over the Kurdish culture and the Kurdish heritage. You are not Kurds, if you do not know your language, understand your music, cannot communicate with your people and barely know your history and traditions! (*It's not "just," it is more important than the armed struggle*, Swedish Forum, June 20, 2010)
>
> Hello dear friends. So what Persian singer do you like?? I listen a lot to Googoosh, now, what about you??? (*Music, Kurdish Forum*, March 3, 2010)

Language has played an important and powerful role among Kurds, which they frequently like to underline. Speaking these three authoritarian languages is seen as a continuation of internal colonialism. Participants have often encouraged each other to sustain their Kurdish language, listen to Kurdish music, attend festivities, and so on, and quite often they also cross borders to other European countries to engage in such transnational events. This, together with the memories of tragedies such as Halabja and other events, was rarely subject for negotiations. The strictness in their approach to persuade their fellow participants to choose, for example, music carefully mirrors the ongoing diaspora struggle for recognition of the Kurdish identity, both inside and outside the ethnic group.

This can be contrasted to the more settled conversations in the Kurdish forum, which, most of the time, was the case across all topics they discussed. Despite the same struggle for international and national recognition of the Kurdish cultural identity, it is interesting to compare homeland-based Kurds with diaspora Kurds. Evidently, long-distance nationalism (Anderson 1992) can be regarded as a strategy of ethnicization of the diasporic populations in these modern and post-industrialized societies. Diaspora Kurds themselves seem to be well aware of the differences in nationalistic endeavours reflected in the words of a male participant: "Many might think these are just a few hundred outside Kurdistan that speak Persian, and that our faithful Kurds in the homeland speak Kurdish. But, NO, the Kurds there are worse (*It's not "just," it is more important than the armed struggle*, Swedish Forum, June 20, 2010). This difference in language use and idioms is an important point that reveals much of the processes of identity constructions among Kurds in both the country of settlement and country of origin. I will return to this aspect, but it is worth noting for the moment these very open differences between the forums.

The problems generated by official repression are compounded by the fact that considerable differences exist between the various dialects of Kurdish, which, in turn, has prevented the development of a standard form of the Kurdish language (Kreyenbroek 1992). Language, in particular, has been seen as a cultural product of Kurdish existence, and impressive efforts have been made to preserve and develop it outside Kurdistan (Kreyenbroek 1992). Med TV is a good example of successful transnational cooperation among Kurds. The TV channel, broadcasting in Kurdish, quickly became popular among Kurds in Europe. These are not small-scale resistance in utterances; rather, they have been supporting the mobilization of Kurdish resistance, which these exchanges highlight by uncovering the enduring significance of colonialism on the diasporic Kurdish community that the earlier post stated under the heading "Belgian police assault Kurdish TV-channel." Endless discussions circulated around renewed assaults on Kurds in diaspora, ordered by Turkish authorities, which Kurds quickly mobilized around online to incite demonstrations against the shutdowns. We see that cultural values, both historical and gendered, as well as language are profoundly contingent upon the consequences of colonialism and homeland images. As seen in the earlier discussions, holding on to language and cultural official expressions—through, for instance, marriage within the ethnic group—is a way of preventing continuation of colonization of the Kurdish culture. This is why teaching a Swede the Kurdish language, or turning a Brit into a Kurd, worked out as a compromise without abandoning Kurdish culture completely.

> As a Kurd in Sweden, it is normal that in many ways that you follow Swedish standards, traditions, that you have become "pretty Swedish". I don't see this as a problem; no Swede has ever tried to deny me the right to my culture, my language and my history. When I started primary school, the state has paid me for me to continue to learn and develop my mother tongue. What I see as tragic is the Kurds who live in Sweden, and who speak Turkish, Arabic or Persian at home. (*It's not "just," it is more important than the armed struggle*, Swedish Forum, June 20, 2010)

One more point on the issues of language is the aforementioned distinction between the Swedish identity politics and those of the authoritarians. This statement, which considers culture in political terms, discloses how much of the contemporary and social multiculturalism conundrum turns to the question of recognition. Recognition of identity, consequently, is largely a question of acknowledging individuals and what we conceptualize as identities. Recognition policies seem to undermine the resistance to adapt to, and employ, the dominant culture's values, artefacts, and other elements within it. This will become clearer later when participants talk about themselves as Swedish and British citizens in their new homelands of Europe.

These post-colonial experiences are important to highlight in order to understand contemporary ethnic relations and how Kurdish constructions are partly based on the rejections of influences from authoritarian states. Language and awareness of historical suffering are important sites of identification of a strong cultural Kurdish identity, and specific strategies—using the Kurdish language in daily life (excluding the antagonist languages, and recognizing major historic and national days)—have been outlined as important by the diasporic Kurds. Preserving the (Kurdish) language as a fundamental part of retaining cultural identity (Anzaldúa 1987; Radhakrishnan 1996) illustrates what Spivak (1990) described as "strategic essentialism." It serves to make strong claims of cultural elements that participants make in relations where the power is unequally distributed. It is the "weapon of the weak" (Clifford 1994), which may, however, alter into a latent form of oppression (Appiah 1994; Ignacio 2005); while the intention may be of "good character,"—to reject oppressive governments—it may at once be a "bad strategy" when it permits violent articulations of exclusivism within the minority group itself in order to uphold a distinct authentic identity (Clifford 1994). We saw tendencies in the previous chapter, but it will become clearer in the following section.

Thus far, these observations confirm previous research on how Kurds (re)construct their Kurdish identities and the awareness they possess around such political and colonial histories of their homeland. In the next part, this will become blurred as we shift focus to internal struggles and othering, and how the change of politics—from addressing exogenous major threats to forming a domestic political system—also changes the rhetoric and discourse of Kurdishness.

SHIFTING GAZE TO THE INTERNAL OTHER

As will emerge from the following interchanges, the question of who is a Kurd and what constitutes the performativities of Kurdishness, move from essentialist understandings to constructionist views. While the earlier posts presented a construction of the Kurdish identity with reference to dominant powers of oppression, I will here show how a closer examination of the exchanges uncovers the subtle fluid and diverse features of identity.

When Kurds identify coethnics by categories of "weak Kurd" or "non-Kurd," they challenge essentialist views of ethnic affiliation and by implication suggest how one should act to be considered an authentic Kurd. The mechanism of internal othering among diaspora Kurds served as a way of suggesting either a weak or strong Kurdish identity, in which participants then circuitously design how one should operate to be identified as Kurd. This methodological approach can examine more closely what takes place in an enclosed setting where internal issues are discussed, and where differences are actively produced through interpersonal engagement

(Schein 1997). The section starts with some of the ubiquitous essential-ist perceptions regarding being a Kurd, mainly gaining legitimacy from injustices, expectations of solidarity, and understandings of how they are distinguished from the external Other. Subsequently, there is a process of internal othering that takes place in different layers, and as specified in each heading.

From Essentialist Claims to Constructionist Notions

What is a REAL Kurd? Please respond to what a real Kurd is and why some people think it is important to be one? (*Real Kurd*, Swedish forum, July 22, 2010)

Am I a Kurd? I consider Kurds to have many languages, not dialects. Dialects differ in the way you pronounce words while languages have dif-ferent words. I feel closer to a Shia Arab than a Kurd, who's not Shia. But still, does anyone have the right to say that I'm not Kurdish? (*Am I a Kurd?* British forum, June 29, 2010)

You are no doubt a Persian monkey. (*Am I a Kurd*, British forum, June 29, 2010, *in response to the post above*)

First of all, these types of questions are rather remarkable per se because they downplay the commonality of ethnicity or nationality imagined among most members at face value. Consequently, they most often led to fierce responses, including insults, name-calling, and flames. Although these types of questions and topics circulating on Viva Kurdistan are embedded in many discussions taking place in different forums, these more straight-forward and bold questions are considered as questioning the Kurdish identity. Broaching these subjects recall the attitudes and treatment Kurds have had to defend themselves against in their regions. The interviewees I spoke with about their decision to become a member of the community, explained that they wanted to meet other Kurds and talk about Kurdish issues and independence. Many of them also made it clear that the ques-tion of what Kurdishness entails has never been brought up for discus-sion before entering this transnational online community. It seemed that the discourse of Kurdishness has been unquestionable, and considering the previous delineations and histories of oppression, this is, perhaps, not surprising. What came as a surprise for participants were, however, these new tackles and dialogues. According to my observations, the nature of such questions was not popular, and many times the posters were verbally attacked. Initial responses would look like the aforementioned third post. Name-callings and trolling of this kind were designed to ruin the discussions, and even resulted in the discussion threads being locked by the online administrators. Having said that, it is also true that such topics became increasingly more common and attracted a large amount of participants engaging in the discussions, which, at times, turned into long, philosophical questions.

> A real Kurd is a proud Kurd who never for one second turns the back on his one people. (*Real Kurd*, Swedish Forum, July 22, 2010, *in response to the post above*)

> [T]o me Kurdishness is not a choice and the way I act, live and will live will be hugely affected because of my identity which I care about. Being a Kurd, it's not a choice, it is part of me and I am very proud of that. (*Am I a Kurd*, British forum, June 29, 2010, *in response to the post above*)

Many posts allude to essentialist notions of Kurdish identity as a fait accompli; emotions, pride, and memories capture the essence of Kurdishness. Participants stated that these feelings are naturally embedded in a Kurd and are "just there," and participants often conferred that such feelings did not need further explanation. The words celebrate an authentic inner essence independent of the circumstances and the processes that Kurds undergo. Given the historical and current background of the political situation in each Kurdish region that has endured physical and psychological violence for decades, these interrogative comments, at times made jokingly, evoked, evoked upset feelings and sometimes aggressive response. Leaving the insults aside, the immediate responses were framed by essentialist opinions, mainly referring to history, culture, and language that are differentiated predominantly from that in Iraq, Iran, Turkey, and Syria. In light of that, participants talk of an essence that journey through history and time and into diasporic spaces. The view that came with natural notions of identity is that either you are a Kurd, or not. In such thinking, there is less space for diversity.

> So what is Kurdish culture? it's probably the most realistic and peaceful culture we have in the middle east and that has a lot to do with our common experience as a people. (*Am I a Kurd?* British forum, June 29, 2010)

> I support pkk and Kurdish independence but I will never support PKK JUST BECAUSE it is Kurdish [...]. We are against Turkish government

and occupation not because they are turks but because they oppress kurds and they have occupied Kurdish land. (*Two Turkish Policemen in Samsun killed by HPG*, British forum, April 21, 2010)

From being a variable of essence, it is now described as a matter of *experience*, which is differentiated from other diasporas' experiences. The historical dimension of colonial rule, oppression, and suppression works as definitional denominators to distinguish Kurds as *a* diaspora from other diasporas. The argument addressing the need for recognition of historical context that creates a diaspora rests upon the changing discourses, meanings, and experiences of being in diaspora. Kurds often refer to themselves as a distinct diasporic group with completely different experiences from that of neighbouring diasporic groups. The points made and embedded in these comments relate to my earlier cautionary note on subsuming groups under a larger semantic category on the basis that they once left their countries. Although this is exactly what diasporic Kurds seem to be aware of since they also put so much effort into it; being a Kurd is initially expressed as something without choice, but is then indicated to rely on certain elements and on certain acts that need to be repeated and upheld. How these converge between online and offline is not always unproblematically translated; although the online environment can strengthen certain elements, it also contradicts and promotes renegotiations from these young men and women. According to Vali (1998), the "obsession" with remaining a distinct group is caused by being consistently unrepresentable. This is also what generates the modality of their relationship with their others. Moreover, this is where Kurdish nationalism also departs from the Western classical form of nationalism produced by modernity with the creation of civil society and democratic citizenship. In the Kurdish context, violence has defined their nationalism.[1]

Kymlicka's (2001) account of the cause and effect of a strong nationalistic agenda explains how discourses about civil rights or a lack of them can place individuals or groups either against or in full support of a country's policies and values. Without overlooking discrimination and dichotomies in Western societies, the right to whatever has been denied harshly in post-colonial history has influenced young women and men on Viva Kurdistan and their position in the society in which they live. These statements explicitly suggest that the denial of one's rights and existence has the opposite effect. While I do believe the cause and effect premise is significant, I have also found a more complex outlook that I demarcate through these different layers of othering.

"I Call You a Turk and a Half Turk"

In January 2009, Kurds and Iraqis went to the polls for provincial elections, which registered more voters than any previous elections. The election that year changed the dynamics of the Kurdish political landscape when a political party opposing the two ruling Kurdish parties, the PUK and KDP, appeared for the first time. The opposition was led by a former PUK leader, Nawshirwan Mustafa, who, in 2007, had created Gorran (the Movement for Change), consisting mainly of disenchanted PUK, but also KDP members (see Chap. 3). The loss of many seats to the new party proved a difficult period for both the Kurdistan Regional Government (KRG) and the relationship between Baghdad and the KRG. The subsequent excerpts took place in the context of the election in Iraq, as the political situation changed dramatically in Iraq and the Kurdish region of Iraq. In these intraconflictual discussions, the new political situation gave way to internal issues that young Kurdish participants were concerned about. Participants repeatedly called for unity in ways that almost required homogeneous acts and ideologies. When these acts went outside what is perceived as the "authentic Kurd," categorizations of "non-Kurd" were made.

> I think that you're acting un-Kurdish now actually no matter how much you hate your Seruk [leader] he is still your Seruk, and he was elected by the Kurdish people. (*Iraqi election*, Swedish forum, March 3, 2010)

> I call you Turk and half Turk because I know your hate against (Barzani/ PDK/Alarengin) [Kurdistan's official flag]. (*Historical perspective: Abdullah Öcalan and Massoud Barzani cooperation!* Swedish forum, May, 28, 2010)

In Saddam's Iraq, the nationalistic agenda by the Ba'ath regime against Kurds dominated the Kurdish agenda. Since 2003, this agenda has been replaced by the rebuilding of infrastructure and by the recreation of an autonomous government in the region. Even if the rebuilding of a nation started already when the USA established the no-fly zone, it was in the post-Saddam period that the Kurdish political dynamics changed. The shift has socio-political implications in terms of the discourse of the Self and the Other. Internal disputes were present earlier, but the region's internal narratives have been badly affected by previous exogenous struggles characterized by a kind of trauma never fully comprehended, nor fully dealt with (Hirsch 1997). In simple terms, categorization, whether by race, gender, or culture, is based on common political agendas. The discussions take place between participants with affiliations to the different politics parties. The naming of "un-Kurd" or "Turk" is considered highly offensive, implying assimilation and a weak Kurdish identity. These name-calling was typically used within the frame of politics, including topics of election, Kurdish leaders, Turkey, PKK, and so on.

The exchanges were lengthy, sometimes up to several hundred posts, and lasted for a long period, occasionally ending with administrators locking the thread, and at times blocking members. These are not occasional terms that Kurds in diaspora use, but are repetitive acts that are discernable in different identificational contexts. It is possible to distinguish the forms of othering along the lines of the Kurdish map, that is, Kurds from Iraqi Kurdistan versus Kurds from the Turkish part, but it would be wrong to claim any firm statements about this here, as many Kurds may find more shared interests or features with other Kurds in the other regions. Moreover, the othering takes place also within the regions, or within the diaspora settled in a nation-state in Europe, demonstrated later in the text. It is more plausible to assume other underlying factors behind the othering of individuals, and while some may be based on imagined notions, others may be shaped by social processes. However, most of these imaginings are disrupted once participants engage in the in-depth conversations that the online community allows.

Karim and Eid (2014) explain that identities within the cognitive frames of Self and Other are shaped by the circumstances of its particular discourse at a particular time. For example, a rival ethnic group is included into a larger Self when relationship changes in the context of foreign affairs. Or, in the aforementioned particular case, we could say that the same Self has become the Other in the contexts of domestic policies. This is, thus, not unique to Kurds, but the diversity was overshadowed by a stronger sense of "us" and "them" (Bhabha 1990), and there was a strong nationalistic agenda against political, social, and cultural inequalities (Kymlicka 2001). With the erruption of the Kurdish struggle against Iraq and its regime once Saddam Hussein was removed, and with more power within their territory, competing internal forces intensified. This tension due to differences is ubiquitous among cultures and people, but we are more locked by the expressions drawn from the dominant languages of the world. The view of the world's civilization as being completely distinct from each other and which can never coexist, or blend, ignores all these mundane interchanges of the Self and Other that take place on the basis of different socio-politico-economic backgrounds rather than categories of ethnic, national, or religious disparities, even if these are not completely absent from it. In the Kurdish forum, the interest in political affairs and the ongoing changes of domestic politics were likewise high (the majority being residents in Kurdish region in Iraq), but the tone and language completely different from that of the diasporic Kurds.

"They've Become European!"

> Why can Kurdish families not keep their values and their religion? And why do some parents pray but their children not? Is that respect, to not listen to their parents? Or do they just want to follow European culture? They've become European! (*Good evening*, Kurdish forum, April 2, 2010)

Cultural and traditional differences have emerged as a key concern for the Kurdish local community (residing in country of origin). The view that diaspora Kurds have had a negative impact on their children was prevalent in the Kurdish community. They emphasized how Kurds in Europe had replaced their culture, habits, and religion with that of the Europeans. Such perceived images also travelled through words of mouth, videos of festivities in different locations in Europe, and other media channels. They were considered to have become culturally and socially "un-Kurdish." The discrepancies between homeland Kurds and Kurdish diaspora were noticeable in two ways. Firstly, the content of the discussion topics varied considerably. While all forums engaged in homeland politics and other questions, diaspora Kurds would also be heavily involved in the current events of their settlement countries. Secondly, it was *how* they discussed different subjects. Depending on contexts, fierce discussions were rather common in the Swedish forum firstly, followed by the British forum, while the tone in the Kurdistan forum was calm with no major conflicts. This is an important aspect that should not be overlooked, as it can be explained by underlying factors that relate to identity issues. My observation of the divergent characters between the forums is shaped by the following posts:

> It would be so interesting if us Kurds, living outside Kurdistan, could participate in the Kurdish forum and create threads in Kurdish, maybe about

things that are taboo to talk about in Kurdistan. (*An idea*, Swedish forum, July 5, 2010)

We'll be honour-killed if we do that haha ;D. (*An idea*, Swedish forum, July 5, 2010, *in response to the post above*)

The Kurdish female based in Sweden implies to the differences between the forums by suggesting an unconventional topic in the Kurdish forum. Such a clear statement speaks to the many topics that related, for instance, to religion and gender roles, which diverged from the other forums in general but from the Kurdish forum in particular. While most of the discussions took a serious tone, participants also framed their puns against the commonly debated issues, many times through self-distance and self-irony. The kind of humour they displayed shows participants' awareness of distinctions across the transnational community. The jokes in the aforementioned posts also imply that the Kurds in the homeland are so different that no one was seriously interested in engaging in a discussion. This is not to propose that none of the participants engaged in the Kurdish forum. They did, and most often it was to gain insights into any new events related to political developments.

Humour, when used, proved to be an unintended tool in the collapsing of the Swedish–Kurdish dichotomies, and more intentionally to close down some of the more frenzied debates. The logic behind it is that when a joke is understood, it affirms the persons to the same membership as, in this case, Swedish-Kurds. The diaspora and homeland tensions became clearer when I interviewed Kurds who had returned to Kurdistan (Iraq) to work and restart their lives there.

"Swedish Kurds are the Worst"

The next quote was originally posted on the Norwegian forum by a Norwegian Kurd, but the post was copied onto the Swedish forum, into a new discussion thread named "Other Kurds' perception of Kurds in Sweden," by a Sweden-based Kurd. As the rubric implies, the participant's intention was to display his discovery in the other forums that did not talk positively about Kurds in Sweden.

> Swedish Kurds are the worst. I've heard many times, and seen with my own eyes. I was at this party in Stockholm … and I was shocked over their style and behavior. Both girls and boys Swedish Kurds forget about their culture too much. This depends on the fact they lived much longer in Sweden than

us. Kurds immigrated to Sweden as early as in the 60–70s. You could say that Kurds there are like the Pakistanis here, but that's really no excuse. Pakistanis haven't forgotten their culture, have they! (*Other Kurds' perception of Kurds in Sweden*, Swedish Forum, June 22, 2010)

Norwegian Kurds can't dress they want because their parents are still freshies, that's why they are bitter. (*Other Kurds' perception of Kurds in Sweden*, Swedish Forum, June 22, 2010)

On Viva Kurdistan, the first and only transnational community of its kind according to the site owners, the diversity among Kurds became more obvious the longer the participants stayed within the community. But beyond the pejorative terms, participants also delved into serious explanations, referring here to the different phases of migration that impact the diasporic formations, which should be noted by anyone who conducts empirical studies about diaspora. Although categorizations can be based on appearances, that is, how Kurds in Sweden are dressed as opposed to Kurds in the UK who are considered to be more modest, they also address how their respective mentalities differ. Comments on aesthetics are made by participants to gauge how well integrated—or assimilated as expressed by some—Kurds in the European countries are. It is worth bearing in mind that the transnational community and the long-term engagement by participants have enabled them to connect with Kurds in other European countries. Many of these participants have been members in the community for three to five years. Although few participants travelled between the different forums, mostly due to language barriers as each forum communicates in the respective country's official language, meetings between the diasporic Kurds across borders was just a click away. Years of various online interactional contexts have thus manifested social differences that have shaped their identities differently. This does not mean that they always led to clashes; one of my interviewees in London explained that they were inspired by each other's activities and impact on their settlement countries. Therefore, while Kurds have been able to gather in a space like this and given the opportunity to unite and mobilize, particularly during critical times, they have equally been observing activities, discussions, behaviours, and attitudes of other diasporic Kurds settled elsewhere and influenced by their settlement country's practices and patterns. These different views are not mutually exclusive in the online space, but the latter perspective has not been given the attention it deserves.

"Imports/Freshies"

> I hear people talking about "imports" all the time. It makes me think of different kinds of people. But what is an import, how does he or she look?? (*Define the word import?* Swedish forum, May 4, 2010)

> I think imports are called imports because of the way they dress, there are people who lived here just over 1 year. (*Define the word import?* Swedish forum, May 5, 2010, in response to the post above)

The term "freshie," or "import" in Swedish, derives from the expression "fresh off the boat" and is applied as a derogatory social marker to distinguish newly arrived migrants from the more integrated diaspora (Eliassi 2010; Franklin 2004; Ignacio 2005; Thangaraj 2015). The term is used to mock new migrants' over-ethnicized appearance "White shoes and white blazer," is a term used to imply an embarrassingly deficient and outdated style. The lack of linguistic proficiency in Swedish and English is similarly caricatured—but this internal othering is also used to condemn more modern approaches as being "too European" by using "snobby" language and being "inappropriately" dressed.

The next two quotes, one from the Swedish forum and one from the British, delve more into the subject and both provide in-depth explanations behind the term. In these first exchanges, the definition of "imports" framed mainly the appearance, acting as a social marker between them. They are pointers of higher economic status and linguistic proficiency in Swedish or English and therefore should not be taken as banal comments as they are helpful in charting the formative years of Kurds in diaspora.

> Those of you who are trying to make it a "Swedish" and "traitor" thing are self-destructive imbecile. A Kurd who took time to learn fluent Swedish, gain a degree from a prestigious school, put their religious fundamentalist views aside, and not be affected by the oppressive politics against us, are much more needed for the Kurds than the Kurds who after several years in Sweden have the exact same tribal, conservative, anti-liberal, religious, reactionary mentality. (*Define the term import*, Swedish forum, May 6, 2010, in response to the post above)

From "freshie" to "traitor", the double-edged sword reflects comparative attitudes as "too ethnic" or "too assimilated," underpinning a changing discourse on individual identity within the intra-ethnic context. They were less fashionable if they were freshies, and if they were too European or too Swedish, they were not decently dressed and exposed too much skin. The respondent quickly cast doubt on the validity of their labelled status by explaining the need for well-educated Kurds that can, implicitly expressed, contribute to the development in the origin countries. This internal othering of the "too ethnic" on the one hand, and the "whitewashed" on the other, was a common feature among Asian Americans (Pyke and Dang 2003). Pyke and Dang (2003) have examined how Asian Americans have been involved in intraethnic othering when children of migrants found that the racial stereotypes of the mainstream society shape their own thinking about their peers and deflect stigma within their own community. In Pyke and Dang's case, some Asian Americans carved out a positive self-identity by showing an "assimilated status" and condescending "other" coethnics as too ethnic. Barzoo Eliassi (2013) describes the same tendencies in his research in which Kurds growing up in Sweden were using these denigrating names when categorizing each other as, "[t]his implies distancing themselves from other 'undesired' and 'unintegrated' people with immigrant backgrounds who have a different way of dressing, behaving, and speaking Swedish (often 'broken')" (p. 161).

These derogatory terms have been given little attention in research on diasporic youth; however, they are also part of the (de)construction of their social and cultural identities in their new settings where they live and work. The terminology that they deploy in the context of identity and ethnicity tells us something about the cultural values and perceptions connected with different identity routes. Pyke and Dang (2003) have understood the case of Asia Americans as internalized racism, "suggesting that their identification with whites signaled progress and superiority over their traditional coethnic peers." (p. 168). While there are denigrating elements in these labels, which include the act of othering each other operating as self-identifications, it leaves unanswered the question of whether these distinctions arose independently or were modes and mimics of the Western representations of the Other. In the context of Kurdish diaspora, such differentiations are however not restricted to old diaspora and the newly arrived migrants, but also appear between the diasporas growing up in different countries in Europe. I believe it is important to look beyond the pejorative terms as the Kurdish men and women are engaged in serious explanations, referring to different phases of migration as well as the social and cultural identity of the settlement country, that has an impact on the diasporic patterns and formations. The following response gives a more in-depth exploration:

> A lot of Kurds have travelled to Sweden in the 70s and 80s and many of the younger generation and even some 30 year olds have been born there, these people have grown up in security and all else. However if you look at some newer migrants myself included we are simply never gonna compete with you on a lot of things because we don't have a foundation and we have to start from scratch, culturally, emotionally, educationally etc., we are simply no different to migrants who have changed places and come from a different world with all sorts of issues which many of you would simply not even dream of if you are not one of those. More so in the past countries have accepted people and people have travelled by planes etc. but for last maybe 15 years many people have come through. (*Kurds*, British forum, April 23, 2010)

The poster attempts to give a more rational description behind the use of the terms by making references to historical and political backgrounds, economies, and to the different migration experiences and policies. It makes informative distinction between the phases of immigration that has led to the differences in the present time among younger generations of Kurds, where newer migrants cannot compete with the old diaspora. This reflection by the participant who belongs to the new wave of Kurdish migrants is a pivotal insight into how changes have occurred among old diaspora Kurds who arrived many years ago. These accounts are immensely important to follow-up, explore, and place in a theoretical framework to understand what they really mean. They go beyond any simple comment and, instead, refer to abstract changes of diaspora, identity, and sense of belonging that become perceptible by other diasporic peers in meetings and dialogues such as these.

Kurds in the UK arrived in larger groups much earlier than Kurds who had settled in Sweden as labour immigrants to a greater extent than as refugees, which was the case for the majority of Kurds in Sweden. What this participant attempts to portray are the divergences between upbringing in a society that equips them with cultural and economic capital, which the newer migrants have not managed. These are excellent observations made by participants themselves in terms of how old diasporic Kurds, who arrived as refugees, have moved from old notions of victims to active agents of their lives. The note on "growing up in security" is, however, debatable if one talks about these old diaspora experiences, as they often mention hardship, exclusion, and other strains during their upbringing in the new societies. Many of them are children to political refugees and arrived in their settlement countries under difficult circumstances. Kurds within these groups may be very active and have developed social, symbolic, and transnational links, but they also remind other newly arrived Kurds of their stories of pain and suffering. They would not be afraid of making those distinctions between themselves as being "more victimized" than their fellow Kurds, who made their journeys under easier conditions. Perhaps, security refers more to the confident, erudite, and secure positions that the old Kurdish diaspora demonstrates. It could possibly also combine influences of different policies and societal accommodation, which differ from recent revisions of multiculturalism models and migration receptions, and the rise of anti-immigrant parties. On the other hand, Kurds faced challenges particularly during the 1980s and 1990s, when the spotlight shifted on them in Sweden after the assassination of Olof Palme (which led to the arrest of several Kurds allegedly involved in the case) and the honour-killing debates.

As Kurdish diasporic individuals articulate their everyday lives through words and expressions, well aware of the differences between them, either by other peers or themselves, the online archives present the complexity of diasporic formations and identifications, and diasporic consciousness. In these reconstructions, the operation of othering shows a terminology that echoes with that of the West–East dichotomy. This is imperative to explore, not to suggest yet another dichotomy but to show how circumstances, changed settings, and histories can interchange the Self and the Other in the present, which, therefore, are not dependent on the outside but on an inside-out manoeuver. The empirical observations in this section show that diaspora are complex societies that relate differently, depending on the phase in which they became a diaspora. Therefore, the differences within a diaspora are significant to explore in depth, as they can present to us the transformative dimensions of the groups. The focus on Kurdish diaspora in Europe has, in particular, been rewarding, as it opens up new insights into the concept, through self-awareness, which adds new material to the debates linked to questions of identity, belongingness, transnationalism, and, in turn, to multiculturalism.

This main strength of this relatively unexplored perspective is how it changes the power binaries between "us" and "them" as a common dichotomy that always places migrants in a passive role and Westerners in the active.

FROM GUESTS TO CITIZENS

The difference between citizenship and belonging is the difference between something formal and something subjective. You may walk around with your piece of paper and say "look I am an Australian", but they can still say "No, you're not". Unfortunately for young people, for any people, it is the subjective, the feeling you get, not the piece of paper that matters the most. It is the difference between being accepted or feeling like an outsider in your own country. (Hage 2011)

The quote by Hage frames, to a great extent, the discussions in this section. Participants share their accounts of how Swedish citizenship is envisioned and experienced. They are mostly drawn from discussions about the Swedish General Election in September 2010, when the far-right party, Sweden Democrats (SD), exceeded the threshold and entered the Swedish parliament. Four years earlier, SD emerged from the right-wing party Moderaterna, and four years later SD became the third biggest party. This came as a surprise to many people in Sweden, although it was part of a wider trend in Europe that was marked by the rise of anti-immigration parties. Elsewhere in European nations such as Austria, Denmark, Italy, the Netherlands, the anti-immigrant parties had already made headway. In the British 2010 general election, the British National Party (BNP) experienced some increase in votes, but it was largely unsuccessful at the polls. In Sweden, characterized by neoliberal restructuring, questions of "race," belonging, and citizenship had become increasingly prevalent in the public debates along with the strengthened neo-Nazi social movements, and the emergence of two parliamentary parties (New Democracy was founded in 1991) in which cultural racism was at the forefront.

On Viva Kurdistan, while many discussions were devoted to homeland politics and affairs, participants were also concerned and engaged with the development of their settlement countries. The discussions have followed a non-linear route, often backtracking and returning to the different sites of origin and settlement country. Along with the manifold links with the land of origin, diasporas develop intricate networks to their settlement country, as well as to other countries where their ethnic communities exist. Online participants give accounts of how Swedish citizenship is experienced, intertwined with their understanding of (neoliberal) globalization and multiculturalism. They are concerned with issues that address both theoretical questions such as attitudes, perceptions, hybrid identities, and the formal aspects of citizenship including rights and responsibilities. They highlighted everyday concerns ranging from the changing political climate and prejudices, to queries about education, youth employment, health, and tax system.

"They Will Throw Us Out Soon"

Can you also sense how the atmosphere against us "wogs" has changed during the past few years? In this year's election there is no doubt that Sweden Democrats will gain seats. What do you think here on Viva, will they one day, just like in Denmark, stop being neutral and openly in the streets shout, "go home you wogs!" They want their country back now. (*Soon they will throw us out*, Sweden forum, April 5, 2010)

Swedes have the right to do whatever they want in their own country, we should be grateful that they accept us and make sure we have our rights. [...] We are strangers in Sweden regardless. If you are not happy with that, you can always go back where you came from. (*Soon they will throw us out*, Sweden forum, April 5, 2010)

The recent changes in the political sphere have been felt by young Kurds in Sweden, and they have often expressed surprise that a liberal society like Sweden had changed dramatically in the past years. It is true that diasporic people experience discrimination, exclusion, and racism, and Kurdish migrants are no different from other migrants in this case. The first poster more or less places belonging in a fixed area of territory; in other words, people belong to a place because they possess the space or because they have been settled there for a long period. The participant envisions belongingness around blood and property. The second quote emphasizes the link between belongingness and blood more. Both participants expose a view that considers the land of Sweden as borrowed territory, and that other ethnicities cannot belong to another nation fully. Membership in the ethnic group of Kurds is followed by the sense of roots, and citizenship is defined by ethnic and geopolitical boundaries. Members and citizens once arrived from another country still suffer injustices and lack some legal rights (Squire 2009). These very personal experiences constitute the distinction between those who really belong and those who do not, and should therefore be "grateful," and if not, should "go back." This unequal relationship that this young man shows between Swedes and Kurdish migrants leads to a sense of "guest–host" relationship (also used in academic writing) to the extent that subordinate migrants should show gratitude towards the hospitality of the society. The feeling springs out of alienation or of not being fully accepted because of the new anti-immigrant nationalism in Sweden and Europe overall."

"I am Swedish as much as a BERTIL and INGA"

Gilroy (1997) has warned us against the victim discourse and that there might be danger in belabouring these narratives. This remark is important simply because diasporic individuals are themselves trying to break away from these victimized discourses. Indeed, Kurds can be regarded as victims of supranational powers both in their countries of origin and of settlement, but these identifications are overtheorized and are challenged by a growing young group of diaspora that implicitly says that no gains in politics can be made by merely being defined by suffering. And, what is even more pertinent is that these victim identities, "while always in process," (Hall 1993, p. 222) have transformed into active and transnational characteristics, which make them represent ways of envisioning community, citizenship, and identity, as they are simultaneously Kurds and Swedes/Britons. This is already embedded in the first post, which, in light of the fear of increasing anti-immigrant parties, implies a life and future in the new homeland through the references to, and concerns for, the future. This challenges the diaspora studies in which general statements and links are made about the definition of diaspora and a return to the homeland. It is said that diasporic members who are removed from the homeland invoke imaginaries and see themselves as exiled and dream to return to the homeland one day. While this might be directed towards the first generation of diaspora, who has a different relation to their homeland, dreaming of a return may be the case, but much of the time the return does not take place. This will be discussed in the context of Kurdish repatriation (in the next chapter), which provided with intriguing insights into this. Therefore, one should ask: Who decides what or where home is? Who defines where diaspora belong? Can diaspora belong to multiple homes? To answer these questions, I move to the next quotes by participants who are shifting focus from the object to the subject within a non-essentialist framework, in which they express ideas about a multivocal sense of belonging. The diasporic individuals bring the imposition of a single idea of belonging to the nation under question (Kalra et al. 2005). I have lined up four posts to more clearly show how each of them identifies key elements in the discourses of post-colonial "us and them," hybridity, citizenship, and imagined commonality.

> Your view on foreigners and immigrants is obsolete and just contributes to US and THEM. I and everyone else here with a residence permit are not guests in this country. I am Swedish as much as a BERTIL and INGA if I decide that I am. And if I and other wogs will never be seen as full Swedes by some people, that's another thing. (*Soon they will throw us out*, Sweden Forum, April 5, 2010)

> But you can be an immigrant and Swede at the same time. Just like you can be half Kurdish and half Swedish for instance. There is no visible read line that goes through half of you. It's 2010, Sweden is NOT homogeneous anymore, Sweden is a multicultural country since 30 years back. (*Soon they will throw us out*, Sweden forum, April 5, 2010)

> What does it take to be Swedish??? We work like them, we study, we pay tax like them, we contribute to the society [...], our culture has already been assimilated to the Swedish society (if that's wrong or right is another question, but this is a fact) the only thing missing is blond hair, blue eyes and white skin, or? (*Soon they will throw us out*, Sweden forum, April 5, 2010)

> "Wogs" have lived in this country for generations, we're in all seams and combinations, criminals, academics, celebrities and so on. A Swedish criminal will find more in common with a criminal foreigner than with a Swede that is working as an auditor and vice versa! We don't live in a Sweden anymore where all Swedes are blond and all foreigners are refugees. We live in a new USA, for good and for bad. (*Soon they will throw us out*, Sweden forum, April 5, 2010)

The sharp reactions to the bifurcation of Swedish citizens and Kurdish guests interconnect with the multiculturalism debates on the one hand, and some of the academic writing on "imagined diaspora" on the other hand, that intersect with conceptualizations such as "hybridity," "body," "onlineness," and the "Self and Other." Firstly, and perhaps somewhat paradoxically in light of earlier othering outlined in the previous section, the participant refuses to acknowledge the "us and them" binary.

If we think of the earlier postulates that cultural identities are followed by scripts, which individuals must act up in order to maintain their cultural values and traditions, then belonging is the achievement—through abstractions and practices—that people present. Achieving residence permit, paying tax, and contributing to the society, as these participants declare, are routines that produce new belongings in Sweden and the UK. Jonathan Boyarin and Daniel Boyarin (1993) concluded in their work that Judaism is not constant, neither essential nor performative, but that these religious and ethnic relationships are performed contingent on the context they find themselves within. In Marie Fortier's (2000) case, the Italian diaspora and their repetitive church visits cultivated their sense of belonging. In the same way, Kurdish diaspora too have adopted new routines, which interrupted old ones.

The second excerpt displays a restless tone, and implies that people need to understand that there is no red line through a body to show the amalgam of cross-cultural influences. Many posts acknowledged that a kind of hybridity is woven into every corner of the everyday life, from popular culture to trendy fusion cuisine, clothes, and not least the multicultural society. The participant is concerned with the singularity of belonging, "you can be an immigrant and a Swede at the same time," and discards the claims of boundedness within the multicultural society, which Sweden has experienced for the last decades, as stated. The poster refers to the hybrid character here as the synthesis of cultural practices, which relates back to what Bhabha (1994) proposed about culture not being defined in and of itself, but rather within a context of construction.

The third poster links the rights of citizenship to the right of belonging, here not only referred to rights but also to responsibilities and allegiance. The extent to which Kurds in Sweden and the UK understand and identify themselves as citizens is measured with factors such as contribution to voluntary work, waged employment, tax involvement, voting rights. These factors contribute to a cultivation of a sense of belonging among the Kurds. The participants have described themselves as Swedish citizens, which, to them, have meant not only to have rights and responsibilities and to be recognized, but also to participate in the debates as full citizens. The performative speeches are statements that expose Kurds' self-identification as citizens, which means the own right to not only be recognized but also to discuss the terms of recognition (Modood 2010). The poster further directs his criticism at the flatness and superficiality of the discourse of citizenship that looks at "blond hair, blue eyes and white skin" as if there is nothing inside the body. His notion of belonging can be understood as already achieved rather than a wish to become, or to belong, as he states that their own culture has already been assimilated. It is worth remembering that these second, third, and even fourth generations of Kurds arrived to Sweden, the UK, Germany, and elsewhere at a young age, together with their parents, seeking asylum. Many of them were even born in Sweden, and they have never seen their origin country. For these Kurds, Sweden is their home, even if Kurdistan has remained as the homeland. The participants use hyphened names, Swedish-Kurdish and British-Kurd, German-Kurd, and American-Kurd to imply a transnational consciousness that includes both nationalities equally.

Among these Kurds, the need to become un-diasporic was not perceivable, but their demands to be treated as equal were declared, and mirrored their references of already being well integrated and successful in Sweden. In the UK, such claims taking were not quite so obvious, although there is indeed an active Kurdish diaspora settled there, not least within academia and the political sphere. But in the Swedish forum, the accounts have not been short of examples of Kurds who have "made it" to the public arena, whether politically or culturally. They would make references to Kurds who have become public personalities that have enhanced the Kurdish identity in these societies, often paralleled with the Fadime context, which depicted them negatively by contrast. Therefore, emphasizing the growing repertoire of Kurdish intellectuals, politicians, artists, and other public figures (see Eliassi 2010) was seen as a recipe for mutual inclusion.

Ontological conceptions of belonging to an origin territory are opposed by diasporic Kurds. Perhaps, the most apt expression of this puncture of imaginings is in the last post in which the participant responds, "A Swedish criminal will find more in common with a criminal foreigner than with a Swede that is working as an auditor and vice versa!" Children of migrant parents are well aware of the difference within their own community despite all efforts to find a common identity, and they have not been reserved about emphasizing that they are formed by the society they grew up in. A Kurdish identity will not be identical to a Kurdish identity in the homeland, many participants contended, paralleling the sociological aspect, "'distance' between the rich of Bombay and the rich in London may be much shorter than the difference between classes in 'the same' city" (Gupta and Ferguson 1997, p. 50).

The physical location and national territory, until now the only grids on which cultural difference have been mapped, need to give way to the multiple grids that allow us to see that connection, diverge according to factors such as class, gender, race, and sexuality, and are in varying degrees available to those in different locations in the field of power (Gupta and Ferguson 1992). This does not mean that identities can be forcibly changed, which is well illustrated by the cases in each and every region of Kurdistan—Iraq, Iran, Syria, and Turkey. Of course, belonging cannot be separated as an individual affair, but materializes in conjunction with the outer world. However, unpacking these abstract concepts and subtle everyday experiences allow us to create or renew the awareness of social relations and their constant transformations.

> But the way I have perceived it, an important part of having an identity is affiliation. A feeling of belonging to a place/people and feeling a responsibility as a "member" to protect your "home". When you live in a place fairly isolated from other Kurds, and the people I once knew back home have all moved on with their lives, that sense of responsibility gradually goes away and you start to worry about your life as an individual. You no longer care about the place you used to belong to and the people you used to care about. Then you get the identity crisis. (*Identity crisis?* British forum, February 1, 2011)

This is a thought-provoking post that unveils the elephant in the room. Much of the academic work on diaspora, in particular on Kurdish diaspora, stresses that young diasporic groups growing up in Europe are deeply engaged in homeland politics and the Kurdish national identity, and that Kurdish identity has been reinforced. Indeed, they have shown a profound interest in the development in their regions through new platforms of communication such as online community, Twitter, Facebook, and YouTube. The aforementioned post, however, complicates such statements, which persuade us to go beyond quantitative assessments of how much young Kurds are involved in these events and ruminate why they are so involved. Is the "crisis" caused by the way life has evolved in Britain, where he or she has been settled during all those years, an indicator to why they so intensely hold on to these discussions? This British-Kurdish citizen more explicitly argue that caring less about the "place you used to belong to" has been replaced by new affiliations and feelings of belonging to a *home* you have committed to with responsibilities. As such, we may need to distinguish between transnational political engagements that aim at improving the situation in the origin country, and the personal testimonies here which at the same time show how the personal changes with new everyday lives, new friends, and new concerns. Wise (2000) describes this as a rhythm of culture, consisting of practices and habits that hold together the culture. They follow cultures as they traverse; they "expand, contract, adjust, adapt, and reproduce themselves," but the adaption to new environments seems to be challenging those who expect the cultures to remain "neat little parcels" (Wise 2000, p. 306). Such statement is confirmed by the quote below by a participant who distinguishes transnational, home-land directed, engagement from new home-making endeavours and personal commitments.

> There is a big difference between supporting the rights of Kurds and lead-ing your own personal life. That you live abroad and are confronted with a lifestyle that is very different from your homeland does not mean you are a "traitor". Many Kurds in diaspora I think have an ID [identity] crisis because they don't know which way to go!!! They might want to develop themselves in a certain way BUT "their culture" that they brought with themselves 20 years ago "doesn't allow this or that". While they are actu-ally in a very luxury position of being able to take the good traits from the culture in their new home country and the experience of their background culture causes this, they've experienced both. (*Identity crisis?* British forum, February 1, 2011)

The identity crisis is the result of the nature of the dialogue between the old, naturalized forms of doing things and the new routines that have been adopted by diaspora, which is reflected in the exchanges by the participants and evinced a somewhat violent nature and sacrifices linked to the production of hybrid identities and diasporic processes. When researchers have talked about "imagined diasporas," they have referred to the changing nature of the homeland while diasporas have been away. The homeland has changed beyond recognition and diasporas are longing for something that does not exist anymore. However, and this is the problem within diaspora studies, this assumes that, firstly, diaspora people are not aware of these changes, and, secondly, that diasporic people remain the same people they were when they once arrived as refugees or migrants in Europe. It implies a disregard for empirical experiences that these dia-sporic individuals clearly face and are not afraid to talk about: "you are confronted with new a lifestyle" and develop a "feeling of belonging to a place/people and feeling a responsibility as a 'member.'" To understand what these young women and men are undergoing is to acknowledge the changes and differences, be it among diaspora or in the homeland. Diaspora becomes the very challenges of difference. Thus, they are not an endpoint as multicultural debates suggest, but an understanding of the construction of these differences and how they can be understood when they cross geographical, political, cultural, and generational boundaries.

The result of this is that culture, in particular diasporic culture, cannot be defined in and of itself, but rather should be viewed within the context of its construction (Kalra et al. 2005).

OFFLINE DELINEATIONS

Although contemporary capitalism is marked by new movements of people, new technologies, and transnational practices, migrants continue to be percieved as rooted in origin nation-states; such consideration of nation-states and national loyalties is at variance with the complexity of the lives of diasporic people. The extracts online have demonstrated how they not only make multilayered links to homeland and settlement countries but also establish distinctions between homeland political engagements and new routines and links to their new environments that pose challenges to the homogeneously built communities. The way in which Kurdish diaspora has engaged in the online space reveals some very important understandings about the ways that transnational migration, coupled with new technologies of communication, is transforming perceptions and notions of individuals as Kurds and as citizens in their new homes, and how they also distinguish between their personal lives and political practices across borders.

The Internet may be a quintessential media for diasporas because it easily bridges distance, but it cannot fully shrink it online as concluded by the members. These new networks and discursive Kurdish-European communities that are emerging have a significant impact not only in the homelands, but also laterally across Europe where Kurds live. The following interview excerpts highlight this further. My first question concerned why they decided to become a member of Viva Kurdistan.

> I thought it was fun to talk with other Kurds in Europe in a Kurdish community. (Interview, male, 25, UK)

> VK reaches young Kurds in Sweden and Europe, and that's why I thought you could use it for making announcements and to share visions and opinions. (Interview, male, 24, Sweden)

> For me it was important that I could come to this place and meet Kurds from all four parts of Kurdistan. And also, I don't know anywhere else to find this kind of platform, where interactions take place like this. (Interview, male, 18, Kurdistan/Iraq)

The online community serves as a network to make new contacts between Kurds in different Western countries to a greater extent than to reconnect with homeland Kurds. It enabled young Kurds to gather in one place and interact in completely different ways as opposed to on the ground. It is interesting to observe the contrast between the Kurdish members of the diaspora and the local Kurds residing in their homeland. For the Kurdistan-based Kurds, it was important to interact with Kurds from different parts of Kurdistan, whereas the Sweden and UK-based Kurds were interested in meeting other diasporic Kurds. The common intention for all members was, however, to meet other Kurds and discuss common interests about Kurds and Kurdistan. Whether this means that they go online to become more Kurdish or because they are Kurds is more complicated than suggested in the interviews, but these components were reflected when they became online members.

> I started to talk with a few and it was "where are you from, which city are you from, not which country", but which town. (Interview, female, 18, Sweden)

> Because when I was younger, my dad always used to say: we are all one, I never really separated myself. (Interview, male, 18, UK)

> I have directed more towards Kurdistan. One's belonging, one's company have become more Kurdish [...] I have done more Kurdish things, because of VK, like attending demonstrations, lectures/seminars and things like that, and that I wouldn't get otherwise. [...] I have felt a bit better, in whom I am. (Interview, male, 23, Sweden)

The dynamics change from offline to online. The question "where are you from?" has, for Kurds, been a sensitive question as the response, "Kurdistan," has evoked many strong reactions, according to the participants. Regardless of who poses the question, they said, there has most often been some sort of follow-up of interrogating questions that declared the non-existence of a Kurdistan. Online, Kurds faced a different reception. Kurdish members used a more familiar terminology that incited a greater sense of one Kurdish nation among new members. Such mutual understanding has been important for Kurds when seeking online groups and communities. These testimonies are often reflective of the early, positive experiences for participants. Other common links made were about jokes and humour that many Kurds could relate to and percieve as mutual understanding as a "Kurdish thing." Moreover, as one interviewee explained, becoming a member of a Kurdish community was considered as a natural step for anyone who was interested in Kurds and Kurdistan, because "we are all one." This shows the different narratives built not only offline and online settings, but also between generations. Most of the interviewees weaved in stories about their parents' experiences, which have been part of building their own memories, which is in the first case not about on-the-ground experiences in Kurdistan but about the stories they have been told. These passages constitute a fourth layer of distinction.

Respondents elaborated this by admitting that they had become more Kurdish, and were doing more Kurdish things than before. Becoming more Kurdish conflated with doing different things, such as attending Kurdish events and lobbying for the Kurdish cause, which consequently restrengthened their belonging to the Kurdish national community. These doings were not limited to the localities but cut across borders as Kurds travelled to attend events, conferences, and festivities, which were linked to Kurds and Kurdistan somehow.

> And also, it started by me being influenced because I could see what they were doing in the other countries and then I would think we should have something like that in London. [...] I wanted to something to represent London Kurds. And we did try something throughout Free Kurdistan campaign, made a YouTube video, went to different demonstrations, we went to the Turkish embassy, Iranian Embassy, and put the stickers outside and just made and an effort to wake Kurds in London up. (Interview, male, 18, UK)

Kurds in different locations explained how influenced they were by other forums and activities they were engaged in, and the successful resonance it had in the public sphere where they were settled. Although the participant, who here talks about campaigns to represent London Kurds, does not understand Swedish, he had found ways to follow the discussions there, which evidently had an impact on him. People, reconnections, cultural artefacts, and services not only travel between the homeland and the settlement country, but are also exchanged in a global web of networks and settlements (Cunningham and Nguyen 2003). For some groups like the Kurdish diaspora, politics in the homeland is of interest, but equally so in other parts of the diaspora is politics an activity of abiding interest, in particular during times of crises (Bunt 2003). These statements resonate in the Kurdish community. Notwithstanding this, while media are often used to mobilize support for the homeland causes (Hassanpour 2003), they have, in this case, also disclosed a "super-diversity" (Vertovec 2007), which, for some Kurds, came as surprise, differing substantially from their offline narratives.

Viva Kurdistan: "A Microcosms of Countries"

Diasporic Kurds tap into different sources such as family or traditional media such as (satellite) television or radio, which play a significant role in their perception of who they are and where they come from. As mentioned in the previous chapter, language is one of the most important attributes of culture and a strategic means in the pursuit of sustaining a sense of Kurdishness. Respondents explained that they were encouraged, or even obliged, to speak their mother tongue at home and Swedish/English outside the home. For instance, the Kurdish channel Med TV has been successful in restrengthening the Kurdish language and appealing to national unity. In the Kurdish case, the lack of an international political curriculum and recognition of a Kurdish state have, perhaps, emphasized the imaginaries of a nation-state. Using concepts of "South" and "North" Kurdistan instead of "Iraqi" or "Turkish" Kurdistan online was reassuring in the making of a virtual state online. Viva Kurdistan played a significant role in that sense. But at the same time, the online community did more than connecting people—it also led to different "splits."

> On Viva Kurdistan, you see a lot of splits, with Kurds, a sort of microcosm of countries. I would definitely say that Viva Kurdistan had an influence … it always seems to be the need, to divide yourself into groups in there, on the forum it would naturally seem to split. I have been on Viva Kurdistan for four years now. (Interview, male 18, UK)

The splits here refer to the different camps that diverged in different ways. The young man described in detail how he decided to become a member, despite its "unserious" reputation, to meet and interact with Kurds in other parts of Europe. What was intended to be a fun experience, instead, became a disappointment, he explained. The London-based Kurd mentioned political affiliation specifically, as dividing Kurds, but also other topics lead to different kinds of splits. While the community had raised awareness and made participants do "more Kurdish things," they would also become painfully aware of the differences among them, not only between homeland-based Kurds and diaspora, but also between the different Kurdish diaspora groups. Most interviewees paralleled their experiences with the narratives they had built before the Viva Kurdistan period. These details can also explain how the online community was not taken seriously by many Kurds—they would view it as "killing time" or "just having fun." Amid transnational engagements, such as replications of campaigns and other activities, online relationships, new friendships, and even trips across and between countries, were notions of the online community as merely "virtual." The interviewees expressed their views of the online site as merely playful, unserious, and separated from the context of "real" everyday life. As mentioned, my own journey from online to offline encounters with the participants allowed me to see how most of the interviewees were active online, and could at times stay online into the early hours, in particular if they were involved in lengthy and in-depth threads about serious issues. Such inconsistencies of how interviewees regard their online participation are important to note, as they have a vast impact on the status of the material and conclusions made.

Going back to how Viva Kurdistan disappointed some members, it shows how online and offline milieus can generate different socio-cultural, political, and economic contours. This, in turn, relates to epistemological and methodological questions of how we, as researchers, understand the everyday realities among diasporic people. This respondent, who had explained to me earlier how his father had narrated a strong unity of Kurds and that he had never separated himself when he was younger, reveals how Viva Kurdistan had disrupted the notions of "us."

> [...] but it [Viva Kurdistan] made me think it's larger than just being Kurdish, we are all human beings. I think it was Ronald Reagan who said, when aliens invade, then we'll know we are brothers on this earth. I could get on with a person who is English much better than I would with a Kurd, but Kurdish nationalism dictates when in a fight, if the Kurds and the English are fighting; I should back up the Kurds. And I just thought, what sense does that make? So, why must this mean that we should automatically feel closer? (Interview, male, 18, UK)

> What is being Kurdish? Is it a way of life? Is it culture? Being Kurdish can't be about traditions and culture only, and if it is, a culture [...] oh you can't get a tattoo, or a piercing, or something like that, then I don't really want to be a part of that. (Interview, male, 21, UK)

For these two young men, not only did Viva Kurdistan encourage more activities where they were settled, but it also encouraged new thinking about being a Kurd. The first interviewee, who earlier told me that his father was part of building his narrative about Kurds, "one nation, one country," describes how Viva Kurdistan made him think more broadly than just being Kurdish. After a long time of social participation online, he reconsidered Kurdish ethnicity as only a shared identity or culture and the role it has in finding commonality among the diaspora group. While listening to this young man, it became clearer that he rejects the notion of ethnicity as a location for people to "automatically feel closer." The ethnic commonality as a component to strengthen a sense of belonging and culture had been weakened online. Other signifiers were listed as more important for him, namely world view, experiences, values, and most of all, an openness to humanity, which is how he explains he could get along better with an Englishman than with a Kurd. His conversation makes me understand that his changed consciousness of what it means to be a Kurd also demonstrates that the ingredients of cultural commonality are not coterminous in the online and offline environments. The re-evaluation does not mean a loss of interest in Kurds, Kurdistan, and related concerns, but he clarifies that myth of descent and nostalgic memories needs to be re-evaluated in light of different experiences.

The other participant shows similar reflections concerning the static notion of identity and culture, and most of all, the restrictions of the concepts that Kurds must follow in order to retain their identity. This illustrates well how he is rewriting his own cultural scripts, if existing ones limit him from conducting himself in certain ways. Questions raised in the online community, what Kurdish culture is and what Kurdishness is, are replicated here, and he implicitly questions any answer to this and wants to leave open for anyone to interpret it in their own way. These are reactions against discrimination within the own culture, or, put differently, the othering of coethnics.

It is important to note that the online experiences do not stand alone in the thinking of young Kurds, but one has to consider a repertoire of ingredients that shape the thinking of young Kurds that involve social aspects, class, education, ideologies, and so on, that are part of the daily life for some of the participants. However, in those cases, I make more distinct parallels along the references they make to the online community specifically. Having talked with the interviewees and listening to their own stories of how they viewed their Viva Kurdistan experiences, it is almost as if they have been engaged in their own ethnographic journey at the intersection of online and offline spaces. New insights, disruptions, contradictions, contestations, and affirmations have displayed multiple consciousnesses among them that are neither romanticizing nor imagining.

Note

1. Some studies (i.e. Eliassi 2010) argue that discriminatory discourses in the settlement country create a national agenda towards the home country and their practice of citizens/ship and exclusivism. This is based mainly on the idea that young Kurds in, for instance, Sweden are either born or have grown up there, and therefore have not experienced the sufferings and injustices to the extent that they base nationalistic sentiments on this.

CHAPTER 7

"My Kurdistan Chapter": Kurdish Repatriation

INTRODUCTION

This brief chapter consists of extracts from interviews I conducted with members from the Kurdish diaspora who have returned to Kurdistan (Iraq) to live and to work. They are Kurdish women and men who were brought to Sweden and the UK by their migrating, first-generation parents at an early age, who years later have decided, for various reasons, to return to the homeland. They are university educated, aged between 25 and 35 years, and are all settled in Sulaymaniyah or Erbil. In the accounts presented, we will follow the returnees' decisions, their experiences, and how they have changed during their stays in the homeland. Such empirical material is valuable and needed in any theoretical discussion about diaspora and their transnational activities. Currently, there is no official census of Kurdish returnees; hence, in the absence of any statistics, it is difficult to estimate how many of the Kurdish diaspora population has resettled in Kurdistan. It is, however, plausible to assume that most returnees travel to the Kurdistan Region of Iraq (KRI) from various different countries where diasporas are settled and with backgrounds from all four Kurdish regions.

One of the main aspects that define a classical diaspora is the desire to return to the homeland. Safran (1991) has described the authentic diaspora in terms of having a vision of an ancestral home, or an ideal home and place for an eventual return. Studies on diasporic returns are numerous, consisting of different cases in different periods of time and

© The Author(s) 2016

J. Mahmod, *Kurdish Diaspora Online*, The Palgrave Macmillan Series in International Political Communication, DOI 10.1057/978-1-137-51347-2_7 to different parts of the world. For example, after the independence of Indonesia in 1949, Dutch Indonesians repatriated from the Dutch East, while "pieds noirs" from Algeria settled in France in the early 1960s (King and Christou 2010). The post-colonial returnees have been called "Europe's invisible migrants," and their numbers are estimated to be between five and seven million (Smith 2003 in King and Christou 2010). Safran (1991) has described diasporic consciousness as being characterized by solidarity and strong links with their origin territories.

This resonates with the expressions online when most of them at times made nostalgic trips to a faraway homeland through their conversations. Some of them do visit Kurdistan during the summer or for holidays, but not everyone does so, and some articulate a wish for a permanent return once the political situation has improved. The desire for a return was, therefore, expressed flamboyantly and conflates with that of the theoretical postulations about diaspora people's myth and dreams of a return to the homeland. However, while being theoretically and ethnographically attentive to the dreams for a homeland and a nation-state that certainly exist among young Kurds in diaspora, the conceptual aim is to question, rather to accept, the underpinnings for self-proclaimed components of attachments (Kuntsman 2009).

The link between a return, myth, and the definition of diaspora is becoming increasingly problematized. The role of nostalgia and return in definitions of who is diasporic seems to assume that they wish to return, but *cannot* (King and Christou 2010). Perhaps, for some diaspora people, this is the case, and it certainly was, and is, for many Kurds due to the political situation in their homelands. Nevertheless, even those complex realities change. As described in earlier chapters, much of the situation in, for instance, Iraq changed with the removal of Saddam Hussein in 2003, which a few years later created the opportunity to repatriate. Needless to say, the situation was also aggravated in many parts of the Middle East, including the Kurdish region of Iraq, in the aftermath of the Arab Spring, and worsened with the rise of Islamic State in 2014. These changes have, however, not affected the returnees. After my interviews, some have moved back to Sweden or the UK, and it was clear that more of them would do so in due course. It is noteworthy that this has less to do with the deteriorating political situation, and more to do with feelings of estrangement in their homeland, identity crisis, and their yearning to go back to their old lives in Sweden and the UK. It goes without saying that are also many of the diasporic returnees outside of this study who intend to stay indefinitely.

As in the online discussions, two dimensions can be discerned in the narratives returnees tell about the homeland. One recognizes a connection and belonging, and another underlines the discrepancies between the homeland and diaspora. It is the latter dimension that has left deep marks on their self-interpretations. Some are more careful in their expressions of alienation, while others are more frank. Once again, it is important to note that interview accounts may, and do, diverge at times from the everyday lives of both Kurdish diaspora living in Sweden and the UK and Kurdish returnees resettled in the homeland. This argument is especially underpinned by my two-year stay in Kurdistan where I had the opportunity to be part of the everyday life encounters of the returnees. This means that the statement about contradictions that have appeared can be explained and justified by the methodological fact that interviewees, to some extent, talk about how they think they experience everyday life rather than how they really experience it (Kendall 1998). The only way to discover such contradictions is by making comparisons. In such a way, my stay in Kurdistan is a methodological undertaking that provides me with more contextual and comparative material, next to the interviews. On the basis of those everyday observations and notes, I have arrived at the following extracts that best describe what many returnees are going through. Needless to say, they are examples of this study and not generalized in order to illustrate the whole Kurdish returnee community. Notwithstanding this, they constitute life-changing aspects of these individuals' lives that have made them reflect, reconsider, and reconceptualize the homeland.

In the following reconstruction of the interviews (most conducted in English apart from one, which was conducted in Swedish), I will highlight differences of "mentality," gender roles, and the notion of home. How is it that young Kurds, who have never lived in their homeland, return alone, independent of their parents and siblings, to resettle there? What were their reactions, and how do they describe their experiences? Do they feel at home? These are some of questions that I posed in my meetings with them, and while the answers are occasionally straightforward, the experiences are much more complicated and contradictory.

Roots, Guilt, and Connections

It is a complicated and at times a confusing journey, both in terms of terminology and geographic movement, when Kurdish diaspora women and men talk about their return to the homeland. Most of the returnees describe their journeys to Kurdistan as "coming back" or "returning home," but while living in Kurdistan, they also talk about Sweden or the UK as home and their wish to return back. Job and career opportunities are better now in Kurdistan, which was one reason for moving back for many of them. Some returned to serve in the government, others to establish businesses, and a few because of personal commitments. Having said that, the return was also influenced by dreams of reconnecting with their roots. Equally, as will be evident later in the chapter, some have also moved back to Sweden and the UK, to their "real" lives. Being "home away from home" was a common statement among Kurdish returnees. These phrasings reflect the state they are in, never feeling quite at home anywhere, but also simultaneously feeling at home everywhere.

> The biggest part of me coming back was to reconnect to my roots. So it was more a personal development, rather than a career, but I could combine those two. I do want to reconnect 100 percent. (Zara, 30, from Sweden)

Although none of the returnees that I talked with had really lived in Kurdistan, apart from making regular visits, it was still indisputably a homeland for them. Many of the underlying reasons seem to be connected with guilt. In terms of a certain mourning and melancholia, some studies suggest that children of diasporic people often inherit guilt and longing from their parents (Gunew 2009). Zara described that her initial experiences in Kurdistan were like "a honeymoon." She made new friends, undertook road trips to the mountains, enjoyed the traditional "seyran" (picnic), wearing traditional Kurdish outfits and listening to old folkloristic Kurdish music. These particular descriptions constitute important loci of their image of their homeland. Therefore, one of the trajectories in the return to the homeland includes these specific visits that they imagined while living in diaspora, which is a common strand among diasporic people (Hatfield 2011). Such visits could include mountains, the house of a relative, or villages like Halabja that constitute an important symbolic meaning for them.

The return to a homeland appears to be more precarious than usually described in academia. The place called homeland will have transformed beyond recognition (Hall 1993), but even more pertinent here, the Kurdish diaspora returnees will have changed beyond recognition, which most often made them feel like strangers in their homeland (see Eliassi 2013 for similar accounts). In the fear of forgetting or never reconnecting with the homeland, however, Zara further explains how guilt plays a role in her decision to return to the homeland:

> There has been something really missing in me, there was a hole in my chest, in my heart. I knew that I had to return to Kurdistan to fill that hole, that gap. I have had bad conscious for not living in Kurdistan during hardship. We did escape during the war, so I had the privilege growing up in Sweden, to get an education and a good life there. Reconnecting has been everything from personally to my relatives but also to not feel the guilt that I had. I have two uncles who were killed when they were very young by the Saddam regime, 16 and 21. That was part of the reason why I was studying what I did study, democracy and freedom of speech. They have been the reason for me coming back here, along with my grandfather who was also executed by the regime. My father was a Peshmerga, and my mother was in the mountains as well. My interest in studying what I studied has to do with that, my personal background. I feel I owe it to them. (Zara, 30, from Sweden)

It is important for children of the forced migrant generation to not become disconnected with the homeland mainly because their parents were engaged with the liberation movement in Kurdistan, struggling to maintain the existence of their homeland. These tragic stories are common among Kurdish returnees, which explain their decision to return. Such narratives have significantly impacted the children in different ways, including education, relocations, and intermarriage, and it is as if the children are feeling undeserving of their opportunities. They carry a burden in terms of unsettled feelings and have a sense of difficulty to fully enjoy their freedom knowing that their parents or relatives could not. In this case, a return to the homeland serves to decrease that happiness, to prevent another disaster, as otherwise it would have been "an insult to the dead" (Boyajian and Grigorian 1991 in Cohen 2002, p. 49). While such unresolved feelings are shared among first-generation survivors who escaped the conflict zones with their children, this "survivor syndrome" (Cohen 2002) is also noticeable among the younger generations. Yet, first-generation parents are less likely to move back to the homeland:

> Kurdistan was just a vision, a blurry vision, somewhere out there, before I came back. But my mother doesn't like it here, and that's someone who lived here for 25 years before they had to leave. When I said I was going to move to Kurdistan, they did support me. But they never thought I'd stay here for two years. My mother doesn't like it here. I've asked her several times, but she has said no, she just can't. They have a distance to Kurdistan, I think in a much healthier way sometimes. (Zara, 30, from Sweden)

Most of the returnees I met with in Kurdistan, and certainly all interviewees I talked with, had returned to Kurdistan on their own, without their parents, which seems to be common among diasporas (King and Christou 2010). As revealed in the above extract, their families had no wish to return to the homeland, and, perhaps, as the young woman describes it, they may have a different view than their children's "blurry visions" of the homeland. In light of the tragedies and sufferings that have been ongoing for years, narratives about the homeland draw from and are shaped through mass media, family, and friends. The blurriness may therefore refer to these more coherent discourses about Kurdistan without having experienced them at all.

But when the honeymoon is over, disappointments and realities set in as the returnees settle in, begin their new jobs, and interact more with the local population. The longer they resided in Kurdish society, the more challenges they faced. This, together with the definition that Zara makes in the extract about her parents having a healthier relationship to the homeland, reflects the different degrees to which imaginings of the homeland have taken place. It shows that parents may be more aware of the difficulties in the homeland. The younger generation's contact with the homeland as well as other Kurds in other nations only started to take place online and during their homeland visits.

> I feel like I have changed. And it's not always good. My identity crisis right now is partly the fact that I feel bad for lack of Kurdish language skills. Part of my personality is not blooming when I live in Kurdistan. (Zara, 30, from Sweden)

While they articulate a "feeling of" change and alienation, it became more obvious that a number of factors contributed to that feeling, including Kurdish language skills, freedom, and gender inequality. The language barrier was one of the main causes of the feeling of alienation, followed by a different "mentality" or mindset. These differences ranged from every-day life details and symbols such as taking "sugar in the tea," or comments about weight (usually being considered as "too thin"), to more significant and overwhelming issues such as changed ethics and norms in their working environment. The adaption to the different ways of living had a profound impact on some of them as they felt they did not know how to behave or interact anymore. Earlier literature on repatriation highlights the challenges that individuals commonly face after the return to the origin country (see Allen and Morsink 1994). In particular, such challenges are noticeable among diaspora people who once were refugees and left civil conflicts:

> Nothing reminds me of my own personality here. In Sweden I was never depressed, I was working from morning until late. I was independent, I had a steady income, and I was free to use my time in the way I wanted. I feel dependent on my husband who is working while I am at home. I'm looking for a job but it takes ages because of administrative issues. But I'm not sure, I have very little in common with people here. I decided I would stay here four or five years before I arrived, but now I don't think I can for that long. If I stay for that long, or even longer, it has to have a very special reason. But I doubt it. (Dalia, 28, from Sweden)

Dalia was settled in Sweden, working as a director at a medical company before she married a Kurdish returnee who has been settled in Kurdistan for the past ten years, also from Sweden. When Dalia married him, they agreed that they would spend the next few years in Kurdistan because of the husband's business, but would eventually return to Sweden. She had even set a time limit for her stay there; however, this had been shortened. For her, losing independence, her occupation, and her freedom in Swedish society was the most difficult part of living in Kurdistan. Dalia had made regular visits to Kurdistan before her return, but only to visit her aunts, not the place itself. For Dalia, who left Kurdistan with her parents and siblings when she was ten years old, a definitive return to Kurdistan is out of the question. She explains that she married a Kurdish man because she felt they shared more traditions and had similar backgrounds. She believes that this would be less current with a Swedish man, while pointing out that she would have considered other Swedes or men from other nationalities if meeting a Kurdish man had proved to be difficult.

By contrast to Zara, Dalia did not express any desire to fill gaps or coming to terms with guilt. There was no extended allegiance in that sense; on the contrary, she pronounced the difficulty of living in Kurdish society with conviction. She listed many differences that made her feel like a stranger not only regarding her homeland, but also with regards to herself. Her personality had changed, and she had turned into someone she could no longer recognize. This loss of identity was a concurrent feeling among all participants, although expressed in different ways and to different degrees.

GOING HOME OR LEAVING HOME?

In the definition of diaspora, or the imagined homeland, migrated people are linked to perceptions of the "original" community. While none of the participants, online or offline, have renounced the importance of some type of alignment with the homeland, symbolically, politically, or transnationally, it is equally fair to say that for most diasporic Kurds, the homeland is not a place they wish to settle in again. For the returnees who have in fact resettled there, their life is neither an entirely affirmative experience nor a fully negative undertaking. However, the women and men I talked with acknowledged many differences, challenges, and difficulties during their stay that impacted them deeply. The homeland has become a place to care about, and not a place they can wholeheartedly belong (Tölölyan 2010); this may be why some of the returnees once again return to the homeland, in diaspora.

During my long conversation spanning for hours with Zara, she explained that she is moving back to Sweden, after one year in London, a few years in the Eastern Mediterranean, and two years in Kurdistan, when she finally decided it was time to move back home:

> I think it's that I am not happy. I am happier in Sweden. The past three months I have been thinking about it, it's been very much up and down, an emotional roller coaster. I feel very tired, chronically. I am emotionally and mentally drained. I don't live like an insider, I'm more of an outsider. It's like you become a foreigner in your own country. (Zara, 30, from Sweden)

The very conceptualization of a return implies a continuation of living. A return by migrants is considered as reuniting the displaced with the origin. Fortier (2000) asks what happens to the homeland in the diasporic imagination when the desire to return is gone. The small-scale doings in everyday life leave a deep mark among Kurdish returnees who feel they change in profound ways that make them unhappy.

Tölölyan (2010) suggests that the instability of national identity in diaspora makes diasporic people believe that the contact with homeland can revive the connections and familiarity. Among Armenians, they use a certain concept to maintain that displaced national identity, which among Kurds is equivalent to the common terms "kurdayeti" or "kurdperwar," which means the performance of Kurdishness. While Tölölyan (2010) argues that the effort fails among Armenians due to the loss of the original traits, Kurds do not completely conflate the terms with identity, but rather connect it to the strength of preserving the Kurdish battle, even if the underlying notion is a preservation of Kurdish identity. The terms were often used online, and were mentioned during the face-to-face counters briefly. It is indeed part of the performance of "kurdayeti" that brings them back to the homeland, even if the economic boom certainly made the decision to move back to Kurdistan easier.

> Diaspora Kurds, especially those in Sweden, they talk so passionately about Kurdistan and independence, if they are so nationalistic about it, why do they not return to their homeland? It is my conviction that we need more diaspora Kurds here, not less. Many of the returnees are actually moving back to Europe now, now when they are needed here the most. (Ari, 34, from UK)

It is my observation that while returnees often questioned the intentions of Kurds in diaspora, who remained in diaspora instead of moving back to the homeland (to contribute to nation building), the local people to whom I spoke to did not make such remarks. On the contrary, local individuals displayed more understanding by asking counter questions such as "Why would they want to return to this place? War, conflicts, and non-functioning government, are not very inviting. They do better by staying there." With that said, they also pinpointed that diaspora returnees have good impact on the local environment.

But perhaps the questions raised by Ari is a valid one in that it seeks to understand why more Kurds did not return to the homeland, especially during the peak years 2010–2011, when they were so intensely involved in long-distance nationalism? It is commonplace that diaspora people in general do not wish to return to the homeland (Mishra 2006; Hammond 1999). Tölölyan (2010) explains that while no one denies the importance of some form of link to the homeland, it is not a place most diaspora people wish to settle. The homeland is not a home any longer. Home is, instead, what academia steadfastly continues to call the "host-land" (Tölölyan 2010), while life there for diaspora people is no longer regarded as a temporary stay. These statements were clearly articulated also by online members, who did not consider themselves as "guests" but considered themselves fully integrated citizens like any other Swedes. This is particularly the case for the female returnees for whom independence, income, and career are important factors that play a major role in the different lives they move between.

> ...the difficult part has been living alone as a woman. There is always some sort of barrier. As a young woman, in her 30s, and as a returnee, I feel like I sometimes pose a threat to my local colleagues or my bosses, who have all been male, and I feel like I haven't been able to speak my mind. There is always been some sort of challenge in work, just because I am a woman. I mean this is the same for local women as well, but I do think returnees face a different kind of challenge, more suspicious.

> And they have some expectations, how you should behave and so on. I have my parents in Sweden basically telling me "You are free to do whatever you like, we support you, but you are still expected as a Kurdish woman to do certain things," a responsibility that I wasn't used to in Sweden. (Zara, 30, from Sweden)

The homeland return has especially been challenging for female Kurds, which accentuated their status as being on the margins of the society. Losing the independent position that Swedish and British society had supported them in gaining was among the difficult new realities to handle. Restrictions on freedom were current also among men, because Kurdish society demanded of them certain behaviours that were different from those that applied in Sweden or Britain. These behaviours refer to a variety of different issues including political awareness of who can talk about sensitive topics concerning the government, and also everyday life performances in terms of how to interact, for example, with women or in their work environment. It is during these recurring moments that Kurds have felt like outsiders, not knowing the social scripts of how to interact properly.

Aside from that, other scholars have observed that returnees, while being considered as a development resource, are also seen as competition for the local community regarding resources, social services, and employment (Hammond 1999).

Women in particular have faced challenges in different contexts, including socially and professionally, and in familial situations. Adapting to local expectations is not only related to upholding a family reputation, but also to the lower status women still have, even if it is much more secular in comparison to neighbouring countries:

> It's difficult to be here as a diasporic Kurd from Britain, but it's even more difficult being a young woman. It's not that I can't wear what I like or go out, I can but it's nothing I do anyway ... but it's the position of a woman here rather, of women who want to progress and pursue a career. I do miss the equality in Europe. It's like they based everything you do on your womanhood and no other sides of your identity. I don't know how much longer I can do this. (Shandi, 27, from UK)

The tangible sense of their minority status, even more than in their settlement countries, had deep-seated impact on their self-identification and self-interpretation, especially among women. In their settlement country, despite the challenges there, they felt more equal and less judged based on gender difference. Drawing on earlier descriptions of the online community and the gender relationship, women were positioned as the minority within a minority, in a way different from local women or expatriates who worked there.

Managing Different Communities Through Transnational Practices

> They [locals] look at us returnees and they think we look dumber than them. There is, not hatred, but mistrust between locals and returnees for different reasons. It can be returnees can have different education from abroad, the locals, they don't have that or they haven't seen the world, they haven't been travelling a lot, and sometimes, even values conflict, mentality and how open or secular or liberal they are. So it depends, I wouldn't go to the street and talk with any person just like that. The locals that are my friends, they are very open-minded. I've become more conservative, less confident, and less social in terms of interacting with other people. (Zara, 30, from Sweden)

One very interesting dimension of their return is how they were treated as partial outsiders. While Kurds in diaspora talked about newly arrived Kurds as "freshies/imports," Kurdish returnees were placed in a similar position in Kurdistan. Firstly, the language barrier was a defining factor for some returnees; although most of them are working in international environments, not being able to express themselves fully had a negative impact on their experience in Kurdistan.

Other moments that created a gap between returnees and the local people are defined by misreading social and cultural codes. While lingua franca constitutes an important aspect of culture and sustains a link to the homeland, as discussed in Chap. 5, belonging also refers to being recognized and understood. However, belonging also refers to being recognized and being understood on an abstract level. To feel commonality is to be aware of socially unwritten collective codes and to make oneself understood through these codes that are part of cultural scripts people enact. In other words, people "speak your language" (Ignatieff 1994).

> It varies—sometimes we have a good laugh, sometimes I feel displaced. They might look at us differently, as if we originate from another country, not Kurdistan. It's a bittersweet feeling here, that's why I can never stay here for longer periods, I need to travel frequently. A couple of months here, and a few months there, that gets me going and in that way I can still pursue my career and lead a personal life. (Karam, 29, from UK)

> I'm going back to Sweden now, I see the two years as my Kurdistan chapter. I will come back here for visits for sure, and it will be much more frequent than before. I won't have gaps of ten years. I will come back as often I can, I do want to maintain the connection and the base that I have here. (Zara, 30, from Sweden)

The returnees' relationship with the Kurdish locals is complex. Their experiences are sometimes characterized by exclusion, marked by condescending comments. While "diaspora nationalism" or long-distance nationalism (Anderson 1992) has enabled mobilization, support, and projects for the homeland, it has also become exhausting and influenced quotidian behaviours, actions, and self-conceptions (Tölölyan 2010). Yet, returnees have found solutions for this by balancing time between the different locations. Karam from Britain strategically divides his time between the different countries, combining his personal life with his professional, which allows him to continue to live in both locations. Spending time consistently within Kurdish society seems to be too tiring for the diaspora individuals. This is confirmed by Zara's account. After two years in Erbil, she has established a solid base, a network of friends and colleagues, which will result in more frequent visits than before. She can go back to Sweden now, the two-year stay was her "Kurdistan chapter"—the "final, mythical return 'closed the circle'" (King and Christou 2010).

Diaspora patriotism converts more convincingly into diaspora transnational practices (Tölölyan 2010) that no longer make the homeland only the symbolic or the physical centre of return. It is now one of two or more locations of return and departure, which maintains the links between the homelands. Hence, transnational activities are not merely directed towards the homeland, but also to the settlement country. It is not strictly about maintaining links with the origin country, but a way of living and combining their lives:

> I try to travel every three months, but it's probably more frequent than that. I have to, I can't stay here for longer periods, it, with respect, can make one go insane. It's important to go away, breath, and then return. I don't find it tiring, it gives me pleasure that we can move with ease now as opposed to earlier. I have family and friends in both locations, and my life is transcending between these and that is quite important as I don't have to lose links to either, and it furthermore is valuable for my work. (Dani, 35, from Sweden)

One thing that most of the returnees repeatedly mention is their state of exhaustion and tiredness. By this they do not refer to their work or physical state, or even the transnational travelling, but rather a state of mind. The strengthening of the shift from diaspora nationalism to transnationalism is not only signalled by physical movements between the locations, but more significantly by changes in attitudes and notions (Tölölyan 2010). Instead of being convinced by the "must" of returning to the homeland and "doing Kurdish things" there, this is a turning point of a changed consciousness open to the possibilities and less restrictive in terms of geographic location. There are many new thoughts that have resulted in a shift on how to manage the homeland community, and although they cannot be discussed further here, one important factor is the experience of the homeland in a more profound way for the first time. By definition, this means that it is also the awareness of where home really is, and that there is no mutual exclusion. However, the two dimensions of their discussions, online and offline, which I have belaboured at this point, are important reminders that the diasporas' experiences, wherever they are, involve no easy state of mind but continue to include contestations and redefinitions.

PART III

Consciousness, Information Technology, and New Directions

CHAPTER 8

Towards a Weakened Imagined Community

INTRODUCTION

The central argument in this book is that the new information and communication technology is challenging the imaginaries of community, identity, and diaspora. The argument is based on observations of how Kurdish diaspora individuals are engaged in transnational activities that have pushed them to rethink and redefine their notions of belonging, identity, and homeland(s). These redefinitions have been preceded by questions such as "Who is a Kurd?" and "What is Kurdishness?" The questions have cut across a range of different themes such as culture, politics, religion, culture, and gender, which, in different ways, have changed the Kurdish identity and diaspora consciousness. While research talks of diasporas as caught between two cultures, I describe Kurdish diaspora as living super-hybrid lives of "Swedishness/Britishness," "Kurdishness," and "globalness" that include other social relations.

I have analysed conversations between diaspora individuals in an online transnational community because "these are the newer communication means and medium for people to gather from all over the place, not only to meet each other but also to discuss a wide range of issues" (Franklin 2001, p. 387). New technologies have become integrated spaces in people's lives, where individuals can make sense of themselves and their surroundings (Morley and Robins 1995; Poster 1995a). As they write,

© The Author(s) 2016
J. Mahmod, *Kurdish Diaspora Online*, The Palgrave
Macmillan Series in International Political Communication,
DOI 10.1057/978-1-137-51347-2_8

reflect, and interact with each other, they have become authors and readers of thousands of online texts over the years that have dealt with serious questions. Being the author of their own texts or scripts has also meant that they have challenged cultural norms of how one ought to behave in order to stay put or change the notions of being, for example, a Kurd, Kurdish woman, or "guest citizen" in their "hostland." By sending these texts to hundreds or thousands of readers, they seek recognition of their new ways of living, which is largely a matter of acknowledging individuals and what we conceptualize as identities.

Two main directions in these discussions are visible. One demonstrates how some features of the Kurdish identity are less likely to be negotiated and redefined. These include suffering and violence at the hands of authoritarian states. Pain, memories, and wounds serve as important sources for staying put as Kurds. The other direction, which is given more attention here, is how other aspects of the Kurdish identity have been contested and rearticulated at the crossroad of new and old societies and online–offline environments. The first section of this chapter offers a more extended description of the two directions. The second section zooms in the second direction by exploring how the different layers conflate with different positions from which Kurds identify themselves. This exploration shows that diaspora consciousness moves beyond the double consciousness that Gilroy (1993) has outlined, and is best described as multiconsciousness. This is an important finding as it breaks away from the duality of the homeland–settlement country. It is also a comment on the differences between traditional media and digital media, and how the latter multiplicity of consciousness is challenging the former national consciousness.

The last section presents *techno-social* aspects. The Internet and its characters have introduced different components that work against the old traditional media, which carries the potential to expose the social order. I will discuss this through some of the components that have had implications for the material that emerged from the online ethnographic work, as well as the emotions conveyed through the online space.

CHALLENGING OLD SCRIPTS AND PERFORMING NEW KURDISHNESS

Like many earlier researchers, I have been confronted with the complex and the contradictory identities among young Kurds. My engagement with Butler's (1988, 1997) theory of performativity and Appiah's (2005) conceptualization of script has been crucial in handling the complex issues that arose from the empirical data. The essential point of departure with the theory of performativity has been that identity is an effect of performance and utterances, and not vice versa (Bell 1999). To that end, the words, reactions, and feelings were in the center of the analysis. Their speeches carry important insights into their identity making as Kurds and Europeans. The idea that identity is not a fait accompli, but is in the making continuously is a crucial start for any empirically grounded micro-level examinations of such abstractions, and even more so among migrants who have left their origin. To understand performativities is to understand the temporal moments of identity making. But forgoing this must be an understanding of what is written in an identity. When young diaspora men and women talk of themselves as Kurds, what do they refer to? What does the Kurdish script compose of, and by implications, what does it exclude? On that basis, I referred the conversations and utterances of related topics to different scripts that come with different categories of how one ought to act as a Kurd, Kurdish woman, Kurdish man, Sunni Muslim, and so on. Scripts help to concretize subtle "doings" in people's daily lives, which otherwise pass by without further reflections. This almost involves a "psycho-analytical" task by going beyond the, often taken-for-granted, conversations to navigate their origins. With this recap of the meaning of the two concepts, I will, in the next step, explain how some scripts are more tightly written than others. This means that some scripts are less subject to negotiations and redefinitions, while others are more likely to change under the pressure of, and desire for, a more contemporary and individualistic lifestyle.

Non-Negotiable Scripts: Suffering as a Source of Kurdishness

One of the two directions pointed to the endeavours and strategies of maintaining Kurdish culture, while the other direction diverged from ideas coupled with a strict sense of Kurdishness. The former has been extensively, and deservedly, explored by Kurdish studies scholars. Such strands include homeland struggles and dreams, suffering and victimhood, human rights and the question of independence. But the new information and communication environment has allowed Kurds to ponder new questions that have been born and swelled during their upbringings in Sweden and the UK. These questions reveal a new direction that points to different ways of understanding Kurdish identity that disrupts old scripts of how to "behave" as a Kurd. The queries produced intense, exciting, and fierce responses that demanded participants to reconsider the acts of Kurdishness that have been rehearsed before arriving to the scene. These scripts contest dominating and static conceptualization of diasporas, illustrating their limitations by demonstrating a diasporic condition that was neither fully Kurdish nor Swedish/British.

As we saw in the early part of the empirical chapters, Kurds in Iraq, Iran, Turkey, and Syria have in different ways been subject to state oppression and cultural marginalization. Their stories resonate with post-colonial views of oppression, statelessness, historical and current injustices (Spivak 1996), as well as the mere denial of their existence and ethnicity (Chatty 2010; Mola Ezat 2000). Despite the fact that many Kurds have adopted language skills such as Turkish, Arabic, and Persian (to a great extent as a result of the assimilationist policies by their states), they do not identify themselves as "Turkish-speaking" or "Arabic-speaking" diaspora. Rather, they have utilized strategic essentialism (Spivak 1990) as a "weapon of the weak" (Clifford 1994) to maintain their Kurdishness in order to end the colonization of Kurdish identity, which Kurds consider is ongoing in diaspora if Kurdish culture is intermixed with those of the authoritarian states. Suffering and grief serve as reminders of why they are in diaspora and where they came from. This explains why identities matter more in some occasions than in other and will demand continuous dialogue (Hall 1993). Expectations of loyalty and solidarity based on common values, historical experience, and future projects are strong repertoires of their sense of Kurdishness. While most of the younger, third- and fourth-generation women and men have not truly experienced war or forced movements, they carry with them the narratives told by their parents and families; trauma is a strong part of a defining feature in contemporary diasporic awareness.

This also means that such narratives, or scripts, are tightly written and less likely to change. They are life stories that are important sources for their sense of being a Kurd. The Kurdish diaspora struggle for recognition of genocide, language rights, and independence will continue to be goals that they work and aim for. Thus, their awareness of being the victim, the Other, of hegemonic nations in the Middle East, in each authoritarian state, has not diminished among Kurds in Europe, but continues to be exercised with determination.

Kurds have also, through their exchanges, disclosed how they are treated as the Other by European states, which has been re-emphasized in the aftermath of each crisis that has taken place. This has been evident especially in the case of honour-killing, when Kurds became a target in the public debates in Sweden, and among Kurds in the UK in the context of migrant debates and the burqa ban. The uncomfortable position they were put in is linked to how unsophisticatedly authorities have approached these questions. This has made Kurds feel more degraded, partly because of how they were spoken about by the authorities, and partly by being completely excluded from the public discussions. Women and men were approached as being the problem—victims or perpetrators—rather than part of the solution. Kurds in Sweden especially found themselves in the position of the Other, portrayed as backward in need of salvation by the modern man (nation). Participants felt that the Kurdish women were manifested as unintelligent minority who do not know what is best for them. In the British forum, while the discussions on honour-killing were more or less absent, they mostly expressed unequal relations in the context of religion, and particularly in relation to the burqa ban question. I will revert to the aspect of religion in a moment.

Contesting Old Scripts of Kurdishness

Gender, sexuality, religion, and political ideologies were frequently contested topics in the online forums. The substantial discussion threads, the character of discussions, and the need for rearticulations show that these engraved scripts were much more exposed to contestations than previous narratives of pain. I have identified the mechanism of internal othering, which was especially evident in Chap. 6 and the discussions about homeland politics, identity, and citizenship, defined in different layers: diaspora Kurds versus homeland Kurds, diaspora versus diaspora, demarcations within diaspora, and different political ideologies that are overwhelmingly following the geographic lines. Apart from this, Kurds have a distinctive awareness of the different patterns among Kurds from different parts of Kurdistan, as well as cross-generational narratives. But the mechanism of othering was also present in many of the dialogues about gender roles. The internal othering cuts across a range of different, but overall interrelated, topics such as gender, religion, culture, and politics that together constitute the Kurdish identity.

Why is this mechanism of othering important to highlight and discuss? What are the implications when Kurds, among themselves, are engaged in identifications of the Self and the Other when such binary carry negative connotations? I argue that this elaboration introduces two important points. The first is how certain collective identity features are contested, which, in turn, shows a changing discourse of Kurdishness. This production, or deconstruction, of belonging and identity is anything but a simple process, yet one that Kurds themselves are demanding. It is in terms of these different positions that Kurds identify themselves when conversing about the juncture of diaspora and homeland and when conversing about "who we are" and what it means to be "who we are" (Mandaville 2001, p. 170). An intervention into internal differences and othering is important in order to create more awareness around the way they talk with each other, which reveals multiple experiences that are important sites for the construction of identity and belonging. We saw how dialogues went from essentialist understanding of the Kurdish identity to constructionist views. At first, the immediate responses to who is a "real" Kurd referred to primordial ideas of identity; being a Kurd is "not a choice" as "it is just there." Blood and soil, and pride and memories framed much of these answers initially, but as they delved into the questions, participants began to talk about identity as the result of experiences. This is where differences started to appear, as their experiences were connected to the common, oppressive memories of the Middle East on the one hand, and to the new diverging experiences in the different settlement countries on the other. As seen earlier, in the framework of history and suffering, such elements of the Kurdish identity have remained solid and unquestionable, while gender and religion were greatly confronted. In these cases, Kurdish men and women presented new characters to their identity, that is, greater awareness of sexuality and more equal gender relations. The "failure" of a performative act is consequently also informing of where the "essence" of the identity, or culture, fails to move further.

Another outcome of the mechanism of internal othering is that it demonstrates that the Self and Other also exist within ethnic groups. This is crucial to demonstrate, as this binary exclusively describes the West and the Orient relationship. This means that differences are imagined to only exist between the West and the Rest, while internal differences are being overshadowed. To accentuate internal differences among ethnic, religious, gendered, and national groups, as well as similarities across them, becomes inevitable when it is empirically evidenced. Internal othering, including online insults, despite derogatory implications, should not simply be waved off as plain rudeness or internal racism. Needless to say, there are occasions when such intentions appear, but online insults should be analysed within the contexts of where such linguistic injury takes place. While I will develop this statement later in the text, the note to make here is that too often class, gender, educational level, social capital, and other socio-economic factors among migrants and diaspora populations are overlooked. Explanations concerning behaviour and attitude are overwhelmingly drawn back to migration, religion, ethnic affiliations, or culture.

The strained relationship between Kurds is not coincidental. There are substantial differences in habitus because of different national socializations as well as different familial patterns. Evidently, the situation in Kurdistan has changed to varying degrees. Many aspects will likewise have changed among Kurdish diaspora, particularly among younger generations. While several participants noted that they were different from each other without being able to articulate in what way, other participants verbalized why differences had emerged between them. They referred to language skills, secular views, and educational levels as contributing factors to why Kurds behave "culturally, emotionally, and socially" in different ways. While this heterogeneity is not new and has been discussed in earlier studies, it is much more enhanced in its new environments and more exposed in its online interactions. This is also why some Kurds find to have more in common with Swedes or Brits than with their coethnics, as one of the interviewees explained to me. Posing the question, "Why must this mean that we should automatically feel closer?" the young man in the UK explicitly questioned ideas about commonality written in ethnicity, and not doings or performativities. If being Kurdish meant that "you can't get a tattoo, or a piercing or something like that, then I don't really want to be a part of that," is a powerful statement against prescribed texts of how to behave to remain a Kurd. These are performativities that go against the "imagined community" and "imagined diaspora" that have implied that diasporas are living in myths of a common culture and identity. The diversity exposed through the new technology, I argue, supersedes the traditional media's homogeneous Self and Other and, in turn, complicates the binary "us" and "them." It is the circumstances that shape the identities within the cognitive frames of the Self and the Other, as Eid and Karim (2014) explain. This exposes more noticeably that the Self and Other are not inherent in ethnic or religious identities. This theoretical interference essentially underlines what we already know but still overlook in diaspora studies, and especially in public debates, that "difference" is imagined and is decisive in the defining of relationships (Vali 2006). What diaspora individuals do is to bring to the fore a consciousness in which both the Self and the Other are situated contextually, referring back to many other factors, which will have meaning in terms of the notions of belonging and commonality.

So, what is at stake, intellectually and politically, in contemporary diaspora debates when these techno-social conversations challenge the established structures of the Self and the Other, us and them? The discourse of internal othering, I contend, has value for (a) how we understand the problematic notion of *difference* as explained earlier, and (b) the consciousness of diaspora, which de facto is a crucial intellectual point that can reveal why the diaspora condition, as a result of forced or voluntary migration, can explain much of the identity conundrum that faces most societies in our contemporaries and in this era of digital technologies, and (c) how old diaspora becomes new transnational, perhaps even cosmopolitan.

Beyond the Duality of Homeland and Hostland

By identifying the different layers where internal othering occurred repeatedly, it becomes more feasible to discern that these are distinctive positions from which Kurds speak and make self-identifications. The positions conflate with multiculturalism and policies (diaspora vs. diaspora in different countries), diaspora formation (diaspora vs. homeland), migration waves (within diaspora; old and new diasporas), and generational shift (between younger generations and immigrant generation). The task is not to make any rigid claims, but to elaborate on tendencies that emerge and that deserve more attention and research in academic scholarship.

Diaspora Versus Homeland

New communication technologies are often described as tools with which, in particular, diaspora people can connect to their origin. This is one way to understand the new media, but the communication tool is not necessarily contributing to such direct links. When young Kurdish diaspora became members of the online community Viva Kurdistan, it was to converse about shared interests such as the Kurdish question, independence, and new homeland concerns. It is a common element within many diasporic people to have nostalgic memories and connection with their parents' birth countries (Wessendorf 2007), who sacrificed much for their homeland. This has infused younger Kurds with feelings of guilt. Many young Kurds talk about a return to the homeland; some do return, while it is out of question for others apart from regular visits they do during the summers.

My first observation during my online ethnography in the context of the link between homeland-based Kurds and diaspora Kurds is that the interactions between those forums were limited. When diaspora Kurds moved between the "diasporic forums" (such as the Swedish or British) and the Kurdish forum, it was merely to gain news updates. Very few members engaged fully in the Kurdish forum with homeland-based members. They were mostly engaged in conversations with fellow Kurds in the same country or in other European nations. Through lengthy discussions about language, gender, religion, culture, and politics, participants have encountered multiple ways of viewing and discussing Kurdishness influenced by both old and new transnational practices. The dialogues have demonstrated how they have detached themselves from certain elements of the Kurdish identity and strengthened others. But it is noteworthy that the contact between young diaspora Kurds and homeland Kurds is much more limited than expected. On the other hand, while young Kurds are prepared to return to the homeland to connect with the origin, first-generation migrant parents are less likely to do that, according to the returnees. The different links are by no means clear here.

Why was there no interest to interact with fellow Kurds in the homeland? There are a few factors contributing to this. First of all, the forums were restricted to communicate in their national languages. This means Swedish in the Swedish forum, English in the British forum, and Kurdish in the Kurdish forum. While most young women and men possess more or less Kurdish language skills, many refrained from conversing in the Kurdish forum because of these restrictions. Reasons for this, according to the participants, were the time-consuming aspect and limitations of terminology to discuss political, academic, and other "serious questions." The second reason emerged from the discussions threads. Their interests diverge considerably, and most diasporic Kurds in the other national forums did not see any gains made by participating in the Kurdish forum. This distance between diaspora and homeland Kurds is also notable among Kurdish returnees in Kurdistan. The common impression among Kurdish diaspora as well as local individuals is that they live in a "diasporic bubble" in the homeland. The social encounters with fellow Kurds in the local community are limited.

Kurds in diaspora feel attached to their motherland, and through links that sense has prevailed. However, we need to also recognize that this does not necessarily mean that the links made are between diaspora and homeland. It is foremost between diaspora and diaspora across Europe, as well as across diaspora and diaspora within the settlement country. Their strengthened notion of a Kurdistan is through such contacts rather than directly with the homeland in this case.

The blurry vision of Kurdistan and the slight contact with local people may be contributing explanations as to why young diaspora Kurds return to the homeland while their parents stay in diaspora. For whatever reasons they return, professional or personal commitments, many of them are not fully aware of what awaits them. The limitations of their mobility and capabilities that were caused by social, political, and cultural issues have, however, changed their visions. While the return serves as an antidote to their guilt, the changes of personality and identity crisis make their stay rather difficult. I observed that men and women, especially the latter, described themselves as almost feeling like a child again. They had to learn certain social codes and norms, and how to behave as a woman. The freedom to move around in the society, or to other cities, was restricted, partly because of security reason, but mainly because they felt more comfortable in the company of someone else.

Considering these components in the experiences of the returnees, a return may very well be understood as another migration process, where estrangement and alienation are factual parts of their experiences. In an examination of the discourse of repatriation, scholars have suggested a removal of the prefix "re" from the term return (i.e. Hammond 1999) when describing this type of migration, because they view it independently and not as a mark to end earlier migrations. Seeing that some returnees do actually return, once again, back to the settlement country, this is a valid point. Also keeping in mind Zara's words that this return was essentially a gap to fill, it was her "Kurdistan Chapter," after which she could return to Sweden, as it is there she feels happy more consistently. Furthermore, there is an important distinction in the character and timeframe of migration with respect to age as well as the character of migration. The diasporic individuals' migration will differ considerably if it takes place at a young age or as adults, in more precarious circumstances, as opposed to their voluntary migration at an older age. Again, this gives reason to why we need to contextualize different types of migrations and dispersals among diasporas.

While most diaspora people sense a connection, a feeling of belonging to the old homeland, the realities on the ground differ. The most striking combat Kurdish returnees found themselves in was the loss of identity. This was especially the case for the female returnees. Independency, confidence, career, gender equality, and freedom to behave differently were factors that made them uneasy with the homeland regardless of reasons for returning there. Abruptly, they were reversely in the position of "freshies," the way new migrants were in diaspora. Subtle but important details such as eye contact, laughter, and habits made them more certain that they missed their homes, Sweden or Britain. This does not exclude their belonging to Kurdistan, or their continuous work and visits.

The new experiences of the homeland illustrate the problematic notion of territory and identity and the imaginaries when children raised outside their origin country return with a different set of rhythms, habits, and tastes. Being legal citizens of the homeland and not marked as foreign by looking "like everyone else," the returnee becomes a foreigner in their *own* land. Of course, experiences vary. For those returnees, as opposed to first generation, this is not a re-turn or re-adjustment. This is a new entry (Hammond 1999).

Between Generations

Research on Kurdish diaspora and media concludes that Kurdish identity has been reinforced by second- and third-generation Kurds, who are presently growing up in Europe (Alinia 2004; van Bruinessen 2000; Curtis 2005). It is said that they tend to be more interested in Kurdish national identity and politics than their parents were. Indeed, young Kurds are intensely involved in transnational engagements towards the homeland.

Because of the rapid and ubiquitous communication technology, such matters can be shared between people across borders in ways never seen before. But the new technology goes well beyond that in some contexts. Young Kurds have also in this study demonstrated regular transnational activities directed at homeland as well as laterally across nations where Kurdish diasporas are settled, which proves of great interest in homeland politics. However, there are nuances that benefit from being explored as they can illustrate other tendencies.

In a thread about life in diaspora and the challenges to Kurdish identity, one participant elucidated how identity changes and homeland politics are not mutually exclusive, "There is a big difference between supporting the rights of Kurds and leading your own personal life. That you live abroad and are confronted with a lifestyle that is very different from your homeland does not mean you are a 'traitor.'" Women and men make a distinction between personal life in their new homelands and the political and cultural developments in the origin land. Intense online debates between the participants confirm the great interest in homeland politics and identity, but we need to be cautious before coming to a conclusion about a strengthened identity, as it may very well be a symptom of the opposite. The cultural critic, Kobena Mercer (1990), has, for example, argued that identity becomes an issue when it finds itself in a crisis. When the imagined fixed thing is placed in an experience of doubt, the crisis emerges. The crisis may be a reflection of new actors, new political subjects, and new socialites (Mercer 1990), and it may happen among Kurdish diaspora, Europeans (with a failure of multiculturalism as a result), or in more conflicted zones where heterogeneous voices challenge the construction of homogeneous national and religious formations.

Younger generations bring along a doubly important perspective in the making of diaspora; they are visibly the living incarnation of both continuity and change, mediating memories of the past with the new living conditions (Fortier 1999). They are charged with duties to preserve some forms of ethnic identity and are called bearers of an "original" culture but with the embodiment of fluidity at the same time. It is especially within migration and ethnic studies that the aspect of generation is commonly addressed to "periodize" the settlement adaption of a population within the settlement country (Fortier 2000). Changes in the cultural lives of migrant communities are typically expressed in terms of generations. The aspect of generations is of immense value as, in line with what Fortier has stated, they punctuate "original" cultures. Some scholars

(Bauböck and Faist 2010) divide this time difference into a phase model where first generation of migrants can be called diaspora and the second generation a transnational community.

Generations, therefore, provide a particular way of speaking of changes within a collectivity, in this case a national collectivity as a whole. We could most clearly see this in how the Kurdish man in London explained, in Chap. 6, that his narrative of Kurdistan as a coherent country with people having common views was produced by his father, as well as through satellite channels such as Med TV. His adopted ideas, however, soon clashed with the online discourse that young Kurds created. This was a much more diverse discourse that comprised of contradictions and irregularities, which made him rethink such essentialist notions. Young Kurds who were either born or brought up in Sweden or the UK have a different relation to the homeland as well as to the countries they are settled in.

Differences between generations emerge as the younger Kurds growing up outside their homelands are, despite them acknowledging the importance of language, less likely to use their Kurdish language in their daily lives. In the different forums in the online community, participants were confined to speak the national language of the country in which they reside. This means that only one forum was communicating in Kurdish. Very few diaspora members participated in the Kurdish forum because of two issues. Firstly, the members, as mentioned, communicate exclusively in Kurdish (using Latin script), and secondly due to the topics and content that diverged from that of the diaspora forums. In addition to this, during the interviews, they would elaborate on this and explain that they would only speak Kurdish with their parents, but even then they could switch to Swedish or English, as it was, occasionally, more convenient. The urge and the emphasis on language in their descriptions of the status of language should therefore not be conflated with how it really appears in their everyday lives. I bring up this particular point on language in this generational context as the intensity and need to discuss Kurdishness, including language and culture, must be contrasted with the everyday realities of young Kurds. There is no clear answer to this, as speaking (or writing and reading) the mother tongue is considered to be a non-negotiable cultural artefact among the members, yet weakened in light of the use of other dominant national languages. Whether the Kurdish language enhances their sense of being a Kurd and belonging to Kurdistan, or whether the "intellectual distance" grows, as at times it is more convenient to speak in other languages, are questions with no clear answer (Hannerz 2001).

Cross-generational narratives are significant encounters between nostalgia and the presence of new realities. This needs to be explored to a greater extent, as especially in Kurdish studies the generational aspect has not been taken into consideration when writing about Kurdish identity. The majority of studies have engaged in first-generation experiences of migration and homeland politics (Eliassi 2013).

Between Diasporas: The Impact of Policies

It is important to note that diasporas do not create their communities in isolation. The active diaspora intelligentsia aside, the nation-state's policies and citizenship patterns play a noteworthy role in creating options for migrants and diasporas (Pföstl 2013; Waldinger and Fitzgerald 2003). This explains, in part, why diaspora patterns may diverge between different countries they are settled in. Sweden is known for its liberal system, which can, to a certain extent, explain the role Kurds have been able to play in the political and cultural arena. Multiculturalism policies in Sweden, more than any other Scandinavian country, have described goals with efforts to avoid any ethnic "Swedifying" strategies, which, for instance, have earlier been directed at its Sami minority to, instead, support minority identities. Kurds in Sweden have been active both in terms of a diaspora engaged in transnational homeland-oriented activities, as well as Swedish citizens contributing to the political, cultural, and social developments in the country. Transnational social activities towards the homeland are especially apparent among the political diaspora who arrived in the early stages of migration from the regions of Kurdistan, and are also laterally engaged in activities across various European countries. Therefore, this shows that political, social, cultural, and economic transnational activities by diasporic individuals do not mean they are distanced from the settlement country; on the contrary, they tend to also be more active in the settlement countries. Claims that migrants and diaspora who are involved in homeland engagements may be less inclined to integrate into the settlement society, as noticed in some migrant debates, should not be simplistically assumed. At the same time, diaspora adaption in the new society is without a doubt an important element of migrant experience as we have seen in the exchanges between old diaspora who arrived in the late twentieth century and the newly arrived diaspora groups.

In Sweden, gender policies and discourse have had an impact on the Kurdish diaspora in two distinct ways. The first has affected the debates and responses to honour-killing. Explanations for the relevant debates are referred to in the country's emphasis on gender equality (strongly emphasized in the Education Act [the law that governs all education in Sweden]) and the strong stance of feminist movements. Women's rights have been a strong marker of Swedish state identity and are strongly promoted in polices. The Swedish gender system also advocates a more open attitude around sexuality, which has an impact on moral values regarding sexual behaviour among its migrant populations. We could see tendencies among the Swedish-Kurdish diaspora online that were more involved in gender discussions, demonstrating a more challenging view. This has also contributed to women's more ambivalent position and their relation to the Kurdish community (see also Alinia 2014).

While gender roles were discussed to a lesser degree in the British forum, there were substantial and lengthy discussions on politics, homeland conflicts, and, to some extent, events on the ground in Britain. Many announcements took place regarding seminars, conferences, demonstrations, Newroz festivities, and other events. Cultural rights among the UK-Kurds have been intensified, especially as the tense Kurdish–Turkish relation is more apparent. It is also in the context of multiculturalism debates that Kurds have had the need to discuss online about, for instance, home-grown terrorism and the burqa ban. This was noticeable as the burqa was discussed to a much greater degree, and equally opposed to much more than in the Swedish forum.

Within Diaspora: Between Old and New Migrants

The reader will by now be familiar with the experiences of the Kurdish people that have forcibly dispersed them around the world, and particularly to Europe, with considerable communities in Sweden, the UK, and Germany. This sense of being a diaspora still prevails among younger generations of Kurds, who, often explicitly, refer to themselves as diaspora. The feeling and awareness of being a diaspora is therefore present, and there seems to be no need or desire to become undiasporic. The question is, however, how their practices and everyday life can suggest other evolving nature of their "diasporicness." If we think about the internal othering that takes place within the diasporic population in the Swedish and British forums, Kurds differentiated one another by the names "imports/freshies" on the one hand, and "assimilated" or "Swedified" on the other hand. Despite the derogatory connotation of the words, these references have a much deeper meaning that involves identity constructions that go beyond ethnicity and include other socio-economic factors. I do not interpret these expressions as simply internalized racism that aims at performing "proud self-identification" as an accepted member of the white society, as suggested by other scholars (Pyke and Dang 2003). In their work on Asian Americans, Pyke and Dang have explained the "intra-ethnic" othering among them as a way to demonstrate identification with the white people that signalled progress and superiority over their "co-ethnic peers." Assimilationist tendencies among migrants presuppose that they leave behind traditions and culture completely, which these young Kurds have clearly demonstrated that they do not. I leave the interpretation to the reader to decide where integration ends and assimilation starts, but in this context, it is the different positions from which Kurdish diasporic individuals talk and identify themselves that I find meaningful to link to other factors such as migration phases, class, education, language skills, and other social experiences. Such parallels were also made by participants online when attempting to give a rational and informative explanation to the integral differences that Kurds display. The participants' discussions reflect diasporas' adoption of liberal values, but also those who may not be as integrated into the new society and instead feel socially and culturally excluded from the society. The participants themselves pinpointed their differences to time of arrival, reasons for migration, and the settlement country's politics.

As described in the earlier chapter, the different migration phases are an indicator of not only the time or location of migration movement, but more importantly, who travelled and under what circumstances (Brah 1996). While I have earlier made a meta-distinction between diaspora people based on the reasons of becoming a diaspora, it is important to make such contextualization also within a diaspora. Among the Kurds who left in the early waves of migration, the majority were either labour migrants (to Germany or Britain), or political refugees (to Sweden and Britain). There are also voluntary migrant Kurds in both settings, who did not share the same migration experiences and specific reasons for leaving the homeland. These are important details to establish in order to view individuals as subjectivities, who carry stories about their lives in their homeland before fleeing or voluntarily moving. Kurds who arrived in the late 1960s, throughout 1970s, 1980s, and early 1990s, have had the time to acquire social and cultural capital, and their contacts with different cultures and other places make these old diaspora populations more trans-national and global in their activities.

The interesting note to make here is that the individuals who belong to the old diaspora arrived in Europe under much more difficult circumstances (war and genocide in Iraq, systematic oppression in Turkey, Iran, and Syria) using different modes of travelling. The later waves of migrants, by contrast, came about during the period associated with modern means of communication (airplanes, telephone, e-mail, and Internet) (Mishra 2007; Spivak 1996). To complicate the terrain of diaspora further, I argue that old diaspora has transformed into new transnational, maybe even cosmopolitan, and global diaspora in the same definition Spivak and Mishra use for new diaspora, with the capacity to move with ease between countries and consciousnesses. Simultaneously, the newer diasporas are in the position of the old diaspora who feel excluded and estranged. Hence, while Kurds are not abandoning the diaspora identification, to address Clifford's question, "When do people cease to be diasporic?" (1994, p. 306), the nature of diaspora changes, demonstrating that the categories of old and new also need to be explored using a critical eye.

This was even more elucidated in the conversations about themselves as "guests" versus citizens in the settlement countries. While a few of the online members expressed a sense of gratefulness to the "hostland," members of the old diaspora strongly opposed being put in the position of a "beggar." The accounts have not been short of examples regarding Kurds who have identified themselves as Swedes as much as "Bertil and Inga," disregarding ethnic boundaries completely. Kurds acknowledged their adopted new routines, different from their parents' that have replaced old scripts. Their right to belong to the new homeland also involved responsibilities that the Kurds had recognized as part of their citizenship, such as tax paying, voluntary work, employment, and so on. The accounts at the same time also address the overtheorizing of diaspora and "displacement," which only leads to the strengthened binary relationship (Fortier 2000); this, in turn, sustains the assumption of the primacy of a placement. Therefore, we may need to reconsider whether young diasporas really are "Suspended between two such terrains (living without belonging in one, belonging without living in the other)" (Mishra 2006, p. 16).

This intervention can markedly impact how we understand the experiences which emerge as an important locus of creating belongings. Indeed, this is an interactive process—continually evolving as one component is repeated and reinforced or reshaped and new associations are created, subsumed, or adapted to. This theoretical point simply informs us that difference, "slow-motioned" in the online space, is contingent on migration experiences, contemporary processes, and new habits that have an impact on how belonging is constructed and deconstructed.

FROM DOUBLE CONSCIOUSNESS TO MULTICONSCIOUSNESS

These identification positions demand us to extend the double consciousness to multiple consciousnesses. Gilroy (1993) has used the expression "double consciousness" to define the state of mind of diaspora in a complex map of cultural and social junction among diaspora and homeland. When striving to be both European and black, the African diaspora required a specific form of double consciousness. By including a lateral point of references, which is the homeland, the double consciousness disturbed the horizontal form of national consciousness, which is produced between the nation and its people. By introducing different layers of internal othering, namely identificational positions, the consciousness proves to be much more complicated and fluid in the Kurdish context than that of the doubleness. Compounded by the awareness of multilocality in different time spaces, diasporic individuals' memories battle with present communities and modernities that go beyond the duality of homeland and the settlement country.

Gilroy's double consciousness has been scrutinized by scholars such as Mishra (2006) for its simple, positive hyper-consciousness, as it has bypassed heterogeneous multiplicity. Mishra also refers to Avtar Brah who writes, "Border crossing does not only occur across the dominant/dominated dichotomy, but [...] equally, there is traffic within cultural formations of the subordinated group, and these journeys are not always mediated through the dominant culture(s)" (1996, p. 209). The double must not be privileged at the expense of the *multiple* in the story of modernity's consciousness. "It is this history [...] that is in urgent need of recovery" (Mishra 2006, p. 76). An emphasis on the multiplicity of experiences and state of mind suggests a "triple consciousness" (Vertovec 1999), which itself is the awareness of the doubleness that is used instrumentally (see also Oonk 2007). In line with such critique, and as the empirical accounts have demonstrated, the double consciousness is not sufficient to describe the state of mind among diasporic individuals in their contemporary intensified transnational engagements online and offline, horizontal but also lateral, between other Kurdish diasporic populations. I argue that an enhanced awareness of their lives, as well as the lives of the "local" population in the homeland whom they met online and during their return to the homeland to live and work, are conclusively shaped by culture and time. Rey Chow (2001) refers to William Safran's explanation that if "diasporic consciousness is an intellectualization of [the] existential condition," of dispersed people from the homeland, then, "diasporic consciousness is perhaps not so much a historical accident as an intellectual reality" (p. 201). Chow's words, that this is about an existential state of which "permanence" itself is an ongoing fabrication (p. 201), and not the transient condition, encapsulate the very essence of the outcome of this book. If identity is changing, and diasporas are a powerful force that disturb the coherent and singular notion of nations and ethnicities, then the processes that diaspora go through, from old victim diaspora to new transnational and active formations, need to be acknowledged.

The multiple consciousnesses have been extended because the imaginings of their homeland, as one nation and one people, have decisively been reshaped by the exchanges online. While the idea of multiple consciousnesses emphasizes a variety of experiences, the concept of double consciousness lends itself well to explaining the imagined community's construction of this duality, where the national consciousness of the homeland and the marginalized notions of the Self and the Other have been at the fore. This type of consciousness was restricted to the condition "here" and "there," and to the social identities that were framed in connection to the two states.

Furthermore, these multiple identification layers mean that the diaspora Kurds have, to an increasing extent, adopted non-essentialistic approach to the understanding of their identities. This in turn implies that they have acknowledged differences among themselves and refer them to specific explanations that address socio-economic capital, including orientation within societies, language skills, and citizenship. Hence, the component of multiple consciousnesses has consequences for how diaspora formation evolves and changes through time and space, which needs to be considered when we talk about multiculturalism, citizenship, and belonging.

TECHNO-SOCIAL ASPECTS

Of course the problem lies with *us*, and not the online community VK. One has to wonder how much Kurds we are when we can see how we are behaving towards each other. I have never seen anything like this, and unfortunately the majority of us, our way of thinking is far away from what it should be as Kurds. You can't see any Kurdishness in the forum, not in the Swedish forum at least. (*Viva Kurdistan*, Swedish Forum, September 6, 2010)

The quotidian use of the new technology has created a new and dynamic information and communication environment, which has cast a new light on the study of migrants and diasporas within the current context of globalization and transnationalism. Perhaps more interesting than to view the Internet and technologies as a catalyst to motion is how the technology methodologically opens up new ways to explore questions of migration, diaspora, and identity. It serves as scene that opens up for new ways of conceiving formations, movements, and contestations that otherwise may not be as easily detected. This has indeed been a valuable way to gain new insights into the case of the Kurdish diaspora. The Internet is a complex terrain that entails a myriad of components that in different combinations can generate different reactions. Any assessment of whether it is "good" or "bad" may, therefore, be complicated. Analysing and understanding the patterns online and the social interactions are needed, and in this section, I will highlight a few of the components of the online community, which, in one way or the other, have had significance for the production of this work and its findings. These include the online anonymity, online insults and flames, and gender aspect.

Online Anonymity and Authenticity

Questions of anonymity and authenticity are frequently raised in relation to the Internet and cyberspace. In the early 1990s, many statements on the Internet stemmed from mystification with the new technologies in which anonymity was a key aspect. From a traditional perspective, this concerned limitations to Internet data; we do not know who the senders and writers of the online texts and posts are, and what their purposes and circumstances are, apart from what is being told. This in turn raised questions of authenticity of members and material, which has become issues of veracity and validity for researchers.

In her early work on the Internet, Turkle (1995) pointed out that people frequently use potential online communities, like multiple-user domains or chat rooms, to deliberately experiment with their own personality, which was potentially liberating. Online personas may not be literally truthful in terms of age, gender, personality, or even interests. Turkle (2011) has later demonstrated an approach that showed online communication as potentially shallow and addictive, which could hinder a more fulfilling interpersonal relationship.

Although the discourse has changed considerably since the first generation of new technology, anonymity is still many times conflated with questions of authenticity and members' intentions, in particular some social media channels. Such arguments are presumably based on an assumption that we are our selves offline, but we can be someone else online as we can "hide" behind a screen. The discourse of anonymity almost becomes a philosophical one, and the question is when are we really ourselves? How do we know when people are their true selves? This aspect of authenticity and being your true self (Goffman 1973) raises questions as to whether individuals can de facto be their "selves" even more while online. Anonymity has allowed for sincere and serious engagements from the participants who have spent hours on a daily basis developing threads into long discussions spanning several pages, which raised questions that were unlikely in the pre-Internet era. Some discussions were academically written with references to prominent theoretical thinkers, and free from grammar and spelling errors. The "discussants" drafted their posts with care and composition in order to read well. They give reasons to think that anonymity conflates with authenticity and that such combination enables the opportunity to freely discuss a gamut of topics in a way previously not seen.

It is useful here to understand the degree of anonymity at different junctures. Members with nicknames and non-authentic information are anonymous in its right meaning: others cannot identify who that person is offline. Having said that, some of these participants have been members of the online community for several years, and they are no longer anonymous to each other. They have, after a while, created a reputation and image of themselves, which may also consequently have an impact on how they participate and how some discussion threads evolve. In that sense, the evolution of a discussion is sometimes just as dependent on the topic-maker as the topic per se. Many of the participants do not feel they are anonymous any more, which does not mean that personal details are exposed, but rather reveals personal thoughts and emotions online. Anonymity here concerns their way of being viewed by others. However, the most valuable aspect of this is the freedom to express and share opinions and views of loaded topics. The service of anonymity "loosens tongues" (Franklin 2004).

A Site of Resistance: Empowering Kurdish Women

The online space, with the anonymity aspect taken into account, has been especially empowering for young women, enabling them to find new expressive spaces, as well as giving voice to participants' opinions and objections to events in the origin country or in the settlement countries with relative impunity. We cannot disregard the importance of the subjects of gender and sexuality when the most frequent and heated discussions have included these issues. The Internet and online community can operate as a site of resistance due to the sensitive character embedded in these subjects, while the everyday offline life has not allowed for such questions to be aired among Kurds. The risks of being labelled have pushed them to test boundaries and make their claims online instead. But even in their online activities, certain tactics had to be taken, recalling the words of a member who said that he can especially understand the female participants for being anonymous online to avoid reputational damage and rumours. Instead, they have found ways to solve such important issues by allowing these hidden questions to surface and to argue for their rights as female Kurds.

These talks commonly place femininity, sexuality, and gender roles at the centre of changing discourses of Kurdishness. They constitute another way of looking at how belongings and constructions are gendered. To a great extent, women themselves initiated talks where they presented new claims of being someone with sexual needs, while being a Kurdish woman at the same time. Such declarations met many reactions. Therefore, while the online community can serve as a site of commonality or sharing memories, it is also at the same time a site of disruptions of imaginaries of national unity or gendered roles (Gajjala 2002; Kuntsman 2009). There were two particular strands that were noticeable within this topic. One delineates how diaspora women are positioned differently towards obligations and rights, and the other how Kurdish females are trying to liberate themselves from old norms of how they should behave sexually.

Earlier research on diaspora and the Internet (Gajjala 2004) has explored the gender imbalance, as male participants outnumber their female counterparts in general, as well as in this study, as the accounts were held overwhelmingly by male Kurds; however, this does not necessarily reflect the gender division in the online interactions, as a large number of members do not participate in the forums, but go online for other reasons. Some of them are lurking and only reading posts, but many were merely interested in encounters for private conversations online. Despite the fact that a male presence dominates online (Miller and Slater 2000; Gajjala 2004; Franklin 2004), it has also been suggested that women are active even if they are in a minority. Bearing this in mind, we also need to examine how other aspects of online forums and their discussion topics distinguish online from offline environments. In earlier studies, this aspect has been discussed (see Alinia 2004; Baser 2011), particularly in terms of how women often become invisible actors in studies on war and conflicts. Accounts on displacement and exile are mostly described from the male's perspective. Interviews conducted with Kurdish women in diaspora have declared how gender issues and inequality are paused and delayed because of the nation-building project (Baser 2011). While these accounts resonate with that of the online participants' experiences, it is against these realities that women online have been able to speak.

Women online have come to test boundaries to a significant degree. Such a statement can also be supported by the interviewees discussed in Chap. 5, who rejected to discuss similar topics and referred to them as unimportant and merely "testing boundaries." This provides an indication of how a "minority within a minority" (Gajjala and Gajjala 2008) negotiates structures in which both racism and cultural norms can be embedded. The new opportunities to raise their voice more boldly online can be reflected in the way they sometimes evoked strong reactions. The reactions within the context of gender and sexual attitudes came from both men and other women online, although many men also supported their stances. On the other hand, their participation in the political topics was questioned mainly by the males who opposed their presence in the political discussions. Nevertheless, it is important to note that these political discussions evoked heated feelings, in general, also between male participants. This takes me to the next aspect, online trolling and insults, which have often been conflated with online mockery rather than other serious intrinsic character that may be connected to changing identities and Kurdishness.

Online Insults

Most discussions about flames (online fights) and trolling (deliberately provocative messages posted with an intention of upsetting) speak of these as negative and disturbing (Kuntsman 2009). Kuntsman has looked into this particular theme and asserts that there is a need to examine violence online as a constituent of spaces of belonging. She suggests that rather than seeing flames as acts of disruptions, they can be forms of being together. In the analysis of my own empirical material, two different types of insults appeared. The first type has a clear, deliberate intention to disturb the discussions, but they were often not long-lasting and participation was shallow, that is, posts consisting of a few sentences only usually lying outside the topic context. The other category of insults that I identify differs from trolling—they are an integral part of the discussion itself and can often be seen in substantial threads. Participants are well aware of the character of the discussions, and the disagreements and insults are often conflated with disunity and the reasons behind the lack of a nation-state.

This distinction can be framed based on Butler's (1997) insightful explanation of the words per se that injure and the mode in which they are delivered, allowing me to go deeper into the meaning and importance of understanding why some words cause such an effect. The interesting question is to map which words succeed in wounding and which do not. Such mapping should also include not only the presence of successful insults but also the failure of certain words to wound, which can help to shed light on a word's meaning and its use in the online community. From this point of view, while the online community and its structure can be said to be the catalyst producing the power to insult, facilitated by the anonymity factor, it is not the rationale behind the insult per se. The questions raised then are as follows: Who insults? Why? When? How? The appearance of injury has something to do with the representation that offends and is responded to in a strong manner. Once we go further and look at the context in which some insults are found, they are connected to important issues of self-identification, strategies of inclusion, and, by implication, also exclusion. In connection to questions such as who is a Kurd, or whether the ethnic identity or religious identity is more important, responses included phrases such as "regarding your looks, you might as well have been Persian, Turk or Arab." Online insults are also an integral part of the internal othering in an effort to imply a weak identity of the discussants. Such name-callings first and foremost upset or annoyed the participants. If we look at the contexts, the modes, and the manners in which the insults are delivered, as Butler advises us, we can see that these acts follow a closer examination about the intimate and political relations between the Self and the Other. The insults work as part of the strategies to "correct" certain behaviours that are new, or not considered to be enough Kurdish, feminine, or religious in some cases. It is for such reasons that it is important to not explain flames as a feature of online space and new technologies, or as plain rudeness, enabled by the online anonymity. This becomes especially insightful in a comparison between the different forums.

The members based in Sweden held by far the most intense, fierce, and frenzied discussions online, followed by the British forum. A skim through the other diaspora forums testified to a rather different atmosphere, although debates occurred. But the most striking in this comparison is that the homeland-based Kurdish participants in their forum had a completely different tone in their discussions. Even the participants of the other forums would note the different attitudes characterizing each forum. What do these observations mean? While previous research refers the intense debates and a strong need to discuss and deliberate Kurdish issues, especially in countries such as Sweden, Germany, and Britain, with their substantial active diasporic Kurds, there may be other latent reasons to explain some tendencies within this discourse.

These fierce discussions indicate how these questions and issues have an underlying meaning in the contestations of identity and belonging in the settlement country. I complicate these interpretations by delving deeper into the linguistic and ethnic stances that are embedded in such acts, and connect them to contestation at the intersection of old and new belongings and a need for reconstruction of Kurdishness in hyper-modern and cosmopolitan societies. The main argument here is that online discussions tinged with insults and rudeness cannot merely be based on these explanations, in particular, considering the context in which they appear. These speech acts need to be penetrated and scrutinized, as they can also constitute important material of other theoretically unexplained phenomena concerning questions of identity, belonging, (the failure) of performativities, and the struggle of staying put. When we look at the contexts and the modes in which the insults and linguistic injuries take place, from a comparative perspective these questions are in closer relation to epistemological issues as well.

The Online–Offline Nexus

The methodological approach to interview the online members after the undertaking of the online ethnography proved to be valuable for a nuanced understanding of the online community and how Kurds made sense of their experiences. To gain further insight, the overarching question was not what the difference is between online and offline, but what people can do online that they cannot do offline? (Orgad 2009).

The Internet and the online community have enabled a platform for internal ponderings and reflections by, and about, Kurds themselves. As one of the Swedish-Kurdish respondents said, "Online, it wasn't which country do you come from, but which city?" While these questions seem self-explanatory, the diasporic online discourse indeed shows a complex mapping at the intersection of a number of passages. This has led to many "messy" discussions, which I have attempted to interpret, understand, and relate to the larger questions. "Messiness" here refers to the explosion of opinions, views, feelings, and contradictions that complicated my work and informed me of a shift in how individuals can liberate themselves from speech restrictions. When young Kurds talk to me as a researcher in an interview, there is a kind of tidiness that wraps up statements and opinions in their formulations. Participants' accounts were seemingly more sanitized face-to-face. It is this online-offline discrepancy that the earlier participant referred to when he urged online participants to ponder their answer to the question "Where are you from" if it takes place outside the "normal situation." I have been able to witness a messiness of online interactions, including insults and offence, enabled by the online structure of anonymity, but explained by other theoretical impetus that shows how certain elements in performative speech acts can be understood as practice of belonging, and contrarily, of detachment. It is where the "I" and "we" are shifting and becoming a "they," also intraethnically.

There is a parallel with similar work by Gajjala and Gajjala (2008), whose work on South-Asian diasporic populations suggests that differences arise in the engagement with the specific interface, which refers to the multiple technologies and the intersection of online and offline. The site as disruptive is also evident in the context of going from offline to online. It is a disruption of memories of the past and the present. As Gajjala (2002, p. 179) asserts, "It is a space where the diasporic stories of the past (often told as if they were stories from the present) and of places left behind can reach the actual physical (socio-cultural in flux) places that are fetishized in the memory/nostalgia of the model native (diasporic) informants." However, these may not be stories from "back home" (which is furthermore not the same place they left, as we have seen in the delineations about "going back" to the homeland), but from a position between there and here.

If the argument has been that identities change and differences develop also within ethnic groups, and similarities grow across them, it is not meant that those are happening online. Yet, it is in the dialogues online that changed dimensions appear, that differences are detected. This is why

I have stated that online space not only changes relations, but it also exposes what is latently and abstractedly happening. As we have seen earlier, all identities have their "others" from which they create their difference. These assertions are usually at the expense of similarities, for example, in the British context, Scottishness and Welshness are often defined in contrast to Englishness, while the differences that are emphasized are not always visible to those "outside" (Weedon 2004). The same can be applied for the relationship between Kurds, Pakistanis, or Germans; they may not be visible to other people, but they become so in the interactions between people online.

A multisited approach is also useful as we can use the Internet not only as a tool opening up new options for accessing social activities, but also because the construction of online communities and digital media offers new ways of interacting and engaging, thereby becoming a natural part of daily experiences and de facto influencing their "selves." Silverstone (2005, p. 6) states how it has become a commonplace in academic writing that the Internet can be investigated on its own terms, as if it was sui generis. This, he considers, is unsustainable as online and offline environments are mutually constituted in everyday life. Silverstone also argues that such mutuality and the necessity to acknowledge the importance of understanding life both online as well as offline, are bases for effective research in the area. Bearing this in mind, as well as the aim of this study, this research project concludes that it is not enough to merely look at online activities and exclude the offline environment, as these are very much interconnected. When George Marcus (1995, p. 199) presents a multisited ethnography, including "following" the people, the thing, the metaphor, the plot, story, or allegory, it is by tracing people that this research project has value in its multisited approach.

CHAPTER 9

Conclusion

Online activities and communications between people and across borders suggest that the new digital media has strong implications for different articulations of identity and belongingness, which open new ways of thinking about the imagined community. The problems of identity, racism, sexism, and other forms of social exclusion have been more exposed in the era of new media, thereby putting increasing pressure on the nation-state and citizenship restrictions. These demands for recognition and political representation are underpinning tensions between citizens and their nation-states and also are influencing the crises we see around the world.

This statement should be placed within the context of wider developments changing the notion of national formation and the national economy that are not new, but have been the subject of lengthy discussion within academic scholarship. The pressure comes from different directions that include the shifting power balance between nation-states, economic decline in Europe, the leaning towards greater internalization of economies, and the capitalist crisis during the 1970s (Hall 1997). As Hall (1997) explains, all of these developments have broken up economic, political, and social fields on which earlier notions of, for example, Englishness have flourished. They are all part of what we call globalization. Enhancing this is the continuous mobility and movement of migrants. Moreover, while there is a growing literature on diaspora and new media within different disciplines that offer different perspectives, the disrupting power that new

© The Author(s) 2016
J. Mahmod, *Kurdish Diaspora Online*, The Palgrave
Macmillan Series in International Political Communication,
DOI 10.1057/978-1-137-51347-2_9

technology brings may speed up the corrosion of structures and systems and deserves much more attention. Theorists who argue that modern identities are breaking up, refer to the structural changes that are changing societies splintering into the cultural spheres of nationality, race, ethnicity, gender, sexuality, and class that had previously provided us with firm positions (Hall 1997). For example, Bauman (1996) says that if the modern problem of identity was how to construct it and maintain its stability, the post-modern problem of identity is primarily how to avoid fixation and to keep options open.

Owing to historical and political reasons, Kurds have already found themselves in such conflicting processes for nearly a century when their land, Kurdistan (although not a nation-state), was broken up into four pieces and distributed between Iraq, Iran, Syria, and Turkey. In that sense, Kurdish identity may be seen as a critique of the concept of identity.[1] With even more scattered Kurdish populations around the world, I believe that Kurds can say much about questions of ethnicity, identity, and transnationalism, not despite their complexity but thanks to it.

IDENTITY DIFFERENCE: THE CONUNDRUM OF THE CENTURY

The book began with an outline of the debates on the perceived failure of multiculturalism in Europe. While there are many different—economic, political, and global—factors that have significant influence on developments, underlying them is a politics that seems to frame the same type of questions, a crisis of identity and difference.

This is not limited to Europe. In the Middle East, harsh violent and assimilation tactics are employed to forcibly include minority identity into the dominant majority group. While uprisings were a serious attempt at changing the political landscape, recent developments have enhanced the tectonic methods for cultural and religious homogenization. In Europe, a crisis has evolved that encircles the same deep-seated questions concerning the coherence of the EU and the nation-states as "swarms of refugees" have threatened national borders. Such media images and depictions have provided ample material for far-right movements who continue to rise since they started winning parliamentary seats over a decade ago across European liberal nations that are generally open to social difference.

A closer look at multiculturalism debates has posed serious questions pertinent to the view of the nation and its indigenous people as the Self and migrants as the Other. Despite the fact that diversity has been hailed, it has also been considered as problematic. Certain terms—"us and them"—have appeared that disclosed rather primordial and homogeneous views of the nation and belonging. Much of the discourse demonstrates a poor analysis of social and multicultural problems as it propounds a view of the nation-state and identity that belongs to the nineteenth century (Blommaert and Verschueren 1998). The crux of the problem is that identity, the Self, is viewed as already complete, fixed by our natures. Given this, it follows that commonality is understood along the lines of ethnic and cultural boundaries. This means a singular view that claims that one ethnic Swede has more in common with another ethnic Swede by default, rather than with any migrant because of their ethnic and cultural difference. Furthermore, the Swede has a natural relationship and sense of belonging to the nation. By the same token, differences are made between religious and gender identities, which reflect the conviction that these "behave" in certain ways in accordance with their categories. The problem with these essentialist views is that they resonate little with the realities on the ground. Firstly, this assumes that identities and cultures are unchangeable, even through the experiences of migration and diasporic life. Secondly, it disregards internal diversity and cross-ethnic commonality. Thereby, it is an indisputable fact of our contemporary world that people have lived by these ideas. People reside in imagined communities, believing that they belong to each other without even having met, and governments in multiple locations have devoted great effort in an attempt to strengthen this notion. It is in the spirit of such larger socio-political ideologies that this book has been written, attempting to address some of the key problems by presenting fresh insights into diasporas and their transnational activities.

Using a case study of diaspora Kurds, young women and men have demonstrated needs, constraints, and a changing discourse of Kurdishness at the intersection of old and new homelands. Keeping in mind that the examples are only one portion of the Kurdish community and the Internet, some concluding remarks can be made.

New Technology, New Consciousness: A Comment on the Human Condition

Diasporas come with different scripts, like any people, and while some scripts are less likely to change, others are influenced by their new homelands and their policies. The statements in this study take the discussion to the point that diaspora people—an old victim diaspora in this case—are also composed of a cultural and political elite that are highly attuned to different cultures, living dual or multiple lives across borders, and travel regularly. Through transnational practices, involving networks, activities, and comparisons, Kurdish diaspora have demonstrated that some exile groups have developed social and political power to advance through different societies and cultures and have begun to establish a transnational and even a cosmopolitan identity (which academic literature tend to refrain from acknowledging). The cumulative effects of the dynamics among diasporas—such as among Kurds at the intersection of online and offline environments—push us to seek alternative ways to understand identity, culture, and belonging. Diaspora dynamics, together with the dynamical structure of the Internet, demonstrates a need to move from intuitive statements and to look qualitatively at diasporic lives. For that, we need to develop new concepts within both academia and multiculturalism models to shape flexible citizenships, thus creating an updated and empirically informed outlook on identity difference. The elastic notion of the diaspora concept that Kurds have opened up places us in a new position to improve our understandings of society, citizens, and imagined differences. This and the multiplicity of diaspora consciousness disclose the inflammatory use of the term "imagined diaspora," which paints any migrated group with a broad brush in order to emphasize their existence away from the homeland and their minority status in the new country.

Diasporic Kurds dismiss socially-produced narratives and notions of how they ought to behave in order to be defined as Kurds, and demonstrate a new, multiple and transnational consciousness channeled by physical places they are attached to, rather than the myths and memories on which the imagined community has been built. Let me underline that this an affirmative idea as it is more likely to emerge when people adopt a non-essentialist approach to identity making. However, both academic scholarship and policies imagine them as remaining the same because of their transnational links to the homeland. Homeland transnational links will remain and even increase in this era of hyper-globalization, but transnational activities among diasporas can also strengthen their activities in their settlement countries. Through online-offline nuances and contradictions, Kurds in Sweden and the UK have learnt that difference and change is the root of their diasporic Kurdish identity. Feeling at home here, with a symbolic homeland there, are not mutually exclusive identificational positions.

It is my conviction that the new communication and information sphere, compounded by its dynamic components, is transforming the rationale and logic behind how identity difference is viewed and how the national community is built. The power of the Internet lies in its borderless and ethnic-blind space where people with different backgrounds gather and unexpectedly find cohesion that challenges the singularities of old media. The online stage forces us to disregard white skin, brown eyes, and accents, because of its structure that shifts power relations, different from offline encounters. On international social media channels such as Facebook, Twitter, and YouTube, this may be more current, as it interlinks people from different ethnic, religious, and cultural groups; however, while it connects people across ethnicities and cultures, it also exposes the diversity within ethnic groups. Surfacing in the post-modern and hyper-mobile era is a "super-diversity" (Vertovec 2007) that challenges both homogeneous and imagined communities.

New Directions

Where we are heading in terms of the future of the nation-state is anyone's guess, but one thing is certain—the nation-state is increasingly changing in character and in its relation to its citizens. Given the current situation around the world with increased conflict regions in the Middle East and North Africa, migration will not go away in a rush. Nation-states have come under pressure after years of forced inclusion of citizens and arrangements along the lines of ethnicities and religious identities. We are witnessing a paradigm shift including "an unchecked slide into an era in which the scale of global forced displacement as well as the responses required is now clearly dwarfing anything seen before," as the UN High Commissioner for Refugees, António Guterres, has stated (UNHCR 2015).[2] It is obvious that for an age of extraordinary forced displacement numbering in millions of people, new and wise responses are needed, both to protect those people living in war zones, those who are fleeing, as well as those who arrive as refugees.

The corrosion of the nation-state, national economies, and national cultural identities is as complicated as it is dangerous (Hall 1997). Powerful entities are dangerous when they are ascending and when they are in decline, and the question is which of these are more dangerous. In the first instance, states "gobble up" everybody, and in the second event, they take everybody down with them (Hall 1997). The first statement may very well conflate with the situation in Europe, while the second statement could conflate with the growing conflicts in the Middle East. In any event, these developments place populations in a precarious situation and there is no way that nation-states are "bowing off the stage of history" (Hall 1997, p. 25). Instead, when the coherence of the nation-state is threatened, its defensive protection will deepen and a return to a defensive national identity will happen, driven by a very aggressive form of racism. It looks as if this is the situation we find ourselves in with a growing far-right movement in Europe. This is what the emphasis on ethnicity, identity, and difference is stimulating more and more.

Leaders may have declared the failure of multiculturalism, but it is now more than ever that we need to talk about multiculturalism (Karim 2006) and renewed policies to better shape attitudes and citizenship in societies. Preceding policymaking, there should be appropriate research and academic involvement, which can build a greater bridge between empirical grounded work and policymaking. It is crucial that we employ appropriate interdisciplinary theories and methodologies for a better compass to guide us through this complex terrain.

While I have attempted to outline the dynamic less talked about in terms of perspectives on new technology and diaspora, it is, of course, also important to recognize the challenges that come with integration of people, in particular diaspora people who were forced to leave their homelands under difficult circumstances, which we have witnessed through the images of desperate refugees taking hazardous routes when fleeing Iraq, Syria, and elsewhere. This disaster, its severity aside, does not stand alone in its media coverage: life jackets, tents in public parks, the body of the drowned toddler Alan Kurdi washed up on the Turkish beach, tear gas and razor-wire fences in Hungary, and police batons in Macedonia (Trilling 2015). The humanitarian crises broadcasted around the world have been concomitant of an increased global solidarity and aid pledges. At the same time, the heightened and accusatory public discussion in European countries has not gone unnoticed.

The Kurdish diaspora in this case study has demonstrated that adaption to a new society is not an effortless process. They come with tragic memories of assimilationist and violent policies, or have experienced attempts at extinction. A forcefully displaced diaspora, like any voluntary migrants to different extents, will not completely abandon their old scripts, traditions and norms.

We need to better understand how cultures evolve, and when they are prevented from changing. Policies have been tightened and new strategies have been incorporated in recent years in Europe, but the political climate is seemingly worsening. We need to learn from counter-productive strategies, for example, in the case of honour-killing, that have led to a backlash reflected in the response by the Kurdish diaspora. Instead, tensions increased, resulting in distance between authorities and its Kurdish migrants. The problem is not that these questions of inequality are being raised, but they cannot be dealt with in the absence of knowledge of the cultural and religious contexts in which they take place. This is relevant for similar questions of forced marriage, burqa and veil, and other gender issues. It is a simple task for dominant cultures to define them as unequal or "barbaric" acts, but this will push away the group targeted. Earlier research (Kymlicka 2001) has described how migrant groups become more nationalistic in a forced systematic assimilation process rather than naturally integrating themselves on their own terms. This is confirmed by, for instance, the treatment of Kurds in those authoritarian states where they have been subject to violent assimilationist policies. In Europe, unequal debates have marginalized women and men in their approach to dealing with inequalities. Political leaders have not shied away from emphasizing the problematic characteristics of differences between the minority and the majority cultures, which, as a consequence, means that they have more or less ignored the changing nature of cultures and identities. Rather than stating differences between cultures as an endpoint, as multiculturalisms often do, this book has embraced the constructive importance of demonstrating how and why differences are produced that override ethic, gender, and national boundaries.

To respond to these deeply embedded issues, this book has attempted to offer new forms of a theoretical language or ideas about diaspora, identity, and difference by illustrating these challenges, and how and where they occur. It is the task of the academic field to describe the vibrant and diverse online space and to rethink fixed concepts and embrace the changing character of diaspora people, who undergo challenging and painful, but also enriching and rewarding, experiences. It is also the task of policies and strategies to change everyday behaviours and attitudes to consider speeches and acts, not skin and origins, as important sources for unity. The book has emphasized a critique and presented empirical data to provide the reader with a framework to consider new directions and to ruminate the implications and potentials. New media is not only changing social relations but also exposing a map of existing socialites and conditions that makes it imperative to explore further in order to better understand the human mind in this digital era of growing migration, transnational and international mobility. Such founding material is also important for education and school curriculum that we seriously need to reconsider in order to find new directions.

NOTES

1. Thanks to Pishko Shamsi for thorough and extensive conversations about these issues from which this expression derived.
2. The UN Refugee Agency, "Worldwide displacement hits all-time high as war and persecution increase," June 18, 2015.

BIBLIOGRAPHY

Abelmann N (2009) The Intimate University: Korean American Students and the Problems of Segregation. Duke University Press

Abu-Lughod L (1991) Writing against culture. In: Fox GR (ed) Recapturing anthropology: working in the present. School of American Research, Santa Fe

Adamo S (2008) Northern exposure: the new Danish model of citizenship. Int J Multicult Soc 10:10–28

Ahmad F (1993) The making of the modern Turkey. Routledge, London

Ahmed S (1999) Home and away: narratives of migration and estrangement. Int J Cult Stud 2(3):329–347

Akkaya AH (2011) Kurdish diaspora: creating new contingencies in transnational space. Paper presented at 4th global conference on interculturalism, meaning and identity, Prague, 11 March. http://www.researchgate.net/publication/264993316_Kurdish_diaspora_creating_new_contingencies_in_transnational_space. Accessed 2 May 2011

Akkerman T, Hagelund A (2007) Women and children first! Anti-immigration parties and gender in Norway and the Netherlands. Patterns of Prejudice, 41(2):197–214, DOI: 10.1080/00313220701265569

Aksoy A, Robins K (2000) Thinking across spaces: transnational television from Turkey. Eur J Cult Stud 3(3):343–365

Aksoy A, Robins K (2003). Banal transnationalism: the difference that television makes. In: Karim HK (ed) The media of diaspora: mapping the global. Routledge, London, pp 89–104

Alinia M (2004) Spaces of diasporas. Kurdish identities, experiences of otherness and politics of belonging. Doctoral thesis, Göteborg University

Alinia M (2013) Honor and violence against women in Iraqi Kurdistan. Palgrave Macmillan, Basingstoke

Alinia M (2014) Gendered experiences of homeland, identity and belonging among Kurdish diaspora. In: Akman H (ed) Negotiating identity in Scandinavia: women, migration, and the diaspora. Berghahn Books, New York

Allen T, Morsink H (eds) (1994) When refugees go home. UNRISD, Geneva

Alonso A, Oiarzabal PJ (eds) (2010) Diasporas in the new media age: identity, politics, and community. University of Nevada Press, Reno

Ammann B (2005) Kurds in Germany. In: Ember M, Ember CR, Skoggard I (eds) Encyclopedia of diasporas: immigrant and refugee cultures around the world. Diaspora Communities, vol 2. Springer, NewYork, pp 1011–1018

Anderson B (1983/2006) Imagined communities: reflections on the origin and spread of nationalism. Verso, London

Anderson B (1992) The new world disorder. New Left Rev 1(193):3–13. http://newleftreview.org/I/193/benedict-anderson-the-new-worlddisorder. Accessed 28 Apr 2014

Anderson LD, Anderson EW (2014) An atlas of Middle Eastern affairs. Routledge, London

Ang I (2001) On not speaking Chinese: living between Asia and the West. Routledge, London

Ang I (2003) Together-in-difference: beyond diaspora, into hybridity. Asian Stud Rev 27(2):149–150

Anthias F (1999) Institutional racism, power and accountability. Social Res Online 4:1

Anzaldúa G (1987) Borderlands/LaFrontera: the new mestiza. Aunt Lute, San Francisco

Appadurai A (2006) Fear of small numbers: an essay on the geography of anger. Duke University Press Books, Durham

Appiah AK (1994) Identity, authenticity, survival: multicultural societies and social reproduction. In: Gutmann A (ed) Multiculturalism—examining the politics of recognition. Princeton University Press. http://veraznanjemir.bos.rs/materijal/multiculturalism._examining_the_politics_of_recognition_-_charles_taylor.pdf. Accessed 12 Oct 2013

Appiah AK (1994/2005) The ethics of identity. Princeton University Press, Princeton

Asad T (2003) Formations of the secular: Christianity, Islam, Modernity. Stanford:University Press, Stanford

Austin JL (1975) How to do things with words. Oxford University Press, Oxford

Ayata B (2011) The politics of displacement: a transnational analysis of the forced migration of Kurds in Turkey and Europe. Doctoral thesis, The John Hopkins University

Banting K, Kymlicka W (2012/2013) Is there really a retreat from multicultural-ism policies? New evidence from the multiculturalism policy index. Comp Eur Polit 11(5):577–598. doi:10.1057/cep.2013.12

Banton M (1994) Modelling ethnic and national relations. Ethn Racial Stud 17(1):1–19

Barr J (2012) A line in the sand: Britain, France, and the struggle that shaped the Middle East. Simon & Schuster, New York

Baser B (2011) Kurdish diaspora political activism in Europe with a particular focus on Great Britain. Diaspora dialogues for development and peace project. Berghof Peace Support, Berlin

Baser B (2013) Diasporas and Imported-Conflicts: The case of Turkish and Kurdish Second Generation in Sweden. Journal of Conflict Transformation and Security, 3(2):105–125

Baser B (2015) Diaspora and homeland conflicts: a comparative perspective. Ashgate, Aldershot

Bauböck R, Faist T (2010) Diaspora and transnationalism: concepts, theories, and methods. Amsterdam University Press, Amsterdam

Baukje P, Saharso S (2006) Cultural diversity, gender equality: the Dutch case. Paper presented at the gender equality, cultural diversity: European compari-sons conference, Free University, Amsterdam, 8–9 June 2006

Bauman Z (1996) From Pilgrim to Tourist—or a Short History of Identity. In: Hall S and Du Gay (eds) Questions of Cultural Identity. London: Sage, pp 18–36

Bay A-H, Strömblad P, Bengtsson B (2010). An introduction to diversity, inclu-sion and citizenship in Scandinavia. In: Bengtsson B, Strömblad P, Bay A-H (eds), Diversity, inclusion and citizenship in Scandinavia. Cambridge Scholars, Newcastle upon Tyne, pp 1–16

Bell V (ed) (1999) Performativity and belonging: an introduction. Routledge, London, pp 1–10

Benhabib S (2005) Borders, boundaries, and citizenship. PS: Polit Sci Polit 38:673–677

Berners-Lee B (1999) Weaving the web: the past, present and future of the World Wide Web by its inventor. Orion Business Books, London

Bhabha H (1990/1994) Nation and narration. Routledge, London

Billig M (1995) Banal nationalism. Sage Publications, London

Blätte A (2006) The Kurdish movement: ethnic mobilization and europeaniza-tion. In: Kleinschmidt H (ed) Migration, regional integration, and human security. Ashgate, Hampshire, pp 181–202

Blommaert J, Verschueren J (1998) Debating diversity: analysing the discourse of tolerance. Routledge, London

Boellstorff T (2008) Coming of age in second life: an anthropologist explores the virtually human. Princeton University Press, Princeton

Borevi K (2014) Multiculturalism and welfare state integration: Swedish model path dependency. Identities 21(6):708–723. doi:10.1080/1070289X.2013.868351. Accessed 12 Nov 2015

Bowen JR (2007) Why the French don't like the headscarves: Islam, the state and public space. Princeton University Press, Princeton

Boyarin D, Boyarin J (1993) Diaspora: generation and the ground of Jewish identity. Crit Inq 19:693–725

Brah A (1996) Cartographies of Diaspora: Contesting Identities. Routledge, London and New York

Braziel JE, Mannur A (eds) (2003) Theorizing diaspora: a reader. Blackwell Publishing, Oxford

Brubaker R (2005) The 'diaspora' diaspora. Ethn Racial Stud 28(1):1–19

Bruneau M (2010) Diasporas, transnational spaces and communities. In: Bauböck R, Faist T (eds) Diaspora and transnationalism: concepts, theories and methods. Amsterdam University, Amsterdam, pp 35–49

Bunar N (2007) Hate crimes against immigrants in Sweden and community responses. Am Behav Sci 51:166–181

Bunt GR (2003) Islam in the digital age: E-jihad, online fatwas and cyber Islamic environments. Pluto Press, London

Burayidi MA (ed) (1997) Multiculturalism in a cross-national perspective. University Press of America, Lanham

Burdsey D (2007) British Asians and Football: Culture, Identity, Exclusion. Abingdon, Routledge

Butler J (1988) Performative acts and gender constitution: an essay in phenomenology and feminist theory. Theatre J Dec 40(4):519–531. https://www.amherst.edu/system/files/media/1650/butler_performative_acts.pdf. Accessed 13 Jan 2010

Butler J (1993) Bodies that matters: on the discursive limits of "sex". Routledge, New York

Butler J (1997) Excitable speech: a politics of the performative. Routledge, New York

Butler K (2001) Defining diaspora, refining a discourse. Diaspora 10(1):189–220

Campbell D (1994) Foreign policy and identity: Japanese 'other'/American 'self'. In: Rosow S, Inayatullah N, Rupert M (eds) The global economy as political space. Lynne Rienner, Boulder

Candan M, Hunger U (2008) Nation building online: a case study of Kurdish migrants in Germany. Ger Policy Stud 4(4):125–153

Cardus S (2010) New ways of thinking about identity in Europe. In: Hsu R (ed) Ethnic Europe: mobility, identity, and conflict in a globalized World. Stanford University Press

Castles S (2003) Migrant settlement, transnational communities and state strategies in the Asia Pacific region. In: Iredale R, Hawksley C, and Castles S (eds)

Migration in the Asia Pacific: population, settlement, and citizenship issues. Edward Elgar, Cheltenham

Chaliand G (1993) A people without a country. ZedPress, London

Chatty D (2010) Displacement and dispossession in modern Middle East. Cambridge University Press, Cambridge

Cho L (2007) The turn to diaspora. Topia: Can J Cult Stud 17:11–30. https://lucian.uchicago.edu/blogs/politicalfeeling/files/2007/10/cho-topia11-30.pdf. Accessed 14 May 2010

Chow R (2001) Leading questions. In: Chuh K, Shimakawa K (eds) Orientations: mapping studies in the Asian diaspora. Duke University Press, Durham, p 201

Christensen M (2011a) Online mediations in transnational spaces: cosmopolitan (re)formations of belonging and identity in the Turkish diaspora. Ethn Racial Stud 35(5):888–905

Christensen M (2011b) Online social media, communicative practice and complicit surveillance in transnational contexts. In: Christensen M, Jansson A, Christensen C (eds) Online territories: globalization, mediated practice and social space. Peter Lang, Bern

Cicek C (2011) Elimination or integration of pro-Kurdish politics: limits of the AKP's democratic initiative. Turk Stud 12(1):15–26

Clifford J (1994) Further inflections: toward ethnographies of the future cultural. Anthropology 9(3):302–338

Clifford J (1997) Routes: travel and translation in the late twentieth century. Harvard University Press, Cambridge

Cockburn P (2014) The Jihadis return: ISIS and the new Sunni uprising. OR Books, New York

Cohen AP (1994) Self consciousness: an alternative anthropology of identity. London, Routledge

Cohen R (1996) Diasporas and the nation-state: from victims to challengers. Int Aff (Royal Institute of International Affairs 1944) 72(3):507–520

Cohen R (2001) Global diasporas: an introduction. Routledge, London

Cohen R (2002) Global diasporas: an introduction. UCL Press, London

Cunningham S, Nguyen T (2003) Actually existing hybridity: Vietnamese diasporic music video. In: Karim HK (ed) The media of diaspora. Routledge, London

Curran J, Fenton N, Freedman D (2012) Misunderstanding the Internet. Routledge, New York

Curtis A (2005) Nationalism in the diaspora: a study of the Kurdish movement. http://www.kurdipedia.org/documents/88599/0001.pdf. Accessed 9 Sept 2009

Dahlström C (2004) Nästan välkomna: Invandrarpolitikens retorik och praktik. Göteborgs Universitet. Statsvetenskapliga Institutionen. Dalkurd. http://pol.gu.se/digitalAssets/1314/1314621_n--stan-v--lkomna.pdf. Accessed 27 Oct 2015

Davis H (2004) Understanding Stuart Hall. Sage, London

Day R (2000) Multiculturalism and the history of Canadian diversity. University of Toronto Press, Toronto

De Santis H (2003) Mi programa es su programa: tele/visions of a Spanish-language diaspora in North America. In: Karim HK (ed) The media of diaspora. Routledge, London, pp 63–75

Eccarius-Kelly V (2008) The Kurdish conundrum in Europe: political opportunities and transnational activism. In: Pojmann W (ed) Migration and activism in Europe since 1945. Palgrave Macmillan, New York

Eid M, Karim HK (eds) (2014) Re-imagining the other: culture, media, and western-muslim intersections. Palgrave Macmillan, New York

Eliassi B (2010) A stranger in my homeland: the politics of belonging among young people with Kurdish backgrounds in Sweden. Doctoral thesis, Department of Social Work, Mid Sweden University, Sundsvall

Eliassi B (2013) Contesting Kurdish identities in Sweden quest for belonging among Middle Eastern youth. Palgrave Macmillan, New York

Emanuelsson AC (2005) Diaspora global politics: Kurdish transnational networks and accommodation of nationalism. Goteborg University, Gothenburg

Entessar N (2010) Kurdish politics in the Middle East. Lexington, Lanham

Entzinger H (2003) The rise and fall of multiculturalism: the case of the Netherlands. In: Joppke C, Morawska E (eds) Toward assimilation and citizenship: immigrants in liberal nation-states. Palgrave Macmillan, Basingstoke

Eriksen TH (2006) Nations in cyberspace. Short version of the 2006 Ernst Gellner lecture delivered at the ASEN conference. London School of Economics, 27 March 2006

Eriksen TH (2007) Nationalism and the Internet. Nations and Nationalism 13(1):1–17

Faist T (2008) Migrants as transnational development agents: An inquiry into the newest round of the migration-development nexus. Population, Space and Place 14(1):21–42

Fawcett L (2001) Down but not out? The Kurds in international politics. Rev Int Stud 27(1):109–118

Fazal S, Tsagarousianou R (2002) Diaspori communication: transnational cultural practices and communication spaces. J Eur Inst Commun Cult 9(1):5–18

Ferris SP (1996) Women online: cultural and relational aspect of women's communication in online discussion groups. Interpers Comput Tech J 4(2–4):29–40

Fortier A-M (1999) Re-Membering Places and the Performance of Belonging(s). In: Bell V (ed) Performativity and Belonging. Sage, London, p 55

Fortier A-M (2000) Migrant belonging: memory, space, identity. Berg, Oxford

Franklin MI (2001) Inside out: postcolonial subjectivities and everyday life online. Int Fem J Polit 3(3):465–490

Franklin MI (2003) I define my own identity. Pacific articulations of 'Race' and 'Culture' on the Internet. Ethnicities 3(4):465–490

Franklin MI (2004) Postcolonial politics, the Internet and everyday life: Pacific traversals online. Routledge, London

Gajjala R (2002) An interrupted postcolonial/feminist cyberethnography: complicity and resistance in the "cyberfield". Fem Media Stud 2:177–193

Gajjala R (2004) Cyber selves: feminist ethnographies of South Asian women. Altamira Press, Walnut Creek

Gajjala R (ed) (2013) Cyberculture and the subaltern: weavings of the virtual and real. Lexington Books, Lanham

Gajjala R, Gajjala V (eds) (2008) South-Asian technospaces. Peter Lang, Digital Formation Series, New York

Georgiou M (2006) Diaspora, identity and the media: diasporic transnationalism and mediated spatialities. Hampton Press, Cresskill

Gilroy P (1987) There ain't no black in the Union Jack: the cultural politics of race and nation. Hutchinson, London

Gilroy P (1993/2005) The black Atlantic: modernity and double consciousness. Harvard University Press, Cambridge

Gilroy P (1997) Diaspora and the detours of identity. In: Woodward K (ed) Identity and difference. Sage, London, pp 299–343

Gilroy P (2005) Multiculture, double consciousness and the 'war on terror'. The cultural politics of multiculturalism. Patterns Prejudice 39(4):431–433. doi:http://www.tandfonline.com/doi/pdf/10.1080/00313220500347899 Accessed 3 Jun 2009

Glick Schiller N, Basch L, Blanc-Szanton C (1992) Towards a transnational perspective on migration: race, class, ethnicity, and nationalism reconsidered. New York Academy of Sciences, New York

Goffman E (1973) The presentation of self in everyday life. Penguin Books, London

Grillo RD (2000) Transmigration and cultural diversity in the construction of Europe. Paper given at symposium on cultural diversity and the construction of Europe, Barcelona

Gunew S (2004) Haunted nations: the colonial dimensions of multiculturalisms. Routledge, London

Gunew S (2009) Resident aliens: diasporic women's writing. Contemp Women's Writ 3(1):28–46

Gunter M (2009) The A to Z of the Kurds. Scarecrow Press, Lanham

Gupta A, Ferguson J (eds) (1992) Culture, power, place: explorations in critical anthropology. Duke University Press, Durham

Gupta A, Ferguson J (1997) Discipline and practice: 'the field' as site, method and location in anthropology. In: Gupta A, Ferguson J (eds) Anthropological locations: boundaries and grounds of a field science. University of California Press, Berkeley, pp 1–46

Gupta T, Hutchinson A-N (2005) Honour based crimes and murders (Working Paper). Law Society, London

Gutmann A (1994) Introduction. In: Gutmann A (ed) Multiculturalism: examining the politics of recognition. Princeton University Press, Princeton, pp 25–73

Habermas J (1984) The theory of communicative action. Heinemann Education, London

Hage G (1996) The spatial imaginary of national practices: dwelling—domesticating/being-exterminating. Environ Plan D Soc Space 14(4):463–485

Hage G (2003) Against paranoid nationalism: searching for hope in a shrinking society. Pluto, Annandale

Hage G (2011) Are 'Multiculturalism' and 'Integration' Dirty Words? Presentation at Symposium. http://www.eccq.com.au/downloads/Publications/Summit/HarpLukePR.pdf. Accessed Aug 23 2011

Hall S (1992) The question of cultural identity. In: Hall S, Held D, McGrew T (eds) Modernity and its futures. Polity, London

Hall S (1993) Cultural identity and diaspora. In: Williams P, Chrisman L (eds) Colonial discourse and post-colonial theory: a reader. Harvester Wheatsheaf, London, pp 392–401

Hall S (1996) New ethnicities. In: Baker HA Jr, Diawara M, Lindeborg RH (eds) Black British cultural studies: a reader. University of Chicago Press, Chicago, pp 163–172

Hall S (1997). The local and the global: globalization and ethnicity. In: McClintock A, Mufti A, Shohat E (eds) Dangerous liaisons: gender, nation, and postcolonial perspectives, University of Minnesota, Minneapolis, pp 173–187

Hall S (2000) Conclusion: the multi-cultural question. In: Hesse B (ed) Un/settled multiculturalisms: diasporas, entanglements, transruptions. Zed Books, London, pp 209–241

Hall S, Critcher C, Jefferson T, Roberts B (1982) Policing the crisis: mugging the state, law and order. Palgrave Macmillan, Basingstoke

Hammond L (1999) Examining the discovery of repatriation: towards a more proactive theory of migration. In: Black R, Koser K (eds) The end of refugee cycle?: refugee repatriation and reconstruction. Berghahn Books, New York

Hannerz U (2001) Transnational connections: culture, people, places. Taylor & Francis, London

Hardi C (2011) The Anfal campaign against the Kurds: chemical weapons in the service of mass murder. In: Lemarchand R (ed) Forgotten genocides: oblivion, denial, and memory. University of Pennsylvania Press, Philadelphia

Hassanpour A (1992) Nationalism and language in Kurdistan 1918–1985. Mellen Research University Press, San Francisco

Hassanpour A (1994) The Kurdish experience, Middle East report, July–August. http://www.merip.org/mer/mer189/kurdish-experience. Accessed 20 Apr 2013

Hassanpour A (2003) Diaspora, homeland and communication technologies. In: Karim HK (ed) The media of diaspora. Routledge, London

Hassanpour A, Mojab S (2005) Kurdish diaspora. In: Ember M, Ember CR, Skoggard I (eds) Encyclopedia of diasporas: immigrant and refugee cultures around the world, Vol. ll diaspora communities, Springer Publishers, Berlin, pp 1011–1018

Hatfield ME (2011) British families moving home: translocal geographies of return migration from Singapore. In: Brickell K, Datta A (eds) Translocal geographies: spaces, places, connections. Ashgate, Farnham

Hellgren Z, Hobson B (2008) Cultural conflict and cultural dialogues in the good society: the case of honor killings in Sweden. Ethnicities 8(3):385–404. Special edition: "Gender Equality, Cultural Diversity"

Hepp A (2009) Transculturality as a perspective: researching media cultures comparatively. Forum Qual Soc Res 10(1):Art. 26

Herring S (1994) Gender difference in computer-mediated communication: bringing familiar baggage to the new frontier. http://urd.let.rug.nl/~welling/cc/gender-differences-communication.pdf. Accessed 22 Aug 2011

Hirsch M (1997) Family frames: photography, narrative and postmemory. Harvard University Press, Cambridge

Hsu R (2010) The ethnic question: premodern identity for a postmodern Europe? In: Hsu R (ed) Ethnic Europe: mobility, identity and conflict in a globalized World. Stanford University Press, Stanford

Ignacio E (2005) Building diaspora: filipino cultural community formation on the Internet. Rutgers University Press, New Brunswick

Ignatieff M (1994) Blood and belonging: journeys into the new nationalism. Vintage, London

Izady M (1992) The Kurds: a concise handbook. Taylor & Francis, Washington, DC

Jensen TG (2010) Making room: encompassing diversity in Denmark. In: Silj A (ed) European multiculturalism revisited. Zed Books, London

Jiwani Y (2014) A clash of discourses: femicide or honor killings? In: Eid M, HK K (eds) Reimagining the other: culture, media, and western-muslim intersections. Palgrave Macmillan, New York

Jones S (ed) (1999) Doing Internet research: critical issues and methods for examining the net. Sage, London

Joppke C (2004) The retreat of multiculturalism in the liberal state: theory and policy. Br J Sociol 55(2):237–257

Joppke C (2013) Legal integration of Islam: a transatlantic comparison. Harvard University Press

Kalra V, Kaur R, Hutnyk J (2005) Diaspora and hybridity. Sage, London

Kamali M (2004) Media, experter och rasismen. In: Larsson S, Englund C (Red). I: Debatten om hedersmord: feminism eller rasism. Svartvitts förlag, Stockholm, pp 20–33

Karim HK (1998) From ethnic media to global media: transnational communication networks among diasporic communities. Paper WPTC-99-02. International Comparative Research Group, Strategic Research Analysis, Canadian Heritage

Karim HK (2006) Nation and diaspora: rethinking multiculturalism in a transnational context International. J Media Cult Polit 2(3):267–282

Kazanjian D, Nichanian M (2003) Between genocide and catastrophe. In: Eng DL, Kazanjian D (eds) Loss: the politics of mourning. University of California Press, Berkeley, pp 125–147

Keles JY (2015) Media, diaspora and conflict: nationalism and identity amongst Turkish and Kurdish migrants in Europe. I.B. Tauris, New York

Kelly L, Lovett J (2005). What a waste: the case for an integrated violence against women strategy. Women's National Commission

Kelly P (2002) Introduction: between culture and equality. In: Kelly P (ed) Multiculturalism reconsidered: culture, equality and its critics. Polity Press, Cambridge

Kendall L (1998) Meaning and identity in "cyberspace": the performance of gender, class and race online. Symb Interact 21(2):129–153

Khayati K (2008) From victim diaspora to transborder citizenship?: diaspora formation and transnational relations among. Kurds in France and Sweden. Doctoral thesis, Department of Social and Welfare Studies, Linköping University

King R, Christou A (2010) Diaspora, migration and transnationalism: insights from the study of second-generation "returnees,". In: Bauböck R, Faist T, (eds) Diaspora and transnationalism: concepts, theories, and methods. Amsterdam University Press, Amsterdam, pp 167–183

Kivisto P (2002) Multiculturalism in a global society. Blackwell Publishing, Malden

Kondo A (2001) Comparative citizenship and aliens' rights. In: Kondo A (ed) Citizenship in a global World: comparing citizenship rights for aliens. Palgrave Macmillan, Basingstoke

Kreyenbroek P (1992) On the Kurdish language. In: Kreyenbroek P, Sperl S (eds) The Kurds: a contemporary overview. Routledge, London

Kuntsman A (2009) Figurations of violence and belonging: queerness, migranthood and nationalism in cyberspace and beyond. Peter Lang, Oxford

Kymlicka W (1995) Multicultural citizenship: a liberal theory of minority rights. Oxford University, Oxford

Kymlicka W (1999) Liberal complacencies. In: Cohen J, Howard M, Nussbaum MC (eds) Is multiculturalism bad for women? Princeton University Press, Princeton, pp 31–34

Kymlicka W (2001) Politics in the vernacular: nationalism, multiculturalism, and citizenship. Oxford University Press, Oxford

Kymlicka W (2010) The rise and fall of multiculturalism?: new debates on inclusion and accommodation in diverse societies. In: Vertovec S, Wessendorf S (eds) The multiculturalism backlash: European discourses, policies, and practices. Routledge, London

Kymlicka W, Straehle S (2000) Cosmopolitanism, nation-states, and minority nationalism: a critical review of recent literature. Eur J Philos 7(1):65–88

Leggewie C (1996) How Turks became Kurds, not Germans. Dissent 43(3):79–83

Livingstone S (2005) Critical debates, in internet studies: reflections on an emerging field. In: Curran J, Gurevitch M (eds) Mass media and society. Sage, London

Lowe R (2006) The Syrian Kurds: a people discovered. Middle East Programme Briefing Paper 6(1):1–17

Lynnebakke B (2007) Contested equality: social relations between Indian and Surinamese Hindus in Amsterdam. In: Oonk G (ed) Global Indian diasporas: exploring trajectories of migration and theory. Amsterdam University Press, Amsterdam

Mahmod J (2005) The boob tube gets smart? An investigation of the democratic potential of the digital TV-channel Medi-TV. MA dissertation, Uppsala University, Department of Media and Informatics, Sweden

Mahmod J (2011) Designing scripts and performing Kurdishness in diaspora: the online-offline nexus. Cult Policy Crit Manag Res 5:72–90

Mandaville P (2001) Reimagining Islam in diaspora: the politics of mediated, community. Gazette 63(2–3):169–186

Marcus G (1995) Ethnography in/of the world system: the emergence of multi-sited ethnography. Annu Rev Anthropol 24:95–117

Masud E (2008) The war on Islam. India Research Press, New Delhi

McDowall D (1992) The Kurds: a nation denied. Minority Rights Group, London

McDowall D (1996/2004) A modern history of the Kurds. I.B. Tauris, London

Meer N, Modood T (2009) The multicultural state we're in: Muslims, 'multiculture' and the 'civic re-balancing' of British multiculturalism. Polit Stud 57(3):473–497

Meer N, Modood T (2013) Beyond "methodological Islamism"? A thematic discussion of 'Islamic' immigrants in Europe. Adv Appl Sociol 3(7):307–313

Meetoo V, Mirza HS (2007) There is nothing 'honourable' about honour killings: gender, violence and the limits of multiculturalism. Women's Stud Int Forum 30:187–200

Mercer K (1990) Welcome to the jungle: identity and diversity in postmodern politics. In: Rutherford J (ed) Identity: community, culture, difference. Lawrence & Wishart, London

Miller D, Slater D (2000) The Internet: an ethnographic approach. Berg, New York

Mishra S (2006) Diaspora criticism. Edinburgh University Press, Edinburgh

Mishra V (2007) Literature of the Indian diaspora: theorizing the diasporic imaginary. Routledge, London

Modood T (2010) Multicultural citizenship and Muslim identity politics. Interventions 12(2):157–170

Modood T (2013) Multiculturalism. Polity Press, Cambridge

Mola Ezat M (1992) The Kurdish Republic of Mahabad: correspondence and documents, vol 1. Apec, Stockholm

Mola Ezat M (1995) The Kurdish Republic of Mahabad: correspondence and documents, vol 2. Apec, Stockholm

Mola Ezat M (1997) The Kurdish Republic of Mahabad: correspondence and documents, vol 3. Kurdistan folkförbund, Stockholm.

Mola Ezat M (2000) The endless journey. Dezgai Serdem, Sulaimaniyah

Morley D (1992) Television, audiences and cultural studies. Routledge, London

Morley D (2000) Home territories: media, mobility and identity. Routledge, New York

Morley D, Robins K (1995) Spaces of identity. Global media, electronic landscapes and cultural boundaries. Routledge, London

Morrell G (2008) Multiculturalism, citizenship and identity. Information centre about asylum and refugees (ICAR). http://www.icar.org.uk/Morrell2008_RightsAndResponsibilities.pdf. Accessed 20 Aug 2015

Narayan U (1997) Dislocating cultures: identities, traditions, and third world feminism. Routledge, New York

Natali D (2005) The Kurds and the state: evolving national identity in Iraq, Turkey, and Iran. Syracuse University Press, Syracuse, NY

O'Reilly T (2005) What is Web 2.0. Design patterns and business models for the next generation of software. http://www.oreillynet.com/pub/a/oreilly/tim/news/2005/09/30/what-is-web-20.html. Accessed 10 Mar 2015

O'shea MT (2004) Trapped between the map and reality: geography and perceptions of Kurdistan. Taylor & Francis, London

Okin SM (1999) Is multiculturalism bad for women? In Cohen J, Howard M, Nussbaum MC (eds) Is Multiculturalism bad for women? Princeton University Press, Princeton, pp 7–24

Ong A (1993) On the edge of empires: flexible citizenship among Chinese in diaspora. Positions 1(3):745–778

Ong A (1999) Flexible citizenship: the cultural logics of transnationality. Duke University Press, Durham

Oonk G (2007) Global Indian diasporas: exploring trajectories of migration and theory. Amsterdam University Press, Amsterdam

Orgad S (2009) How can researchers make sense of the issues involved in collecting and interpreting online and offline data? In: Markham AN, Baym NK (eds) Internet inquiry: conversations about method. Sage publications, Los Angeles, pp 33–53

Østergaard-Nielsen E (2003a) The politics of migrants' Transnational political practices. Int Migr Rev 37(3):760–786

Østergaard-Nielsen E (2003b) Transnational politics: the case of Turks and Kurds in Germany. Routledge, London

Parekh B (2000) Rethinking Multiculturalism: cultural diversity and political theory. Macmillan, Basingstoke

Pföstl E (2013) Diasporas as political actors: the case of the Amazigh diaspora. In: Seeberg P, Eyadat Z (eds) Migration, security, and citizenship in the Middle East: new perspectives. Palgrave Macmillan, New York

Phillips A (2007) Multiculturalism without culture. Princeton University Press, Princeton

Portes A, Guarnizo LE, Landolt P (1999) The study of transnationalism: pitfalls and promise of an emergent research field. Ethn Racial Stud 22(2):217–237

Poster M (1995a) CyberDemocracy: Internet and the public sphere. http://www.humanities.uci.edu/mposter/writings/democ.html. Accessed 12 Oct 2014

Poster M (1995b) The second media age. Polity Press, Cambridge

Pyke K, Dang T (2003) 'FOB' and 'whitewashed': identity and internalized racism among second generation Asian Americans. Qual Sociol 26(2):147

Radhakrishnan R (1996) Diasporic mediations: between home and location. University of Minnesota Press, Minneapolis

Radhakrishnan R (2003) Theory in an uneven world. Blackwell Publishing, Oxford

Rattansi A (2011) Multiculturalism: a very short introduction. Oxford University Press, Oxford

Razack S (2004) Dark threats and white knights: the second Somalia affair, peacekeeping, and the new imperialism. University of Toronto Press, Toronto

Razack S (2008) Casting out: the eviction of Muslims from western law and politics. University of Toronto Press, Toronto

Rear M (2008) Intervention, ethnic conflict and state-building in Iraq: a paradigm for the post-colonial state. Routledge, New York

Rheingold H (1993) The virtual community: homesteading on the electronic frontier. Addison Wesley, Boston

Romano D (2002) Modern communication technology in ethnic nationalist hands: the case of the Kurds. Can J Polit Sci 35(1):127–149

Romano D (2006) The Kurdish nationalist movement: opportunity, mobilization and identity. Cambridge University Press, Cambridge

Romano D, Gurses M (eds) (2014) Introduction: the Kurds as barrier or key to democratization. In: Conflict, democratization, and the Kurds in the Middle East: Turkey, Iran, Iraq, and Syria. Palgrave Macmillan, Basingstoke

Runsten PS (2006) "Hedersmord", eurocentrism och etnicitet ('Honour killings', eurocentrism and ethnicity). In: Mediernas vi och dom (Us and them in the media). Government report SOU, 21, pp 189–225

Russell-Johnston LD (2006) The cultural situation of the Kurds. Report to the Committee on Culture, Science and Education. Council of Europe

Parliamentary Assembly Doc. http://assembly.coe.int/nw/xml/XRef/X2H-Xref-ViewHTML.asp?FileID=11316. Accessed 15 July 2016

Safran W (1991) Diaspora in modern societies: myths of homeland and return. Diaspora: A Journal of Transnational Studies 1(1):83–99

Said E (1978/2003). Orientalism. Penguin Books, London

Sainsbury D (2012) Welfare states and immigrant rights: the politics of inclusion and exclusion. Oxford University Press, Oxford

Sater J (2013) Citizenship and migration in Arab Gulf monarchies. In: Seeberg P, Eyadat Z (eds) Migration, security, and citizenship in the Middle East: new perspectives. Palgrave Macmillan, New York, pp 27–42

Savelsberg E (2014) The Syrian-Kurdish movements: obstacles rather than driving forces for democratization. In: Romano D, Gurses M (eds) Conflict, democratization, and the Kurds in the Middle East: Turkey, Iran, Iraq, and Syria. Palgrave Macmillan, New York

Schein L (1997) Gender and internal orientalism in China. Modern China 23(1):69–98.

Schein L (2000) Minority rules: the miao and the feminine in China's cultural politics. Duke University Press, Durham

Schierup CU, Ålund A (2011) The end of Swedish exceptionalism? Citizenship, neoliberalism and the politics of exclusion. Race Class 53(1):45–64

Schlesinger P (1991) Media, state, and nation: political violence and collective identities. Sage Publications, London

Schlytter A, Linell H (2009) Girls with honour-related problems in a comparative perspective. Int J Soc Welf 18:1–10

Schnapper D (1999) From the nation-state to the transnational world: on the meaning and usefulness of diaspora as a concept. Diaspora 8(3):225–254

Seeberg P, Eyadat Z (eds) (2013) Migration, security, and citizenship in the Middle East: new perspectives. Palgrave Macmillan, New York

Seib P (2007) New media and the new Middle East. Palgrave Macmillan, New York

Seib P (2012) Real-time diplomacy: politics and power in the social media era. Palgrave Macmillan, New York

Shachar A (2015) When law meets diversity: implications for women's equal citizenship. In: Vertovec S (ed) Routledge international handbook of diversity studies. Routledge, London

Sheffer G (1986) Modern diasporas in international politics. Croom Helm, London

Sheikhmous O (1990) The Kurds in exile. In: Fuad K, Ibrahim F, Mahvi N (eds) Yearbook of the Kurdish academy. Ratingen, Germany, The Kurdish Academy

Sheikhmous O (2000) Crystallisation of a new diaspora: migration and political culture among the Kurds in Europe. Centre for research in International Migration and Ethnic Relations. Stockholm University, Stockholm

Sheyholislami J (2008) Identity, discourse, and media. Doctoral thesis, School of Linguistics and Language Studies, Carleton University

Sheyholislami J (2010) Identity, language, and new media: the Kurdish case. Lang Policy 9(4):289–312

Sidaway J (2000) Postcolonial geographies: an exploratory essay. Prog Hum Geogr Dec 24:591–612

Silverstone R (ed) (2005) Media technology and everyday life in Europe. Ashgate, Aldershot

Slater D (2002) Social relationships and identity online and offline. In: Lievrouw L, Livingstone S, (eds) Handbook of new media: social shaping and consequences of ICTs. Sage Publications, London. pp 533–546

Smith LT (1999) Decolonizing methodologies: research and indigenous people. University of Otago Press, Dunedin

Somer M (2005) Failures of the discourse of ethnicity: Turkey, Kurds, and the emerging Iraq. Sage Publications. http://home.ku.edu.tr/~musomer/research_files/Somer%20Sec%20Dialogue%20article%20final.pdf. Accessed 10 May 2015

Soysal YN (2001) Postnational citizenship: reconfiguring the familiar terrain. In: Nash K, Scott A (eds) The Backwell companion to political sociology. Blackwell, Malden, MA, pp 333–341

Spevack E (1995) Ethnic Germans from the East: Aussiedler in Germany, 1970–1994. German Polit and Soc 13(4):171–91

Spivak GC (1990) The post-colonial critic: interviews, strategies, dialogues. Routledge, London

Spivak GC, Landry D, MacLean G (eds) (1996) The spivak reader: selected works of Gayatri Chakravorty Spivak. Routledge, New York

Squire V (2009) The exclusionary politics of asylum. Palgrave Macmillan, Basingstoke

Stansfield G (2014) Kurds, persian nationalism, and Shi'i rule: surviving dominant nationhood in Iran. In: Romano D, Gurses M (eds) Conflict, democratization, and the Kurds in the Middle East: Turkey, Iran, Iraq, and Syria. Palgrave Macmillan, New York

Stier OB (1996) The propriety of holocaust memory: cultural representations and commemorative response. Doctoral thesis, University of California, Santa Barbara

Stone AR (2001) The war of desire and technology at the close of the mechanical age. MIT Press, London

Taylor C (1994) The politics of recognition. In: Gutmann A (ed) Multiculturalism: examining the politics of recognition. Princeton University Press, Princeton, pp 25–73

Tejel J (2009) Syria's Kurds: history, politics and society. Routledge, London

Thangaraj S (2015) Desi hoop dreams: Pick-up basketball and the making of Asian American masculinity. New York University Press, New York

Thapar-Björkert S (2011) Conversations across borders: men and honour-related violence in the UK and Sweden. In: Idriss MM, Abbas T (eds) Honour, violence, women and Islam. Routledge, Abingdon, pp 182–200

Tölölyan K (1996) Rethinking diaspora(s): stateless power in the transnational moment. Diaspora 5(1):3–36

Tölölyan K (2010) Beyond the homeland: from exilic nationalism to diasporic transnationalism. In: Gal A, Leoussi A, Gal A, Smith AD (eds) The call of the homeland: diaspora nationalisms, past and present. Brill, Amsterdam

Tsagarousianou R (2004) Rethinking the concept of diaspora: mobility, connectivity and communication in a globalised world. Westminster Papers in Communication and Culture (University of Westminster, London) 1(1):52–65. DOI: http://doi.org/10.16997/wpcc.203

Tsaliki L (2003) Globalisation and hybridity: the construction of Greekness on the Internet. In: Karim HK (ed) The media of diaspora. Routledge, London, pp 162–176

Turkle S (1995) Life on the screen: identity in the age of the Internet. Simon & Schuster, New York

Turkle S (2011) Alone together: why we expect more from technology and less from each other. Basic Books, New York

Turner BS (2006) Citizenship and the crisis of multiculturalism. Citiz Stud 10(5):607–618

Vad Jønsson H, Petersen K (2012) Denmark: a national welfare state meets the world. In: Brochmann G, Hagelund A (eds) Immigration policy and the Scandinavian welfare state 1945–2010. Palgrave Macmillan, Basingstoke. pp 97–148

Vali A (1998) The Kurds and their others: fragmented identity and fragmented politics. Comp Stud South Asia Afr Middle East 18(2):82–95

Vali A (2006) The Kurds and their 'others': fragmented identity and fragmented politics. In: Jabar FA, Dawod H (eds) The Kurds: nationalism and politics. SAQI, London

Vali A (2014) Kurds and the state in Iran: the making of Kurdish identity. Palgrave Macmillan, New York

van Bruinessen M (1999) The Kurds in movement: migrations, mobilisations, communications and the globalisation of the Kurdish question (Working Paper No. 14). Islamic Area Studies Project, Tokyo, Japan, p 20

van Bruinessen M (2000) Transnational aspects of the Kurdish question (Working paper). Robert Schuman Centre for Advanced Studies, European University Institute, Florence http://www.hum.uu.nl/medewerkers/m.vanbruinessen/publications/transnational_Kurds.htm. Accessed 15 Aug 2010

Vanly IC (1992) The Kurds in the Soviet Union. In: Kreyenbroek KP, Sperl S (eds) The Kurds: a contemporary overview. Routledge, London

Verschueren J (2000) Culture vs. cultures: an irreverent approach to conceiving and working with diversity. Paper presented at the Symposium Cultural Diversity and the Construction of Europe, Barcelona, 13–16 December 2000

Verschueren P (2005) From virtual to everyday life. In: Carpentier N, Servaes J (eds) Towards a sustainable information society: deconstructing WSIS. Intellect & DEFAE, Bristol, pp 169–184

Vertovec S (1999). Three meanings of 'diaspora', exemplified among South Asian religions. Diaspora 6(3):277–300. University of Oxford. http://www.transcomm.ox.ac.uk/working%20papers/diaspora.pdf. Accessed 10 Jan 2010

Vertovec S (2000) Religion and diaspora. Institute of Social & Cultural Anthropology, University of Oxford, Oxford

Vertovec S (2001) Transnational challenges to the 'new' multiculturalism. Paper presented to the ASA Conference, University of Oxford, WPTC-01-06

Vertovec S (2007) Super-diversity and its implications. Ethn Racial Stud 30(6):1024–1054

Vertovec S, Wessendorf S (eds) (2010) The multiculturalism backlash: European discourses, policies and practices. Routledge, London

Wahlbeck Ö (1999) Kurdish diasporas: a comparative study of Kurdish refugee communities. Palgrave Macmillan, London

Wahlbeck Ö (2010) The concept of diaspora as an analytical tool in the study of refugee communities. J Ethn Migr Stud 28(2):221–238

Weedon C (2004) Identity and culture: narratives of difference and belonging. Open University Press, Maidenhead

Wessendorf S (2007) 'Roots-migrants': transnationalism and 'return' among second-generation Italians in Switzerland. J Ethn Migr Stud 33(7):1083–1102

Wikan U (2003) For aerens skyld. Fadime til ettertanke (For the sake of honour: Fadime for consideration). Universitetsforlaget, Oslo

Wise JM (2000) Home: territory and identity. Cult Stud 14(2):295–310

Woodward C (ed) (2004) Identity and difference. Sage Publications, London

Yildiz K (2005) The Kurds in Turkey: EU accession and human rights. Pluto Press, London

Yuval-Davis N (1993) Women, ethnicity and empowerment. ISS Working Paper Series / General Series (Vol. 151, pp. 1–20). Erasmus University Rotterdam. http://hdl.handle.net/1765/19113. Accessed 14 May 2010

Yuval-Davis N (1996) Women and the biological reproduction of "the Nation". Women's Stud Int Forum 19(1–2):17–24

Yuval-Davis N (1997) Gender and nation. Sage Publications, London

Zeydanlioglu W (2008) "The white Turkish man's burden": orientalism, kemalism and the Kurds in Turkey. In: Rings G, Ife A (eds) Neocolonial mentalities in contemporary Europe? Language and discourse in the construction of identities. Cambridge Scholars, Newcastle upon Tyne

Zubaida S (1992) Introduction. In: Kreyenbroek P, Sperl S (eds) The Kurds: a contemporary overview. Routledge, London, pp 1–7

ELECTRONIC SOURCES

BBC News (2010) Damian Green says burqa ban would be 'un-British'. 18 July 2010. http://www.bbc.co.uk/news/uk-10674973. Accessed 29 May 2012

BBC News (2011) State multiculturalism has failed, says David Cameron. 5 February 2011. http://www.bbc.com/news/uk-politics-12371994. Accessed 10 Jun 2011

Committee to Protect Journalists (2013) Second worst year on record for jailed journalists. 18 December 2013. https://cpj.org/reports/2013/12/second-worst-year-on-record-for-jailed-journalists.php. Accessed 20 Apr 2015

Council of Foreign Relations (2015) http://www.cfr.org/about. Accessed 15 Sept 2015

Guardian (2003) A veil drawn over brutal crimes. 3 October 2003. http://www.guardian.co.uk/uk/2003/oct/03/ukcrime. Accessed 20 Apr 2012

Guardian (2011) A new kind of riot? From Brixton 1981 to Tottenham 2011. 9 December 2011. http://www.theguardian.com/uk/2011/dec/09/riots-1981-2011-differences. Accessed 28 May 2012

Guardian (2015a) Turkey election ruling party loses majority as pro-Kurdish HDP gains seats. 7 June 2015. http://www.theguardian.com/world/2015/jun/07/turkey-election-preliminary-results-erdogan-akp-party. Accessed 3 Aug 2015

Guardian (2015b) Refugee rhetoric echoes 1938 summit before Holocaust, UN official warns. 14 October 2015. https://www.theguardian.com/global-development/2015/oct/14/refugee-rhetoric-echoes-1938-summit-before-holocaust-un-official-warns. Accessed 3 Nov 2015

Hage G (2011) Are 'multiculturalism' and 'integration' dirty words? Presentation at the symposium. http://www.eccq.com.au/downloads/Publications/Summit/HarpLukePR.pdf. Accessed 23 Aug 2011

Human Rights Watch (2014) Turkey: Internet freedom, rights in sharp decline. 2 September 2014. https://www.hrw.org/news/2014/09/02/turkey-internet-freedom-rights-sharp-decline. Accessed 13 Feb 2015

HRW (2015) Human Rights Watch submission: world development report on Internet for development. 26 August 2015. https://www.hrw.org/news/2015/08/26/human-rights-watch-submission-world-development-report-internet-development. Accessed 10 Oct 2015

Internet Live Stats (2015) http://www.internetlivestats.com/internet-users/. Accessed 10 Nov 2015

Request More (2015) Refugee rhetoric reminiscent of pre-Holocaust sentiment—UN human rights chief. 14 October 2015. https://www.rt.com/uk/318656-refugee-migrant-rhetoric-holocaust/. Accessed 13 Aug 2015

Slate (2012) Sweden's gender-neutral pronoun: Hen. 11 April 2012. http://www.slate.com/articles/double_x/doublex/2012/04/hen_sweden_s_new_

gender_neutral_pronoun_causes_controversy_.html?tid=sm_tw_button_toolbar. Accessed 20 May 2010

Svenska Dagbladet (2010) Reinfeldt och Sahlin i debattduell. 27 January 2010. http://www.svd.se/nyheter/inrikes/reinfeldt-och-sahlin-i-debattduell_4162613. svd. Accessed 29 May 2012

The Atlantic (2015) The global refugee crisis. 14 October 2015. http://www. theatlantic.com/notes/all/2015/08/the-global-refugee-crisis/402718/. Accessed 20 Oct 2015

The Economist (2007) In praise of multiculturalism. 14 June 2007. http://www. economist.com/node/9337695. Accessed 23 Oct 2014

The New York Times (2009) Sarkozy backs drive to eliminate the burqa. 22 June 2009. http://www.nytimes.com/2009/06/23/world/europe/23france. html?_r=0. Accessed 15 Jul 2011

The New York Times (2015) Beirut, also the site of deadly attacks, feels forgotten. 15 November 2015. http://www.nytimes.com/2015/11/16/world/middleeast/ beirut-lebanon-attacks-paris.html?_r=0. Accessed 20 Nov 2015

The Telegraph (2011) Nicolas Sarkozy declares multiculturalism had failed. 11 February 2011. http://www.telegraph.co.uk/news/worldnews/europe/ france/8317497/Nicolas-Sarkozy-declares-multiculturalism-had-failed.html. Accessed 10 Jun 2012

The Telegraph (2015) We are watching the death of open frontiers in Europe. 26 October 2015. http://www.telegraph.co.uk/news/worldnews/europe/ 11955742/We-are-seeing-thelast-dying-days-of-open-frontiers-in-Europe. html. Accessed 29 Oct 2015

The UN Refugee Agency (2015) Worldwide displacement hits all-time high as war and persecution increase. 18 June 2015. http://www.unhcr.org/558193896. html. Accessed 12 Oct 2015

Transparency (2015) Request: removal request, January 1–June 30, 2015, https://transparency.twitter.com/removal-requests. Accessed 1 Nov 2015

Trilling, D. (2015) What to do with the people who do make it across? London Review of Books 37(19):9–12. 8 October 2015. http://www.lrb.co.uk/v37/ n19/daniel-trilling/what-to-do-with-the-people-who-do-make-it-across. Accessed 29 Oct 2015

INDEX[1]

[1] Note: Page numbers with "n" denote notes.

© The Author(s) 2016
J. Mahmod, *Kurdish Diaspora Online*, The Palgrave
Macmillan Series in International Political Communication,
DOI 10.1057/978-1-137-51347-2

GPSR Compliance
The European Union's (EU) General Product Safety Regulation (GPSR) is a set
of rules that requires consumer products to be safe and our obligations to
ensure this.

If you have any concerns about our products, you can contact us on

ProductSafety@springernature.com

In case Publisher is established outside the EU, the EU authorized
representative is:

Springer Nature Customer Service Center GmbH
Europaplatz 3
69115 Heidelberg, Germany